Judaism in Society

Judaism in Society

The Evidence of the Yerushalmi

Toward the Natural History of a Religion

Jacob Neusner

The University of Chicago Press

Chicago and London

The University of Chicago Press, Chicago 60637
The University of Chicago Press, Ltd., London

© 1983 by The University of Chicago
All rights reserved. Published 1983
Printed in the United States of America

90 89 88 87 86 85 84 83   5 4 3 2 1

Library of Congress Cataloging in Publication Data
Neusner, Jacob, 1932–
    Judaism in society, the evidence of the Yerushalmi.

    Bibliography: p.
    Includes index.
    1.   Talmud Yerushalmi—Criticism, interpretation, etc.
I.   Title.
BM498.8.N48   1983   296.1'2407   83–4916
ISBN 0–226–57616–7

JACOB NEUSNER is University Professor and the Un-
gerleider Distinguished Scholar of Judaic Studies at Brown
University. Among his many books are *Take Judaism, for
Example, Stranger at Home*, and *Judaism: The Evidence of
the Mishnah*, all published by the University of Chicago
Press. He is the editor of the thirty-five volume translation
of *The Talmud of the Land of Israel*.

For
John Updike

Contents

Preface

Imagine for the moment that a hillside cave in Galilee, carved open to the light for the first time in nearly two millennia, yielded a vast library of hitherto unknown writings of ancient Judaism. Pot after pot of documents on blackened leather came forth. Once deciphered and published—a labor of many years—these leather pages turned out to discuss a known document but to say quite new things about it, to speak in an unfamiliar idiom about already established rules. Consider in your mind's eye the sensation such a discovery would cause, the scholarly lives and energies that would flow to the new find and its explication. Converging interests in not merely philology and history, but also the study of religions and the analysis of the roots of Western culture, would contrive to make the new Galilean library a centerpiece of scholarly discourse for many decades. To call the contents of that hillside cave a revolution, to compare them to the finds at Qumran, the Dead Sea, or Nag Hammadi, or to any of the other great contemporary discoveries out of ancient times, would hardly be deemed an exaggeration.

The Yerushalmi (also: "Palestinian Talmud," "Talmud of the Land of Israel") is such a library. Comprising thirty-nine tractates, it fills many hundreds of pages of barely intelligible writing. Famous for its incomprehensibility, the document has come before the scholarly public in bits and pieces, odd pages snatched from an otherwise inaccessible *Geniza*. A paragraph here, a sentence there—these have been made to serve as representations of this odd and difficult work. The result is that the Yerushalmi as a whole, with its remarkably coherent and systematic statement, has yet to win sustained attention. Its testimony to the world view and way of life of the people who made it up has gone unnoticed. The few who took an interest sedulously protected their monopoly of knowledge, declaring all outsiders unclean for entry into the sanctum of learning. Accordingly, with the completion of the first full translation of the Yerushalmi as a whole into a Western language (the French translation skips difficult passages), the Yerushalmi comes forth for the first time to the light of day to be viewed whole and complete by the generality of learned people. While, as I said, a handful of Talmudists have long had access to bits and pieces, they mined underground, alone and in deep and barely accessible passages. They traded in a mysterious, closed market whatever nuggets they retrieved. Few in any case spent much time in the depths of the Yerushalmi. With the breaking open of a strip mine, however imperfect for the moment, the whole vein for the first time is open to the light for all to see and plunder in the name of learning.

Known for sixteen hundred years, from the time, generally assumed to be the end of the fourth century and beginning of the fifth, of its closure and redaction, the Yerushalmi has suffered an odious but deserved reputation for the difficulty of making sense of its discourse. That reputation is partly apropos; there are many passages that are scarcely intelligible. But there are a great many more that are entirely or mainly accessible. And the document is now becoming available in a complete, if preliminary and occasionally uncertain, translation, on the basis of which I here propose to accomplish the first historical-religious study of the document as a whole. Of necessity, as I shall explain, that study is little more than an original labor of classification. Taxonomy is required so that we may assess the contents of the Yerushalmi as a whole, in their fullness. So we make use of those contents in exercises pointed toward the history of Judaism, worked out within the classificatory method and program of natural history: taking up specimens and comparing them to other specimens, both among the known and among the unknown, of the same and of similar classifications. This book is then a work of preliminary description and interpretation of an old text, freshly examined.

In giving to my translation the adjective "preliminary," and in explaining why it will require substantial revision in time to come, I have paid full respect to the difficulty of understanding the Yerushalmi. At the same time, I also have demonstrated that vast stretches of the Yerushalmi are quite accessible and comprehensible. Having translated all of the texts adduced here in evidence as specimens of the Yerushalmi, I have used only those passages, and they are many, in which there can be no doubt about either the wording of the text, the meanings of the words of the text, or the message and intent of the passage as a whole. The Yerushalmi is no longer in that inaccessible hole, known only to a handful of adepts, those agile miners able to squeeze into the tiny aperture of the cave. It is now out in the open, for all to see, and for many to work to understand and interpret. From the viewpoint of the study of ancient Judaism, therefore, the Yerushalmi here comes to the fore as if it were a newly discovered text. As I said, it is to be compared in its originality and immense importance to the Qumran library, for Judaism, and the Nag Hammadi library, for Christianity.

The Judaism to which the Talmud of the Land of Israel testifies forms one plank in the bridge that leads from antiquity to the beginning of the Middle Ages, from the Middle East to Europe, from the end of the classical age to the nascent moment of our own time and place. Circa A.D. 200, the Mishnah, on which the Yerushalmi rests, looks to classical times. It describes an orderly world in which Israelite society is neatly divided among its castes, arranged in priority around the center that is the Temple, systematically engaged in a life of sanctification, remote from the disorderly events of the day. The Talmud, circa A.D. 400, portrays the chaos of Jews living among gentiles, governed by a diversity of authorities, lacking all order and arrangement, awaiting a time of salvation for which, through sanctification, they make themselves ready. The Mishnah's imaginary Israel is governed by an Israelite king, high priest, and Sanhedrin. The Talmud's flesh-and-blood Jews lived under rabbis near at hand, who settled everyday disputes of streets and households, and distant archons of a nameless state, to be manipulated and placated on earth as in heaven. The Mishnah's Judaism breathes the pure air of public piazza and stoa, the Talmud's, the ripe stench of private alleyway and courtyard. The image of the Mishnah's Judaism is evoked by the majestic Parthenon, perfect in all its proportions, conceived in a single moment of pure rationality. The Talmud's Judaism is a scarcely choate cathedral in process, the labor of many generations, each of its parts the conception of a diverse moment of devotion, all of them the culmination of an ongoing and evolving revelation in the here and now, a snare for Heaven's light. The Mishnah is Judaism's counterpart to Plato's *Republic* and Aristotle's *Politics,* a noble theory of it all.

So when we study the Mishnah, we contemplate a fine conception of nowhere in particular, addressed to whom it may concern. When we turn to the Talmud, we see a familiar world, as we have known it from the Talmud's day to our own. We perceive something of our own day, as we who study Judaism recognize self-evident continuity with those times. So the Mishnah marks the end of the ancient and Near Eastern, the Talmud the beginning of the modern and the Western (as well as the Near Eastern) epoch in the history of Judaism. That is why the Talmud of the Land of Israel deserves attention, in the setting not only of the history of Judaism but also of the formation of the civilization of the West in the place and period, circa 200–400, to which this Talmud attests.

Let me first define the terms at hand, beginning with Judaism. The Talmud of the Land of Israel testifies to the formation of the kind of Judaism paramount and normative from its time to this day. Called "Rabbinic," because of the honorific title of its principal authority, the rabbi, or "Talmudic," because of the main document on which it is based, this particular version of Judaism proved lasting beyond its formative years. So at issue is a moment in the birth of Judaism.

As to the time, as I have indicated, at the beginning, the period is marked off by the completion of the Mishnah, about A.D. 200, and, at the end, by the closure of the Talmud of the Land of Israel, about A.D. 400. These tumultuous centuries witnessed the transition from late antiquity to early medieval times. The Roman Empire became two, dividing east from west, turned from pagan to Christian, from the mode of being we know as classical to the one we identify as medieval. The birth of Judaism thus forms a chapter in the history of the movement of the West from its Greek, Roman, and Israelite beginnings, to its full expression in Christianity, for the generality of Europe; (later on) in Islam, for Africa and Asia; and in Judaism, for the margins of both worlds. True, the birth of Judaism in context fills little more than a paragraph out of the long chapter of the movement from classical to medieval civilization, both east and west. But in the end it may prove a suggestive chapter, exemplifying in its accessibility much that may otherwise lie beyond our capacity for detailed description and explanation, the social world of village and private life. In what is small we may discern large things, in detail, the configuration of the whole.

Let us now define what changes, what marks the turning of the way. It is evoked, in literary terms, in the transition from the Mishnah to the Talmud of the Land of Israel. As I said, from the strict and formal classicism of the Mishnah, like Plato's *Republic* describing for no one in particular an ideal society nowhere to be seen, in its day the Judaism described by the Talmud of the Land of Israel turned to the disorderly detail of the workaday world, the crowded streets below the Parthenon, so to speak. If Aristotle's *Politics* had been written as a gloss to Plato's *Republic,* amplifying and extending piece by piece the once whole and coherent writing of Plato, we should have a rough analogy to what the Talmud does with the Mishnah of Judah the Patriarch (henceforward: Rabbi). If, further, many philosophers took up the fantastic account of the *Republic* and out of its materials, and other writings, worked out new *Republic*s, so bringing diversity to what had been a single conception and book, we should find a possible precedent for what happened from 200 to 400 in the move, in Judaism, from the ancient to the medieval mode: theoretical to practical, monothetic to polythetic, uniform to diverse, cogent to chaotic, and system to incremental tradition.

We come now to the rich literary context of the Yerushalmi. The second century yielded a single document of Judaism, the Mishnah. The dawn of the fifth century witnessed the beginnings and formation of many and the completion of one. By that time, the Talmud of the Land of Israel, a vast amplification of the Mishnah, neared closure. The Tosefta, a supplement to the Mishnah's materials in the Mishnah's own idiom and structure, was taking shape. The Sifra, a compilation of exegeses pertinent to Leviticus, with special interest in the relationship of the Mishnah's laws to those of Leviticus, would soon follow. In the hundred years beyond the closure of the Yerushalmi a quite different mode of collection and organizations of sayings, represented by the compilations of exegetical remarks on Genesis and Leviticus, called Genesis Rabbah and Leviticus Rabbah, would come to full expression. Nor may we silently pass by the other, greater and more influential, Talmud, the one created in Babylonia, generally thought to have come to its final condition in the two centuries after the Yerushalmi's closure. Accordingly, the Mishnah, a single document, stands at the head of many paths. Numerous roads lead forward, out of the Mishnah. But none leads backward from it, except the leap to Sinai conveyed in the proof texts of Scripture. Among these paths onward from the Mishnah, the Palestinian and the Babylonian Talmuds and midrash collections mark the principal way forward.

For its part, the Talmud of the Land of Israel testifies to the existence of a coherent world view and way of life embodied in a distinct and distinctive society, the rabbis—masters and disciples—or estate of Jews of the third and fourth centuries in the Land of Israel. This book amply describes and illustrates principal traits of that world view and way of life, so far as the Yerushalmi portrays them. But, as I must emphasize, before us in the Yerushalmi is no complete system of Judaism contained in a single document. This presents a contrast to the Mishnah, which provides a full and exhaustive account of its system and its viewpoint. So while whatever we know about the Mishnah's system is in the code itself, the Yerushalmi is quite different. The Judaism to which the Yerushalmi testifies defines the matrix in which, among other documents, the Yerushalmi came into being. But the Yerushalmi does not constitute the sole, or the one important, corpus of evidence about that kind of Judaism. Nor is there a single document that expresses that whole. Accordingly, the Judaism *in* the Talmud of the Land of Israel is not the Judaism only *of* that book, in the same way in which the Judaism to which the Mishnah testifies is expressed within the Mishnah, whole and complete.

Our problem therefore is quite different from the one addressed in my earlier book *Judaism: The Evidence of the Mishnah*. It follows that this book and that one have in common a similar goal, therefore the title, but nothing else. The evidence of the Yerushalmi about the Judaism attested in its pages must be described in a way quite different from the way in which we lay out evidence of the Mishnah about the Judaism expressed within the Mishnah. The one, it is clear, gives evidence of a world beyond itself, a world of which it is an important component. The other gives evidence only about itself and the world view contemplated within its words.

The Yerushalmi and the Mishnah interrelate like a vine and a lattice. But the vine is separate from the lattice. The Yerushalmi in its fundamental literary traits and modes of thought is so unlike the Mishnah that a single mode of description of the two documents is unimaginable. Since I have devoted an entire book (*Talmud of the Land of Israel,* vol. 35, *Introduction: Taxonomy*) to the differences between them and to an account of how they relate to one another, I need here underscore the simple fact that describing and interpreting the Yerushalmi's picture of Judaism requires one set of procedures and questions, Mishnah's a different set.

The salient trait of this book remains to be explained. First, let me specify the character of this book, then explain the setting of the work. The subtitle defines the methodological context in which I choose to work: "toward the natural history of a religion." To contribute toward that goal, I work in the way in which, it appears to me, the founders of natural history had to do their work. I have now to unpack this simple explanation of the way I have done the work in terms of the way in which others do much different work.

To provide an account of how the Yerushalmi attests to Rabbinic Judaism, I adduce in evidence a very sizable corpus of texts. These give the book the character of an anthology. But this is not an anthology. The texts serve to exemplify the traits of many other texts in the document as a whole. They constitute, in selection and arrangement, a sustained argument. That is why I present them. What we learn from them permits us to describe as a whole that part of the rabbinic system of which the Yerushalmi forms a principal component. The reason is that the Yerushalmi is a remarkably uniform document, as I shall explain in Chapter 2; it speaks about many things with a single voice. Its modes of discourse are not much differentiated, in particular, when a passage of the Mishnah comes under analysis. Then we find a limited range of repetitious rhetoric of patterns through which any passage of Mishnah exegesis will unfold.

In *Talmud of the Land of Israel,* vol. 35, *Introduction: Taxonomy,* I have already shown the remarkably limited repertoire of exegetical initiatives available to the framers of the Yerushalmi's discussions of passages of the Mishnah. They are likely to choose and carry out one of only a handful of procedures. Indeed, these may be reduced to two: explain the simple meaning of a passage, or expand and theorize about one passage in the light of other passages (or of a problem commmon to several passages).

Exegesis may therefore take the form of (1) explanation of the meaning of a given pericope of the Mishnah, or (2) expansion upon the meaning. It follows that if we understand what the Talmud does with a single item, we also may confidently claim we can describe and make sense of what the Talmud is apt to do with a great many such items. Citation and analysis of a few instances, claimed to be representative, therefore allow us to describe the mode of exegetical thought of the framers of the Yerushalmi in general. (At a later stage in the argument, also in Chapter 2, I shall suggest why I think these framers encompass only a small number of sages living in a circumscribed period, though I do not know how many years or decades, toward the end of the process in which our Talmud came into being in its units of discourse and ultimate redaction and closure.) For the present it suffices to explain, and I hope justify, the fairly extensive inclusion in this book of illustrative texts. These illustrate because they are typical and so exemplify traits of the document as a whole. At the end the reader should have in hand not a few snippets, an anthology of this and that, but a complete account of the system of the document as a whole, as seen through representative and important illustrations of its definitive conceptual characteristics.

The issue of context and comparison is fundamental to the exercise of natural history. To describe the text specimen in hand, we have to deal with the entirety of its ideas and perspectives. That labor becomes possible because, for the first time, the whole of the Yerushalmi has been translated into a language other than its original one, and so has been subjected to the first systematic heuristic exercise beyond phrase-by-phrase exegesis.[1] By setting the whole into the context of another language entirely, I have begun the inquiry into the comparison of the text with the larger context of culture. That is, I have begun to see the text of the Yerushalmi from the outside rather than from the inside, now from the perspective of a language other than its own. Only when one moves a text from its original setting to some other, meaning, to begin with, from its original language into another, is the perspective of the outsider pertinent and possible. Then exegesis transcends the urgent issue of small-scale study of words and phrases and their *ad hoc* and particular meanings, moving to the still more pressing issues of contextual sense and cultural meaning.

Just as the work of natural history is to collect specimens and to classify them, so the work of the natural history of a religion, in its primitive stages, is to collect what is specific and to classify those data, hence to place what is particular into the context of what is general and already intelligible. When the text is located in some context other than its own uninterpreted set of statements, with their self-evident and predictable meanings and implicit logic, it may become intelligible to someone who does not already know what it means. By itself and so lacking all connection to something outside of itself, by contrast, the text forms a closed system, opaque and private. To turn what is closed and particular into something intelligible and accessible, we have to compare one thing with something else, to establish a common frame of meaning for two (or more) otherwise unique and incomparable things. So, as I said, we collect specimens of one thing and bring them into juxtaposition with the specimens of some other thing. We attempt to discover classifications capable of making place for both things and of rendering each meaningful and comprehensible in terms of the other. For the study of religions, as much as of fish or rocks, the work is to uncover resemblances and differences. That is, when we see how something is like something else, we also become able to perceive how something is different from something

1. This book is composed on the basis of my translation of twenty-four of the thirty-four projected volumes, and my students' completed translation of yet another three (in all, thirty-two of the thirty-nine tractates). Since the findings over the bulk of the Yerushalmi proved to be uniform, I think it unlikely that there will be much to change in this preliminary account. My students' completed translations are these: Tzvee Zahavy, *Berakhot;* Martin Jaffee, *Ma^caserot;* Peter Haas, *Ma^caser Sheni.* In addition, I used more than half of Alan Avery-Peck, *Terumot.* My colleague, Edward Goldman, supplied the first part of *Rosh Hashanah.* Entirely omitted are Yerushalmi tractates Peah, Demai, Kilaim, Shebi^cit, and Pesahim. I have completed the translation of Yerushalmi tractates Hallah, Orlah, Bikkurim, Shabbat, Erubin, Yoma, Sheqalim, Sukkah, Besah, Taanit, Megillah, Hagigah, Mo^ced Qatan, Yebamot, Ketubot, Nedarim, Nazir, Gittin, Qiddushin, Sotah, Baba Qamma, Baba Mesi^ca, Baba Batra, Sanhedrin, Makkot, Shebu^cot, ^cAbodah Zarah, Horayot, and Niddah.

else. The work of comparison may then move onward and upward to the more subtle and parlous labor of interpretation.

These general remarks serve to account for the title and subtitle of this book, explaining the text under discussion and the context that I seek in this preliminary work toward what will eventually constitute a natural history of formative Judaism. In defining this first approach to the study of the Yerushalmi as a document of Judaism, I mean to replicate precisely that experiment in the description and interpretation of religion already invented by Jonathan Z. Smith, in his essays, *Map Is Not Territory: Studies in the History of Religions* (p. ix). Describing his essays as "a comparative enterprise within closely adjacent historical, cultural, or linguistic units which insists that comparison be between a total ensemble rather than between isolated motifs," Smith explains the purpose of his papers as follows:

> Such comparative endeavors have a double thrust. They seek both to situate a text within a "family of resemblances" and to clarify the complexity and limits of this "family" by examining a specific document. They are exercises in that most rudimentary but also most basic, of scholarly procedures: classification. I take seriously the oft-repeated remark that, in the history of a discipline, such a taxonomic enterprise is more indicative of a "natural history" than a "science;" indeed, as an *historian* of religions, I am content that this be so. The former stage appears to be the necessary precondition for achieving the latter.

In *Imagining Religion* (p. 8), Smith further states:

> Classification is but a stage in natural history; it is not yet science. For that, explanation is required. But classification is a necessary prerequisite. As F. Max Mumuller insisted, more than a century ago, "All real science rests on classification, and only in case we cannot succeed in classifying the various dialects of faith, shall we have to confess that a science of religion is really an impossibility."

This brief definition suffices to provoke many long studies indeed.

In the case of this book I seek first to situate the Yerushalmi within its larger context in the Roman world (Chapter 1). Then, in Chapter 2, I ask where the document is to be situated in the history of the Jewish people and in relationship to other works of the larger form of Judaism of which it is a part. The text here speaks for itself, as I attempt to account for its uniform and monotonous voice. I propose, third, to describe the principal points of insistence, the things on which the document lays emphasis throughout all of its points of inquiry, each of its exegetical initiatives (Chapter 3). These two matters—external setting in Judaism, internal context of discourse—define the Yerushalmi's particular and definitive characteristics. The work is wholly inductive. The text standing alone suffices. No further information, by definition, is necessary or possible.

Turning outward to the matrix, that larger framework in which the text is to be located, that is, the other writings by the same sort of Judaic authorities, rabbis, I propose, fourth, to describe what the text in hand tells us about its own sponsors, its picture of the social role of the particular kind of figure who speaks both here and in other books of the same place, time, and type of Judaism (Chapter 4). That seems to me the necessary first step in comparing the document to other documents, that is, to discover what it has in common with other documents of its texts belonging to the same subdivision of its larger classification.

I then, fifth, try to point to the purpose of the document, the message put forward by this text, in the name of its authorities, for the larger world of Judaism (Chapter 5). Here I ask about the points on which the Yerushalmi's framers insist, why what they say matters.

Accordingly, as is clear from the table of contents, the progression of description moves from context, to text, to matrix. The opening part presents the question of the book, the relationship of the document to its age. The answers are adduced in the two steps of Parts Two and Three: first, inductively, through a close reading of the recurrent traits of the text itself, second, not entirely deductively, through an account of those traits of the text congruent to traits of other rabbinic texts (not here presented) of the same class as this one.

I am reticent to spell out the net result, because I think it is obvious. The following seems ample. The questions with which Chapter 1 concludes are answered in the points of insistence and emphasis revealed in the repertoire of extracts of the next four chapters: a reasoned, uniform discourse (Chapter 2) yielding (1) certainty about God's will (Chapter 3), (2) authority for the rabbi (Chapter 4), and so, (3) salvation for Israel (Chapter 5). Given the calamities of the later fourth and early fifth centuries, in which the document at hand came into being, and the uncertainty about what was to follow, we shall hardly be surprised to discover a document aimed on every page at the reaffirmation and validation of the faith of Judaism as the rabbis had framed it. In an age of deep self-doubt, the Yerushalmi's framers spoke confidently about the basis, in revelation accurately transmitted and logically understood, of Israel's true salvation through the Torah as the rabbi represented it. That is the meaning of the Yerushalmi's Judaism, deriving from its context, the traits of its text, and its larger matrix.

It seems to me, then, that these are the primary, the absolutely basic, steps toward the natural history of the genus of Judaism of which the Yerushalmi constitutes a principal species. By specifying what I find to be the distinctive attributes of this particular text, I say how the specimen differs from others, how it is to be defined against its context, treated in Chapter 1. By then making explicit what I believe to be the hallmarks of the text (Part Two) and the shared or complementary traits of this text within its larger context (Part

Three), I place the specimen into relationship with others of the same classification. That is the entire program of this book.

Before proceeding to explain the way in which the book presents the data, let me revert to Smith's statement, which I mean to illustrate and advance in this study. In response to the proposal to "situate a text within a 'family of resemblances'" and to clarify the complexity and limits of this "family" by examining a specific document, I propose to situate the Yerushalmi in its larger setting within the vast corpus of rabbinic writings of late antiquity. Thus, I ask first about the limits of the text by comparing it to the one that precedes and generates it, that is, by relating the Yerushalmi to the Mishnah, upon whose framework the Yerushalmi is constructed. That effort to examine a specific document leads me next to address the family of resemblances between this document and others of its larger classification, that is, the ways in which the Yerushalmi is a specimen of Judaism. These at the foundations seem to me two: first, social, second, theological. The former inquiry leads us forthwith to the social expression of the document, the things it claims about its own political and societal context, purpose, range of power and influence (Chapter 4). The latter draws us to the purpose and goal of the document, evidence of why people want to do things in just this way and not some other, make these particular statements and not other statements (Chapter 5). To define that purpose and goal, I simply ask how the document tells us its own purpose and goal, the sanction and, especially, salvation. What will happen if everything demanded in the text is adopted and realized in context (Chapter 5)? The four studies, of Chapters 2 through 5, therefore, are meant, in Smith's language, "to clarify the complexity and limits" of a "family of resemblances" by examining a specific document. As is clear, Chapter 1 describes, to begin with, the natural habitat of the speciman at hand—the temperature of the seas around the Galapagos, the fauna and flora of the islands.

In all, therefore, I continue a labor of classification, a taxonomic enterprise directed toward the formation of a "natural history" of Judaism. Such a work, when it has advanced, should contribute to the science of religion, though in itself it cannot yet be called part of a science of religion in general, only a prior labor in the history of a particular religion. I do not see how Judaism can take its rightful place within the science of religion until its natural history has been outlined and the issues attendant upon the classification of its data been addressed and partially settled. What this task of classification involves, finally, is defined by Jonathan Z. Smith (p. ix, n. 2): "Classification . . . is a polythetic grouping or clustering procedure which requires temporal specificity." That simple sentence amply defines the work at hand.

The way in which I carry out the work through this book is now easily understood. I quote an immense volume of sources (in my own translations).

A visit to any museum of natural history will provide an ample understanding of why I cite one specimen after another, patiently working my way through the principal categories and problems of classification by extensive presentation of the stories and sayings that, all together, constitute the corpus of data. While the book presents a thesis and an argument, the principal work of the book was to figure out what to select and lay out for the full articulation of the thesis and statement of the argument. At first, I considered simply alluding to sources, rather than citing them as fully as I do. I rejected that option because it would not materially advance the work of detailed classification but only hinder it. Since one fundamental claim of this book is that the Talmud speaks in a single, uniform voice, a vast repertoire of extracts, not merely allusions, was necessary. Since, moreover, I claim to provide an account of the Judaism of the Yerushalmi, it seemed to me necessary that the data of that Judaism be made conveniently accessible to readers. Who beside me is going to wade through thirty-four volumes of translation? Since these will appear in stately procession, a few a year from now to nearly the end of the century, were I not to give ample extracts, people would have to wait for close to two decades to check whatever references I might give, or, if they knew Hebrew and Aramaic, to make sense of what I do with a given passage. Accordingly, the only suitable way is the one I take.

This is the right way, moreover, for a substantive reason. Every item is meant to exemplify; none is a singleton. I make no effort to catalogue all passages that say the same thing. My model is the great naturalist, Charles Darwin, who took samples from Galapagos, but did not take home with him every turtle he ever saw. People back in Cambridge had to believe only that in his account he described something more than a species consisting of a single turtle, that each specimen represented a species. My exhibition in this book therefore is in the model of a museum of natural history, which lays forth a range of examples of a given type of species, each instance available for contrast and comparison with the others.

I give two or at most three examples of each "species." Perhaps one would have sufficed, and if the reader finds the extracts uncommonly tedious, skipping the second or third instance of essentially the same thing will do no material damage to the larger understanding of the book. But I do have to establish among a variety of instances, drawn from diverse tractates (different islands of the archipelago, if we may return to Darwin's Galapagos), the claim to lay out a true species of a still larger genus. One item may be idiosyncratic; three are apt not to be. Still, I cannot claim to be certain that every extract is equally necessary, and if I have erred, it is on the side of giving too many. At a few points I have cited a paragraph or two of the writings of other scholars (Morton Smith, Michael Avi-Yonah, Peter Brown), rather than paraphrasing them. I always prefer to rely upon others to express their own ideas in their own way, particularly when I claim no competence in the fields about which they expertly speak. No paraphrase can do justice to Smith and Brown in any case. Here too I beg the reader's indulgence, and I hope the work is engaging and not tedious.

My fundamental taxa governed the selection of specimens. As I explained, these are (1) the time and circumstance; (2) traits of the evidence as a whole; (3) the principal social form exhibited by the document; and (4) the primary appeal, the sanction and teleology, of the document's system as a whole. This refers to what makes the Yerushalmi's Judaism work, what its system works to accomplish. So this natural history consists of an account of text and context: the turtles and the seas in which they swim. True, I knew what I wanted to know before I opened my volumes of translation and went in search of data. My classificatory scheme was in mind. But I did not pretend to know what I should find out, in answer to my four questions for the Yerushalmi. So I admit that the reader may find it difficult to muster adequate patience for the long sequence of sayings and stories which comprise half of the book. But these are the data of the Judaism at hand. To be sure, being not only a historian of religions but also a Talmudist, I cherish them all. But my claim in behalf of each is that it is typical and thus suggestive beyond itself. So none is to be skipped. All are to be seen as I have chosen and arranged them, to form a totality, a statement and a message.

Since the claim of this book is to describe the world view of the framers of the Yerushalmi in particular—that is, authorities who flourished in the later part of the fourth century and perhaps the earliest decades of the fifth—the reader must ask why I have sidestepped pressing questions of history. Specifically, I have not worked out a system for assessing whether a saying in the name of an earlier figure informs us about ideas held, or conditions prevailing, in the time of that figure, prior to the age of redaction itself, circa A.D. 350–400. The reason is that I could find no suitable system for demonstrating that something assigned to an authority assumed to have lived in the third or earlier part of the fourth century actually was said by that authority, or at the very least in the time when that authority flourished. Because of the character of the Rabbinical movement, moreover, were I to solve the problem of assessing the historical work of the document for the periods prior to its closure, I should not gain very much for the labor of the history of Judaism. Let me spell out why the difficulties seem formidable, and the potential success in overcoming them of somewhat limited consequence.

When I took up the study of the Mishnah, I found it possible to trace the history of some of the ideas of the Mishnah back from the point of its closure about A.D. 200 to their starting point nearly two centuries before. Accordingly, for the Mishnah's system of Judaism, it was possible to relate some sizable part of the end product to conditions prevailing prior to the formation and redaction of that end product. Specifically, I claimed to relate some of the Mishnah's laws and ideas to the period before the destruction of the

Temple in A.D. 70, some to the period between that event and the Bar Kokhba War three generations later, and, finally, some from the end of that war to the completion of the Mishnah itself. The reason is that the Mishnah is so arranged as to make possible the study of sequences of ideas. The tractates are internally cogent and carefully laid out. There is little overlap among them.

The Yerushalmi's layout is quite different, because it is suspended from various particles of the Mishnah, having no inner coherence whatsoever. It is exceedingly difficult systematically and comprehensively to demonstrate that any statements in the names of the authorities of the Yerushalmi testify to conditions prior to the point of closure of the document as a whole. While a few initiatives, not yet attempted, seem promising, the encompassing and systematic work done on the Mishnah—I stress, possibly because of the very character of the Mishnah—as yet has not been attempted on the Yerushalmi.

Furthermore, I do not regard the labor as promising. Should the work flourish and we discover ways of determining which attributions are more, and which less, reliable, our gain would be minimal. So much of the Yerushalmi—I estimate 90% in volume—consists of close exegesis of the Mishnah itself that the bulk of the result, for the history of the ideas of Judaism, would be of only modest interest. That is, I cannot think why it matters to know much about the sequential unfolding—the "history"—of the exegesis of the various discrete passages of the Mishnah, unless we are able to determine, also, that factors quite remote from the inner tensions and logic of the passages of the Mishnah themselves come into play. If I am able to relate Mishnah exegesis to the circumstance in which the exegesis is carried out, then the work may prove suggestive beyond itself. If not, the work seems to me arid and merely academic.

I dwell on this matter, because my negative judgment determined my strategy for this picture of the Yerushalmi's Judaism, so different from the one followed to gain a picture of the Mishnah's Judaism. Accordingly, the character of the evidence has to be made clear. The Talmud of the Land of Israel consists of passages of the Mishnah, each followed by two or more units of discourse (complete and cogent discussions of a single theme or problem) generally pertinent to that passage. These units of discourse had taken shape prior to their construction as the Talmud as we know it. The work of closure and redaction was separate from the work of formulation of the several units of discourse. The units themselves, moreover, normally are made up of a conglomerate of materials. These originated in diverse ways, in that various names are associated with the sayings at hand.

The unsolved problem, as I said, is how to come to an assessment of the ways in which the components of the Talmud of the Land of Israel may serve to describe the period from the closure of the Mishnah, in circa A.D. 200, prior to the age of the conclusion of the Talmud, in circa 350–400 (or 425). So the particular problem at hand is to find out how, if at all, we may learn from the Talmud about the period from A.D. 200 to 350. The evidence awaiting analysis has to be specified. Specifically, what basis do we have to suppose that anything in the Talmud Yerushalmi testifies to the state of affairs prior to redaction? The answer is simple. Numerous sayings in the Talmud come with the names of sages alleged to have composed those sayings, or to endorse the views contained in them. There are, moreover, numerous allusions, throughout the Talmud, to what various named authorities said and did. It would be difficult to point to more than a handful of units of discourse in the entire Talmud in which we do not find names of sages who are assumed to have flourished between the time of the closure of the Mishnah and that of the conclusion of the Talmud. These clearly are supposed to attest to the existence and authority of the materials in which the names occur, especially where what is attributed to a given sage takes account of completed discourse and comments upon it. So the question of treating the Talmud as a corpus of information on a period prior to that of its closure turns upon the simple fact that most of the units of discourse are assigned to specific named authorities. Without those names nothing is possible.

But what do we do with the names? Short of simply accepting the accuracy of these attributions and so assuming that if the Talmud says Rabbi X made a statement, he really did make it, we must construct a mode of evaluating the data provided by the available names and sayings. First, are there truly reliable ways by which we may test the assertion that a given saying really was said by the authority to whom it is assigned? The answer is that there surely are, but we simply do not have them. If we had not only the Talmud, with its third-person references to rabbis, but also writings, compiled and preserved by a given rabbi in his own hand or among his own disciples, we might then test the allegations of the Talmud. We should know how to sort out valid from pseudepigraphic attributions, verifying the one, falsifying the other. But the only evidence we have about the rabbis of the Talmud—a collective, anonymous document—is what the Talmud itself tells us. There is nothing personal; there is nothing outside of the document itself. Accordingly, we have no way whatsoever of investigating whether a given rabbi really said what was attributed to him.

If we do not know whether a rabbi really said what is ascribed to him, then what do we learn from the fact that a name of someone assumed to have flourished at a certain time is attached to a specific saying or story? It is the indisputable, but paltry, fact that someone, sometime after that named authority, assumed and persuaded others to believe that the named rabbi had said or done what the later sage alleged. On the face of it, then, we may state the Talmud's historical claim very simply. It is one of authority and tradition. If we have a saying that Rabbi X said or did something, then someone, sometime after the moment, alleged that that had happened. Unless we accept the authority of tradition, we can never assess the facts of the matter. We do have in hand the fact that someone believed and transmitted as authoritative the stated assertion as to the facts of the matter. This historical claim is somewhat different from the one we have set aside. That is, we do not know that Rabbi X said or did what is alleged, but we do know that someone at some point thereafter—a day? a century?—believed that he had said or done it.

The criteria, suited to internal evidence, by which we may test the historical allegations—that is to say, the claim that we may differentiate among sayings and assign some to an earlier, others to a later, period—have now to be specified. What criteria can I suggest?

1. *Adherence to intelligible criteria, consistently revealed.* In evaluating the policies behind the assignment of sayings to a given name, the first question must be whether the practice is consistent or capricious. If we are able to show that a coherent set of principles is associated with a given name, then we can claim to validate or falsify the attribution, to that name, of opinions on diverse subjects pertinent to a single principle. On that basis, we may show that a given saying either is, or is not, consistent with other ones in that same name. The upshot is the possibility of demonstrating that an intelligible and coherent set of reasons stands behind the use of names for the differentiation of sayings. But this need not be based on interest in historical accuracy, since at issue is authority behind a given opinion, a judgment wholly *post facto*.

2. *Progression of principles from simpler and more fundamental to more complex and derivative, parallel with succession of authorities from an earlier to a later generation.* Alongside the issue of consistency of the ascription to a given name comes a second consideration. If what is assigned to an early authority takes for granted issues or facts otherwise attested only in the name of later authorities, then on the face of it the ascription in the former instance is dubious. Since we cannot suppose we are dealing with prophets, we have to suppose that what is attributed to an earlier authority, incomprehensible except in light of what is otherwise known only to later authorities, is in fact pseudepigraphic. Here too there is the possibility, then, of verifying or falsifying attributions. In this case we do have some measure of hope to determine what comes earlier and what later in the formation of units of discourse or of ideas in their successive layers.

If these two criteria were to be systematically applied, we should have some slight basis on which to estimate how the Talmud may serve for historical purposes for the period prior to redaction. That is to say, we might interpret the implications of the Talmud's consistency of ascriptions to a given authority, of the movement of discourse from primitive to developed in close tandem with the movement of the period of the sages to whom discourse is assigned from earlier to later times. On this basis a history of the ideas of the document might come into view. But just what sort of ideas might then be shown to have a history? As I said at the outset, since the bulk of the document provides *ad hoc* and episodic observations about the meaning of a brief passage of the Mishnah, the upshot would be tiny histories indeed, sherds and remnants of thousands of jugs from how many potteries we do not know. I am not sure the result would be worth the effort.

No one would maintain that the work of analysis of the literary and conceptual traits of the document, leading to a picture of which passages come first and which come later, is without promise. On the contrary, a more sophisticated grasp of how the document came into being and the relationship between what people really said and did and what the Talmud's framers claim they said and did would open many paths of inquiry and interpretation. But, as always, the best is the enemy of the good. Just as I have provided a preliminary translation of the Talmud of the Land of Israel, all the while pointing to the many passages requiring much more work, so I here offer the first account of the Judaism to which the Talmud of the Land of Israel provides testimony. The value of the work will be measured by its early obsolescence, as further progress unfolds along the lines I here try to lay forth. Here, in my book, the systematic and encompassing descriptive and analytical work begins. More than that I need not claim.

The upshot is that, since we speak of a document universally assumed to have come to closure in the last part of the fourth century, we study the Judaism of the Land of Israel of that age. We cannot show, so we do not know, whether or not the document tells us about its form of Judaism prior to that time. Accordingly, we must find pleasure in what we can do, even while acknowledging what we cannot yet achieve.

To conclude: My purpose is to offer a set of generalizations about the definitive religious traits of the Yerushalmi's structure of Judaism, seen as a whole, just as in the companion volume, *The Talmud of the Land of Israel,* volume 35, I have tried to give a few fundamental generalizations about the literary-exegetical traits of the Yerushalmi, viewed as a complete document. These two books, parallel in their way to my *History of the Mishnaic Law of Purities* (vol. 21, *The Redaction and Formulation of the Order of Purities in Mishnah and Tosefta,* and vol. 22, *The Mishnaic System of Uncleanness*), are meant to open many paths, but to close only one. It is no longer possible to take the view that the Yerushalmi is simply a potpourri of this-and-that, sentences but not paragraphs, paragraphs but not chapters, random thoughts but not a system. The very exercise of generalization proves that, in Mishnah and Yerushalmi alike, we possess not merely anthologies of information but, rather, immense achievements of soaring intellect and imagination; whole systems exhibiting structure, order, and sense; applied and practical reason to sanctify Israel in a world of salvation without end.

Part One

Context

1

The Yerushalmi's Judaism in Its Late Antique Setting

The Land of Israel within the Roman Empire

The Talmud stresses the themes of certainty, consensus, and authority. These points of insistence also express a general concern to overcome doubt, confusion, diversity, and civil chaos. When we look up from the Talmud's pages to the time and place in which they were written, we should not be surprised to discover that at the same time—the later fourth century—the world was emerging from an age of disorder. After a half-century of disaster, the old order had given way to a new one. A very brief account of the principal historical traits of the third and fourth centuries allows us to form a picture of the Talmud in its world.

To state matters simply, the third century produced collapse, the fourth century, reconstruction. In the third century the old order crumbled. In the fourth, the rubble of the classical age was reshaped into the foundations of the medieval world. The world of circa A.D. 200 stood continuous with a long and stable past. The age of circa A.D. 400 looked forward to a long and continuous future, with institutions stretching onward to Europe and the Middle Ages. The Eastern empire was so strongly founded that it endured for another thousand years. But in-between, behind, and near at hand, in the interim, one could see only the abyss—a lost past, an uncertain future, a difficult present.

What had happened, in brief summary, was that, at the beginning of the third century, the centuries-old principate, under which the Roman empire had flourished, came to an end. For two-and-a-half centuries, the Augustan political structure had sustained a vast empire with peace and consequent prosperity. From 235 to 285, by contrast, the government fell apart in civil wars. From the murder of Alexander Severus in 235 to the victory of Diocletian in 284 (Smith, p. 185), there was anarchy. The twenty years of peace provided by Diocletian from 285 to 305 were followed by further civil war. It was Constantine who in the earlier fourth century reunited the empire and reestablished government. The causes of the century of collapse and ruin need not detain us. What is important to know is that, for the world at large, the fourth century proved a time of reordering and reconstruction of stability. Establishing his capital in the East, at Byzantium, Constantine rebuilt a sizable administration, capable of raising money to pay for an army and bureaucracy.

Let us proceed to somewhat more detail. The frontiers of the Roman Empire cracked open in the middle of the third century, admitting armies of marauders east, north, and west. The task of the later third- and fourth-century emperors, east and west, then was to stem the tide, reconstruct a defensible border, and reestablish effective government over vast territories. This they did in ample measure in the east. Accordingly, the history of the Land of Israel as part of the Roman Empire of the third and fourth centuries is the story of crisis and remission, calamitous collapse, and painful reconstruction. When the Empire suffered assault on all fronts, a long sequence of hapless emperors proved unable to protect the homeland and defend the frontiers. The Empire was saved, toward the second half of the third century, by a military revolution (Brown, *World,* p. 24), which reorganized the Roman army and prepared it for the more flexible "defense in depth against barbarian raiders" (Brown, *World,* p. 24) that was now required. The military revolution threw back the barbarians everywhere: In Yugoslavia and northern Italy in 258 and 268, at the Danube in 269, in the eastern provinces in 273, and on the Iranian front in 296 (Brown, *World,* p. 25). The army then produced talent required to reorganize the government itself. Sons of freedmen, cattle herders and pig farmers in the countryside rose to power and reestablished the Empire that the old aristocracy had been unable to save. An aristocracy of service, in the time of Constantine from 324 to 337, completed the restoration of the civil service and bureaucracy, so government once more became possible (Brown, *World,* p. 27).

All of this manifest history happened at the surface of the world. Underneath, the old and established order continued its slow and majestic progress. The latent or subterranean history, to a corner of which the Talmud testifies, was considerably less dramatic but no less important. Great landowners, the educated upper classes of the towns and countryside, retained their estates and long-term power (Brown, *World,* p. 29). In these classes there was a systematic exercise of nostalgia as various groups sought to regain roots in the past, patronized scholars, restudied the classics. As Brown puts it (*World,* p. 21): "As the Mediterranean receded, so a more ancient world came to light. Craftsmen in Britain returned to the art forms of the *La Tène* age. The serf of late Roman Gaul reemerged with his Celtic name, the *vassus.* The arbiters of piety of the Roman world, the Coptic hermits of Egypt, revived the language of the Pharaohs; and the hymn writers of Syria heaped on Christ appellations of Divine Kingship that reach back to Sumerian times." In this context, the reversion of the heirs of the Mishnah to the ancient Scriptures in their search for authority forms part of a larger movement back to roots and tradition rediscovered and invented at one and the same time.

In 312 Constantine achieved power in the West, and in 323 he took the government of the entire Roman Empire into his own hands (Lot, p. 26). In 313 he promulgated the edict of Milan, in which Christianity attained the status of toleration. Christians and all others were given "the free power to follow the religion of their choice." Constantine himself became a Christian sometime thereafter. In the next decade Christianity became the most favored religion. Converts from Judaism were protected and could not be punished by Jews. Christians were freed of the obligation to perform pagan sacrifices. Priests were exempted from certain taxes. Sunday became an obligatory day of rest. Celibacy was permitted. From 324 onward Constantine ceased to maintain a formal impartiality, now intervening in the affairs of the Church, settling quarrels among believers, and calling the Church Council at Nicaea (325) to settle issues of the faith. He was baptized only on the eve of his death in 337. From the viewpoint of the affairs of the East, his most important act was the founding of Constantinople, the second Rome, destined to become the guardian of classical civilization for a thousand years. Reaching his decision in 324, Constantine had the notion of turning ancient Byzantium into a city that was wholly Christian (Lot, p. 37). The city was inaugurated in 330 and became the effective capital of the East. Over the next century the pagan cults were destroyed, their priests deprived of support, their intellectuals bereft of standing. The issues of the day were to be debated within the agenda of Christianity; the goal of the day was to attain orthodoxy. Harmony was to be attained by "authority, through a long series of acts of force" (Lot, p. 42). In consequence, Lot says (p. 42):

> . . . individuals and countries which refused to adopt this or that creed were bound to resist not merely the spiritual authority of a particular bishop or Council, but the Emperor who made the creed his own, and desired to impose it on all. Political rebellion was the inevitable consequence of religious opposition.

In the time of Constantine, the result of the engagement of the state, through the emperor, in affairs of the Church, first became clear in the protracted Athanasian-Arian controversy. In the end, the Church changed in character, becoming all-powerful even within the lifetimes of men who had faced persecution and death in its cause. Unprepared for a role in civil and political life, Christianity had promised a kingdom of Heaven, but gained its realm in the here and now. Using the state to fight its enemies, it became subservient to the state as well (Lot, p. 50). So Constantine first legitimated, then adopted Christianity. He began by bringing to an end the intense persecution undertaken in 303 by Diocletian, rescinding his decree in the West in 306, and arranging the toleration of all religions in 312. He ended up by seizing the property of pagan temples and endowing Christian churches, lavishing upon the clergy valuable rights as well.

The character and position of Christianity in the fourth-century empire are described by Smith (pp. 194–195).

> The bishops' powers were increased by increase of the funds they controlled. Civil and criminal law was also revised in Christian interest and more or less according to Christian standards. Sunday was made a holiday as "the day of the sun," so pagans as well as Christians would observe. Celibates were permitted to inherit property. Divorce was made more difficult (for women, almost impossible), concubinage and pederasty outlawed, illegitimacy penalized. Gladiatorial games were prohibited— though they continued in the west until the beginning of the fifth century. Beside expropriation of the lands and treasures of pagan temples, animal sacrifice was prohibited, but this prohibition, too, remained a dead letter. A few temples were destroyed. Obstacles were put in the way of conversion to Judaism. Finally Christians were favored in appointments, benefaction, petitions, and appeals. The upper administration became largely Christian. Christianity was not merely the cult of a new god (or gods—the Christians were not clear on this point). It was an *organized* cult in a way that none of the pagan cults had been. It was also an *intolerant* cult, not only intolerant of those who worshiped other gods without the state's permission (this paganism had often been), but intolerant, by inheritance from Deuteronomy, of anyone who worshiped any other god at all, and thence, by theological extension, of anyone who practiced Christianity "incorrectly." These two characteristics were complementary: the intolerance had done much to build up the organization; the organization made the intolerance effective . . . . Now, for the first time, there were two great powers within the empire—state and church. No longer were priests civil officials in charge of religious affairs, as they had been by Greco-Roman tradition. They now belonged to an organization essentially different from the civil government, one claiming a different (and higher) authorization. The bishops were happy to accept Constantine's patronage and willing, in return, to follow his directives. They would also use their influence in the service of the state—with the fourth century begins their condemnation of Christians who refuse to perform military service. But they did not become members of the imperial council, nor did they normally invite imperial officers to participate in their councils. From now on, these two organizations, civil and ecclesiastical, were to live side by side, through conflicts and alliances.

We see, then, that the fourth century was "the age of the restoration." Even coins called it by that name: *Reparatio Saeculi* (Brown, *World*, p. 34). It was a time, described by Brown (*World*, p. 34), as "the background of a rich and surprisingly resilient society, that had reached a balance and attained a structure significantly different from the classical Roman period." The age was marked by a widening gulf between rich and poor and by confiscatory taxes (a third of a farmer's gross produce), inflexibly applied and ill distributed. A further trait was intense provinciality. Leaders came out of their own society and stayed there. Officials governed provinces in which they owned large tracts of land (Brown, *World,* p. 36). Ruling groups therefore knew their territories well and could govern effectively, as in the case of the Jewish patriarchs of the Holy Land. The great man—the patron or boss—interceded for his clients but also told them what to do. At the end we shall see how the rabbi emerged out of the same mold. Smith describes the political and administrative reforms of the fourth century in the following way (Smith, p. 192):

> The nature of the new government was reflected in the new titles, trappings, and rituals of the court. These, like the government, had their beginnings in earlier periods, but only now were developed consistently. Everything that had to do with the emperor become "sacred": he no longer wore the old Roman toga, but a purple triumphal robe, embroidered with gold and jewels, and a diadem, symbol of hellenistic kingship, studded with pearls or with the rays of the sun god; he was surrounded always by a military escort; his ministers and officials customarily wore military uniform; he was hailed as "King" and "Autocrat."

Brown for his part lays emphasis on personalization of politics led at the top to the elevation of the person of the emperor (*World,* p. 42). Loyalty was to persons, not to institutions, especially in the East. The shift from Temple to rabbi as the focus of piety epitomizes this same phenomenon.

From politics, we turn to social questions. The crisis of the third century had destabilized society. Unsettled conditions created opportunities for change, both downward and upward. Hereditary positions in life no longer seemed necessary (Jones in Momigliano, p. 34). The anarchy led to war, famine, plague, and so to the decline of population. There was a manpower shortage. The movement of population made possible by the need for labor threatened collection of poll taxes and land taxes, as people moved about and land fell fallow (Jones in Momigliano, p. 35). The response of the state now, in the fourth century, was to propose to maintain a caste system, in which a person's station in society was made both permanent and hereditary. As Lot says (p. 100), "It was a state of siege, for life or perpetuity." The most striking expression of this caste system was in the creation of the colonate, that is, a huge group of people tied to the estate on which they were born as serfs. These were farm workers for life, bound to remain on the soil. So a sizable portion of the population was tied to the land and not free to leave it. The serf possessed the land only as he was possessed by it; the landowner or landlord collected the dues, the tenant performed fixed and defined duties. The *colonus* was free to marry, make a will, engage in disputes about his tenure, so he was not a slave. But he was tied through his property to his lord or patron. The class of free farmers, who rented land on a short lease for money, disappeared. Estates were then divided by the landowners among their clients or *colonists.* This system extended upward into a hierarchy of functions, with each one required not only to continue in his occupation but also to pass it on to his children.

If the third century marks the end of the old and the fourth the beginning of the new in politics and religion, the third century itself had prepared the way for economic patterns well established by the earliest Middle Ages. The most important events were the movement of the economy from money to barter, with debasement of the coinage, and the chaos of prices in the long period of political instability. A domestic economy, in which, as Lot says, "exchange values exist[ed] hardly or not at all," was established in which estates attained self-sufficiency for families and their dependents. The "household" and "householder" to which Talmudic law refers represent such estates. Products in kind were the medium of exchange, including payment of taxes. In the Greek east, nearly eight hundred years of a monetary economy thus drew to a close, and the feudal system dawned. Lot cites the judgment of Albert de Broglie (p. 85):

> In the fourth century, Rome could neither feed her citizens, provide for the upkeep of her administration, nor pay her troops; every year her peoples were becoming more impoverished, and her burdens heavier, while at the same time her forces were becoming less.

To conclude: For nearly everyone in the Roman world the most important event of the period in which the Talmud of the Land of Israel was coming into being was the legalization of Christianity in the aftermath of ferocious persecutions, followed very rapidly by the adoption of Christianity as the state's most favored religion. The astonishing advent of legitimacy and even power provoked the rewriting of Christian and world history and the working out of theology as reflection on this new polity and its meaning in the unfolding of human history. A new commonwealth came into being (Jones in Momigliano, p. 6), taking over the old and reshaping it for the new age. The Church at just this time emerged as an organization competing with the state (*ibid.*, p. 9) and attracted some of the aristocracy and some remarkably creative intellectuals—Ambrose, Jerome, Hilary of Poitiers, Augustine in the West, Athanasius, John Chrysostom, Gregory of Nazianzus, Basil of Caesarea, in the East (*ibid.*, p. 9). On them, Momigliano comments, "They combined Christian theology with pagan philosophy, worldly political abilities with a secure faith in immortal values. They could tell both the learned and the unlearned how they should behave, and consequently transformed both the external features and the inner meaning of the daily existence of an increasing number of people." So too did the rabbis of our Talmud and the Babylonian Talmud. By the end of the fourth century, with Theodosius' law of A.D. 392, the practice of paganism had been outlawed. The great city, Rome, fell to barbarians in 410. There never was a more momentous century in the history of the West. On all of these immense events, the Talmud of the Land of Israel, a document of the very same years, maintains perfect silence.

The Jewish Nation in Its Land

Let us begin our brief survey of the Talmud's setting in the history of the Jews in their own country with the geographical question: What, exactly, was the Land of Israel? Everyone knew where *Palestine* was, for the frontiers of the province enjoyed clear demarcation at all points in the history of the third and fourth centuries. But what Jews, or rabbis in the Talmud in particular, meant when they spoke about "the Land of Israel" was hardly self-evident. Indeed, in the end "the Land of Israel" must be seen as a state of mind, rather than a political and territorial entity. For defining the geographical context of the Talmud of the Land of Israel is less simple than would appear at the surface. Jews lived side by side with gentiles. Only a few towns, such as Beth Shearim, Lud, Sepphoris, and Tiberias, appear to have been inhabited mainly by Jews. But there were "Aramaeans" (that is, "others") in those towns too. Important cities, such as Caesarea and Acre (Akko), as well as towns throughout the area supposed to be Israel's land in particular, possessed gentile majorities. For purposes of assessing cultic cleanness, that is, designating properties deemed to fall within the holy land and so to be cultically pure, as distinct from properties deemed to lie outside of it and so to be unclean by reason of corpse-uncleanness, the rabbis knew very precisely the borders of the land. But these were imaginary. They bore slight consequence to Jews except for priests, who alone were eager to maintain cultic purity as much as possible.

For political purposes, therefore, it is difficult to say there actually was a "Land of Israel." In the period of which we speak, Jews lived in and under multiple polities, of which their own ethnarch, the patriarch, was only one. (As we shall see later on, this ethnarch, called *nasi*, patriarch, ruled the Jews of the Land of Israel from the second century until the beginning of the fifth. The rabbis served as his clerks and bureaucrats, and the Mishnah was his constitution and code.) Accordingly, a map of Jewish settlement in the territories imagined by our Talmud to constitute "the Land of Israel," marking each town with a color appropriate to its ethnic majority, would be speckled. The Jewish plots on the map would call to mind not the evenly spaced spots of a leopard nor the stripes of a zebra but the blotches of the springer spaniel. Some heavy concentrations were in Galilee, on the one side, and in the region called "the South," around present-day Lod, on the other.

Such was the Land of Israel as a geographical and political realm. Accordingly, the geographical definition no more corresponded to concrete reality than did the political one. The "Land" was nowhere in particular, rather it was scattered about in general; there was no Jewish sovereignty in one contiguous area, but much authority here and there. No wonder that the Talmud's rabbis, like others in the Jewish world, in dealing with obedience to the law of the supernatural Torah, laid so much emphasis on inwardly accepting, in the heart, the outer yoke of the commandments and the yoke of the kingdom of Heaven. When the rabbis described the inner, imaginary state of Israel, they merely repeated the traits of the outer state of the nation: sovereignty based upon an act of supreme will, overcoming the facts of geography and politics alike.

Yet these imagined facts indeed corresponded to the realities of power, which tended to favor the local over the regional, let alone the imperial authority. On the one side, it was difficult to move troops about, except by having them walk from place to place. Accordingly, it was easy to build a large state, since little ones could not very easily cooperate to defend themselves. But the superstates, once formed, found it difficult to control their components (Smith, p. 230). Smith states (p. 321), "Imperial organization was balanced by the intense parochialism of the city-states. Even the power of Rome occasionally failed to prevent the cities of Asia Minor and Syria from going to war with their next door neighbors . . . . Thus unification without uniformity . . . resulted from lack of transportation." What this meant is that the inner discipline exerted by people who believed in a law in common proved more effective in establishing a uniform policy then the formal discipline of contiguous territory or autochthonous government and army alike. So Israel the nation existed in the mind and soul of the Jewish people, with the consequence that the Land of Israel as an entity took on substance and meaning otherwise called into doubt or denied by the ordinary facts of life.

A continuous survey, year by year, of the history of the Jews in the Land of Israel is neither necessary nor possible, because our principal document, the Talmud of the Land of Israel, is essentially ahistorical. Such tales and fables as it does tell us are disconnected, notoriously difficult to interpret as accounts of things that really happened on some one day. In any event they always are reshaped for the didactic or theological purposes of the storyteller. On the basis of independent evidence, not a single one of them can be verified or falsified as to the main point they choose to relate or the dramatic narrative they claim to provide. Using the Talmud in order to discover manifest history—what was really happening to the Jews of the Land from one period to the next—is not possible. The Talmud's information is of another order entirely.

The indifference of the framers of the Talmud to events that strike us as important is easy to prove. As I said just now, to take a single stunning example, the conversion of Constantine to Christianity must be regarded, as Lot says (p. 39), as "the most important fact in the history of the Mediterranean world between the establishment of the hegemony of Rome and the setting up of Islam." The Talmud nowhere refers to that event, scarcely gives testimony to its consequences for the Jews, and continues to harp upon prohibited relationships with "pagans" in general, as though nothing had changed from the third century to the fourth.

The Talmud not only fails to provide any sort of continuous narrative history of the Jews of whom it speaks. It does not even tell us about important events, of which its framers surely were informed. For example, as we shall note in a moment, some maintain that there was a sizable rebellion in Galilee under Gallus in 352 (Jones, p. 342). While there are some references here and there that may be associated with that rebellion, we have no more of a sustained account of that event than we do, in the same document, of any other political or military happening. We know as fact that certain laws were enacted to restrict Jews' activities. As we shall note below, Theodosius I prohibited marriage between Jews and Christians. Laws from Constantine's time onward forbade Jews to circumcise slaves, to buy Christian slaves, or to own Christian slaves (Jones, p. 342). There is no record of such laws in the Talmud, nor any hint that they had any impact upon the Jews. In the early fifth century, at which time the Talmud was drawing to a close, Jews were excluded from the civil service. No word of the matter finds it way into the discourse of our document. On the other hand, Jews enjoyed the right to practice their religion and live under their law. Synagogues could not be used for billets for soldiers; Jewish clergy were exempt from curial duties. Jews could not be served a summons on the Sabbath. Jewish clergy ruled affairs among Jews (Jones, p. 342), as bishops did among Christians. The Talmud takes for granted that a state of affairs allowing Jewish religious and limited political freedom did prevail. But at no passage can we find evidence of how the system really worked, nor do we find concrete evidence that the framers of the Talmud knew, or cared to know, details of the imperial system, or systematically and routinely interacted with imperial authorities.

Yet in its way the Talmud's silence on what appear to us events of the first magnitude is hardly surprising. For so far as the Jews of the Land of Israel were concerned, not much changed at Milvian Bridge in 312, when Constantine conquered in the sign of Christ. Legal changes affecting the Jews under Constantine's rule were not substantial. Jews could not proselytize; they could not circumcise slaves when they bought them. As I said above, Jews could not punish other Jews who became Christians. Jews, finally, were required to serve on municipal councils wherever they lived, an onerous task involving responsibility for taxes. But those who served synagogues, patriarchs and priests, were exempted from civil and personal obligations (Avi-Yonah, p. 163).

In the reign of Constantius III (337–361), further laws aimed at separating Jews from Christians were enacted, in 339 in the Canons of Elvira (Avi-Yonah, pp. 174–175). These forbade intermarriage between Jews and Christians, further protected converts, and forbade Jews to hold slaves of Christian or other gentile origin. Avi-Yonah adds (p. 175):

> Another law of Constantius III, published in 353, prohibited the conversion of Christians to Judaism; the proselyte lost all his property. This

law was slightly less harsh than the former one as far as Jews were concerned; a pagan proselyte was not punished at all, whereas the earlier edict punished Christians and pagan proselytes alike.

The law forbidding Jews to assault a coreligionist who adopted Christianity is supposed to have come about because one of the members of the council of the patriarch at Tiberias, head of the Jewish community throughout the empire, was attacked when he became a Christian. This man, Joseph, was given the title of *comes* and a pension by Constantine. He founded churches at Sepphoris and Tiberias. The Jewish population of Galilee was unaffected (Jones, p. 47). This story, told by Epiphanius, is summarized by Avi-Yonah (pp. 167ff). It is an odd account, worth following, in Avi-Yonah's summary, at length:

> About the middle of the fourth century, in the reign of Constantius III (337–361), a young Christian priest, named Epiphanius, happened to pass Scythopolis (Beth Shean). This Epiphanius was of Jewish origin, and was born at Beth Zadok, in the vicinity at Eleutheropolis (Beth Gubrin). The city of Scythopolis was in these days almost wholly Arian, for this sect was then in favor at the imperial court. Epiphanius, who was himself a pillar of orthodoxy, found refuge in the house of an old man of seventy years or more, who lived isolated in the town because of his orthodox beliefs. In his house there lived also an Italian bishop who had been exiled to Scythopolis by order of the emperor.
>
> The owner of the house was called Joseph. He told Epiphanius the story of his life, mixing, as old people are wont, truth and fantasy. Joseph was originally one of the great men at the court of the patriarch at Tiberias. He acted as counsellor to the patriarch Hillel II and was a guardian of the minor, Judah IV. In Tiberias he read the Christian books kept in the patriarchal archives—undoubtedly because they could serve in disputes with the *Minim*. Later on Joseph learned that the name of Jesus had a magic influence and that it could be used for healing, especially in the cases of sickness of the soul. He thus became a believer in Christ. While on a mission in Cilicia on behalf of the patriarch his conversion became public. He was expelled from the Jewish community and took refuge at the court of the emperor Constantine. There he was honored with the title of *comes* ("companion of the emperor," Count). With imperial protection he returned to the Jewish cities in Galilee and began to build churches there. In Tiberias he used for this purpose the unfinished Hadrianeum; he built also at Sepphoris, and in the Judaeo-Christian centres Capernaum and Nazareth. His aim was to revive the almost defunct Judaeo-Christian communities in these places. The imperial favor and his official title protected Joseph against the attacks of the Jews, but he could not achieve his principal aim. In the end he left his residence at Tiberias and passed his last days at Scythopolis. There he lived alone, shunned by the local Christians. As most converts, Joseph wished to justify his change of faith. He therefore told Epiphanius that even the patriarch Hillel had on his

death-bed adopted Christianity. According to his story the local bishop had visited him in the disguise of a physician, and baptised him.

A more public event of the same period, Avi-Yonah maintains, was a Jewish revolt against Gallus Caesar. This uprising, he says, did not enjoy support from "the mainstream of the community" (p. 178). The revolt began in 351. It did not last long. The rebels seized the armory at Sepphoris and won some initial successes, taking Lud, in the South, and enjoying some support in Tiberias. The revolt, he says, was put down without much difficulty. But Lieberman, for his part, denies the authenticity of sources on a Jewish uprising in Palestine in 352 or 353 (p. 337). He observes that contemporary rabbinic writings know nothing of a supposed destruction of Sepphoris, Tiberias, and Lud, in which the rebellion was alleged to have taken hold. What happened, Lieberman maintains, is that the Jews of Sepphoris "raised (perhaps with the help of the Roman garrison itself) a certain Patricius to the royal power. This Patricius might have been a heathen Roman officer whom the Diocaesarean [Sepphorean] Jews preferred to the extremely cruel Gallus, who, like the emperor, was a devout Christian" (Lieberman, p. 340). All of this was insignificant. Lieberman concludes (p. 341), "The incident had no serious consequences for the community in general, because the majority of the Jews were not involved." Lieberman further states unequivocally (p. 342), "There is absolutely no direct reference in the entire rabbinic literature of the third and fourth centuries from which we might legitimately conclude that the Roman government deliberately persecuted the Jewish religion during this time." Constantius began to curtail certain Jewish rights, but Jews were not forced to transgress their laws; rabbinic literature, Lieberman adds, "does not refer to the limitations of Jewish rights imposed by the first two Christian emperors." Jews complained because of exploitation by tax collectors, who did not discriminate but seized what they could without regard to race or creed. Still, Lieberman's principal argument is the silence of sources that ordinarily preserve silence about events of this sort. Accordingly, I should not be so rapidly inclined to dismiss Avi-Yonah's picture.

The reversion, to paganism, of the emperor, Julian, about 360, involved a measure of favor to Jews and Judaism. He permitted the rebuilding of the Temple at Jerusalem, but died before much progress could be made (Avi Yonah, pp. 185–207; Bowersock, pp. 120–122). From the time of Julian, for nearly three quarters of a century, there was, in Avi-Yonah's words, "the great assault on the Jews and Judaism." But he observes that in the first part of this period, 363–383, no important changes affected the status of the Jews. From the accession of Theodosius II in 383 to the death of his son, Arcadius, in 408, there was an "energetic attack on Judaism by the leaders of the church, mainly through pressure on the imperial government. The government ceded here and there but did not cause serious injury to the

Jewish community as a whole or to Jews as individuals" (Avi-Yonah, p. 208). Only in the final period, from the accession of Theodosius II to the publication of his third Novella, 408–438, were Jews' rights both as individuals and in communities "seriously curtailed. The patriarchate was abolished" (*ibid.*). We shall return in the next unit to the pertinence of those facts to the document under study.

Theodosius I from 392 to 395 issued a number of laws protecting Jews. From 398 to 404, there were laws contradicting one another in policy, some confirming, some abrogating the same right. But from 404 onward, anti-Jewish laws tended to limit Jewish rights. The basic policy was to isolate Jews, prevent them from growing in numbers, lower their status, and suppress their instruments of self-government (Avi-Yonah, p. 213). Laws against intermarriage posed no problem to the Jews. The ones limiting proselytism and those protecting converts from Judaism, did not affect many people. But the edicts that reduced Jews to second-class citizenship did matter. They were not to hold public office, but had to sit on city councils responsible for the payment of taxes. Later, they were removed from the councils, though still obligated, of course, for taxes. Between 404 and 438 Jews were forbidden to hold offices in the civil service, represent cities, serve in the army or at the bar, and they ultimately were evicted from every public office. These were hardly of much practical importance (Avi-Yonah, p. 216).

In the earliest decade of the fifth century, however, Jewish self-governing communities retained their autonomy. Avi-Yonah (pp. 217–218) provides a convenient summary:

> The legal change as regards the communal autonomy occurred in 415. Till then the Roman government followed the traditional line of supporting the Jewish self-governing communities. In 392, while promulgating laws against the Jews in the matters of mixed marriages and proselytism, the emperors were still defending the Jewish courts instituted by the patriarch. They discouraged for instance appeals to the civic courts against excommunications pronounced by these courts. In 396 all intervention by strangers in Jewish markets which aimed at interference with the free movement of prices was forbidden. In 397 the community officials, who were under the authority of the patriarch, were freed from the *curiae*. If the patriarch dismissed them, they would lose the privilege; in this way the power and authority of the patriarch were much enhanced by the Roman government. In 398 a law was made which seemed *prima facie* to subject the Jews to the authority of the Roman court and their laws. In fact it left a loophole, in that it authorized the Jews to have recourse to courts of arbitration in civil matters. The rabbinical courts continued to act in the guise of arbitrators and the civil courts were instructed to carry out their decisions. In 412 the right of Jews not to appear before the civil courts on Sabbaths and Jewish holidays was confirmed. It seems that many Christians had great confidence in the uprightness of the rabbinical courts. They asked such courts to judge their cases, especially if the defendant was a Jew. In 415

this practice was forbidden. All cases between Christians and Jews were henceforward to be tried by the ordinary civil court. This was the first real infringement of Jewish judicial autonomy.

In 404 the privileges of the patriarchate were confirmed. A decade later, accused of building new synagogues, causing Christian slaves to be circumcised, and judging litigations of Christians, the patriarch was reprimanded by Theodosius and deprived of his status. Christian slaves were freed. New synagogues were destroyed (Avi-Yonah, pp. 227–228). When Gamaliel VI died, the patriarchate came to an end. In 429, the right to appoint Jewish communal officials was vested in two Sanhedrins, functioning in two of the three provinces into which Palestine was then divided: *Palaestina prima*, meaning Judaea and Samaria, the coastal plain, and the Peraea, east of the Jordan, and *Palaestina secunda*, meaning Galilee and the Decapolis. There was also *Palaestina salutaris* or *tertia*, the Negeb and southern Trans-Jordan (Avi-Yonah, p. 228), but Jews lived only in the first two. Tiberias remained the Jewish center for the entire country.

To conclude: the situation of the Jews (and Samaritans) in the Roman empire from its Christianization is summarized by Smith as follows:

> Judaism and Samaritanism. . . . They were protected by the tradition of Roman law, which authorized their practices. Also, the god they worshiped was recognized by the Christians as one of the "persons" of "the true God." Again, Paul had predicted that "Israel according to the flesh" would eventually be converted; this was part of God's plan; therefore some Jews (and Samaritans?) had to be kept on hand for conversion. Another factor may have been the separation of church from state. While persecuted, Christians had preached tolerance. Tertullian, a distinguished apologist, had insisted that the civil government had no right to compel belief. Christian emperors forgot this doctrine in dealing with pagans, Manichees, and heretics; but it may have influenced their treatment of Jews and Samaritans. At all events, both cults remained licit, but only for persons born of Jewish or Samaritan parents. Conversion to them was prohibited. Christian vandalism, moreover, went beyond the laws; destruction of synagogues followed destruction of temples. Early in the fifth century erection of new synagogues was prohibited; thereafter Jews and Samaritans, like pagans, were expelled step by step from civil service and army, from all public dignities, and from practice of law.

The Talmud in Its Age

A document so reticent about events in its own day clearly wishes to claim that it be read as if composed in a vacuum. That claim on the face of it has to be resisted. Merely because people pretend something has not happened, we cannot conclude that an otherwise well-attested event has not occurred.

Insistence that nothing has changed never changes the facts of the matter. All that happens is that that pretense becomes one of the facts. What we learn is about people unable to cope except through massive efforts at feigning indifference. So, paradoxically, we observe a profound response indeed. On the basis of the evidence of the Talmud, ample though it is, we could scarcely prove the existence either of the Roman empire or of Christianity. Accordingly, we may scarcely be guided by the insistence of the Talmud that it declare what does and does not demand attention. Part of the Talmud's powerful mode of coping with and shaping reality is that very insistence.

A brief account of the principal events of the later third and fourth centuries, as they affected the life of the Jews of the Land of Israel, must now lead to reflection upon the relationship between those events and the paramount points of emphasis of the Talmud of the Land of Israel. True, no one can claim that people made up the Talmud to deal with distant happenings, however crucial such happenings turn out to have been. Nor shall we reduce the profoundly inner-turning discourse of the Talmud, preoccupied as it is with its own faraway issues, to a rather general message about the nature of the world and of Israel in it. At the same time, a simple reading of the ups and downs of the age (for Israel, mostly downs) surely is to be drawn into relationship with an equally unprepossessing account of the Talmud's own stresses, its matters subject to insistence: Scriptural and textual certainty, rabbis' authority, Israel's salvation.

As I see it, in the review just now completed, there were five events of fundamental importance for the history of Judaism in the period in which the Talmud came to closure. All of them are beyond cavil and were well known in their own day: (1) the conversion of Constantine; (2) the fiasco of Julian's plan to rebuild the temple of Jerusalem; (3) the depaganization of the empire, accompanied by attacks on pagan temples and, along the way, synagogues; (4) the Christianization of the majority of the population of Palestine; and (5) the creation and closure of the Talmud of the Land of Israel. To state matters simply at the outset: the Talmud came into being in an age of high hope succeeded by disaster. During the age of the Talmud's closure Jews who left Judaism surely had found the messianic hope, as it had been framed, to be a chimera. So it was a time of boundless expectations and bottomless despair—much like the age in which the Mishnah, on which our Talmud is constructed and suspended, was made up. Admittedly, the Talmud says nothing about Constantine or Julian, the proposed Temple, the devastation of synagogues, let alone mass apostasy (if that is what happened). But these things did happen, all of them. Everyone knew about them. Nothing that came in their aftermath can be perceived and interpreted wholly outside the realm of reality they define. Like famine, earthquake, plague, invasion, so too despair, disappointment, and disengagement with the old Israel—these are facts. They set the stage and the scene for all actors, whatever their dialogue. While defiance takes many forms, in my view the chief among these is normality, serene reason in spite of all. In context we see that this was the Talmud's response: triumph over despair.

Let us begin with a brief review of the four events that framed the setting for the fifth, starting with Constantine's conversion. The first point is that we do not know how Jews responded to Constantine's establishment of Christianity as the most favored religion. But in the Land of Israel itself, his works were well known, since he purchased many sites believed connected with Israel's sacred history and built churches and shrines at them. Accordingly, the topography of the Land of Israel itself bore the marks of the emperor's new faith. The Land of Israel became the Holy Land, a map of faith. But every time they handled a coin, Jews had to recognize that something of fundamental importance had shifted, as the old images were blotted out and the Christian emperor and symbol took their place. The Christians, for their part, were well able to take over the world that had miraculously fallen into their hands. In the preceding century, as Brown says, "The leaders of the Christian Church, especially in the Greek world, found that they could identify themselves with the culture, outlook and needs of the average well-to-do civilian. From being a sect ranged against or to one side of Roman civilization, Christianity had become a church prepared to absorb a whole society" (*World*, p. 82). That, then, is what began to happen in the fourth century. There is no way Israel could not have known.

Indeed, Brown says, "The Christian Apologists in both Latin and Greek presented Christianity not merely as a religion that found a *modus vivendi* with the civilization that surrounded it. They presented it as something far more than that. They claimed that Christianity was the sole guarantee of that civilization—that the best traditions of classical philosophy and the high standards of classical ethics could be steeled against barbarism only through being confirmed by the Christian revelation; and that the beleaguered Roman empire was saved from destruction only by the protection of the Christian God." We have then to observe that Judaism as we know it presented no equivalent message to the world, because it did not have to. Judaism in the Land of Israel itself is represented by no extant writings in Greek. We do not have a theory, equivalent to Christianity's, on the relationship of Judaism and the people of Israel to the rest of the world. No one could imagine that the world would flow into Israel, surely not in this-worldly terms. Nor was there need for a theory about how the civilization of the world, that is, of Rome, depended upon realization of the Torah as the foundation of it all.

Perhaps the messianic hope, associated as it was with a radical caesura of the natural world, made such a theory unthinkable, since, in any case, the Messiah could be trusted to attend to all those problems. But I think it more likely that the Jews of the Land of Israel looked out upon the world through the eyes of a besieged garrison, seeing friends only rarely, and then motionless, on inaccessible, far-distant hilltops—or in heaven. Israel's language, Aramaic, was not the language of the world to the north, northwest, and southwest. There people spoke Greek. Those who spoke Aramaic included many deemed by Rome, including Christian Rome, to be the other side. People on the margins do not worry about civilization, but about survival. Living in Aramaic, rather than in Greek, with good connections to the enemy side of the contested eastern frontier, the Jews thus formed part of the third world, the one sandwiched between the Greek-speaking West of the Near East, and the Semitic-, Armenian-, or, mainly, Iranian-speaking East. Along with other Semites, Armenians, and diverse linguistic and cultural groups, the Jews of the Land of Israel had no interest in guaranteeing the civilization that had conquered them and wiped out their Temple. It is scarcely possible to point to a single document of the second, third, or fourth centuries in which a Jewish writer identifies with the civilization of Rome or regards the invasions from the east (let alone the north) as a world-historical threat. Siege was calamity, not the end of civilization.

That is why Judaism bore within itself no theory of the world beyond its imaginary borders. Israel in its mind's eye saw no need to claim to provide the foundations of a world philosophy and an international ethics that Judaism, for its part, viewed as null and degraded. So, in a word, Jews appear to have been both more insular than their neighbors and also less fearful of the strange peoples beyond the horizon. While the Greek-speaking citizen of the town feared the awful alien, not only invasion and siege, from which all suffered, but also a nameless chaos, a general collapse of worth and sense, the Jew, not identifying himself with the present order anyhow, did not. Accordingly, Christian Apologists appealed to fears not felt by Israel. The upshot is that Judaism as represented by the Talmud of the Land of Israel confronted the succession of one vision of empire by another, with little to say about the relative merits of either one.

We come now to the paramount trait of the new world: the process of Christianization. The single most profound shift in the context of the Judaism of the West from ancient times onward to the nineteenth century, took place when the world in which Jews lived passed from pagan to Christian auspices and dominion. That shift took place in the period and domain in which the Yerushalmi came into being. When Judaism along with the rest of the world moved from the authority of the pagan Diocletian, persecutor of Christianity, to the rule of the Christian Constantine, everything familiar fell away. A new age, stretching downward nearly into our own century, began. In many ways the new faith bore salient traits of the one out of which it had been born, Judaism in its several forms of the day. Brown's discussion (*World,* pp. 65–66) of the relationship of the Christian Church to the world describes with slight variation the view of Judaism toward the world:

> The Christian Church differed from the other oriental cults, which it resembled in so many other ways, through its intolerance of the outside world. The cults were exclusive and, often, the jealously guarded preserve of foreigners; but they never set themselves up against the traditional religious observances of the society round them.

What changed now for Judaism, to be sure, was not clear at the outset. Perhaps that is why the Talmud makes so little of the changes. Intent on constructing a reality insulated from the vagaries of history, the Talmud's great philosophers proposed to make little of the outer changes represented by the wars and dynastic struggles of the day. These happened far away. Judaism for its part had long enjoyed licit status and had only to maintain its separation from the world at large to continue to endure until the foreordained end of time. No one could foresee the progressive shift in the status of Judaism, and with it that of Israel, as Christianity moved from persecuted to persecutor in not much more than one generation.

The reason is that the conversion of Constantine brought no palpable changes in the circumstances in which Jews in their Land lived out their lives. The world-historical meaning Christians attached to the event speaks eloquently in all their writings. If Jews said nothing about the event, that provides no indicator of what they were thinking. We cannot doubt, given the unchanging nature of Judaism's reflection on the meaning of events, that Jews, as much as Christians, tried to fit the event into some larger pattern or scheme of things. The special problem posed by the establishment of Christianity as most favored, then governing, religion, for Jews was the view that Christianity was a kind of heresy of Judaism, based on a wrong reading of the Torah, so to speak. A move of the empire from reverence for Zeus to adoration of Mithra meant nothing; paganism was what it was, lacking all differentiation. Christianity was something else. It was different. It was like Judaism. If so, the trend of sages' speculation cannot have avoided the issue of the place in the messianic pattern of this remarkable turn. Since the Christians celebrated confirmation of the faith—Christ's messiahship—and, at the moment, Jews were hardly prepared to concur, it falls surely within known patterns for us to suppose that Constantine's conversion would have been identified with some dark moment to prefigure the dawning of the messianic age. That conclusion goes far beyond idle speculation, though it also cannot rise to the level of confirmed fact. If, however, the events of the day, about which Jews were amply informed and the point of which was joyfully, forcefully, and ubiquitously proclaimed by their Christian counterparts, failed to excite messianic speculation among Jews, then we deal with a unique moment in the entire history of Judaism. Worlds do not change orbit, but Israel watchfully scans the horizon for a new star. All that showed up was a meteor.

If people were looking, then, for a brief dawn, the emperor Julian's plan to rebuild the ruined Temple in Jerusalem must have dazzled their eyes. For while Constantine surely raised the messianic question, Emperor Julian decisively answered it. In 361 the now-pagan Julian gave permission to rebuild the Temple. Work briefly got underway, but stopped because of an earthquake. The meaning of the plan was explicit. Julian had in mind to falsify the prophecy of Jesus that "not one stone of the temple would be left upon another" (Bowersock, p. 89). We may take for granted that, since the prophecy had not been proven false, many will have concluded that it indeed had been shown true. We do not know that Jews in numbers then drew the conclusion that, after all, Jesus really was the Christ. But, as we shall see, in the next half-century Palestine gained a Christian majority. The Christians, at any rate, were not slow to claim their faith had been proved right. We need not speculate on the depth of disappointment felt by those Jews who had hoped that the project would come to fruition, whether priests looking forward to a return to power through the reinstatement of the cult, or ordinary folk who took for granted that the rebuilding of the Temple would mark the coming of the Messiah.

The threat to Church and Christian state alike presented by the advent of a pagan emperor such as Julian made urgent the formation of a new and aggressive policy toward outsiders; caught in the net was Judaism too. Jews were perceived as an enemy, but a negligible threat. They were to be protected but degraded, as we have already noted. As to paganism in its institutions and expressions, however, matters were otherwise. The Christian emperors who succeeded Julian, and, in particular, Theodosius II, made certain that the Christian empire would never again face a mortal threat such as Julian ("the apostate") had posed. This they did by rooting out the institutions and rites that had sustained the enemy within. First and foremost, the temples were closed and sacrifice prohibited. The process is described as follows (Peters, p. 715):

> In A.D. 391 Theodosius enacted, perhaps under pressure from the militant Ambrose, the first general edict forbidding sacrifice and closing the temples throughout the Empire, and he followed it in the next year with a law that made even private non-Christian cults illegal. This was the official attitude expressed through the normal legal channels, but even earlier crowds in the cities and the countryside took matters into their own hands and destroyed pagan temples, frequently with a great deal of bloodshed, since the temples also had their defenders. Probably the most spectacular of these incidents was the destruction, sometime about A.D. 390, of the great temple of Serapis in Alexandria. For the Egyptians it seemed like the end of an era, and indeed it was, and in more senses than one. Along with the temple, the crowds put to the torch the great library that had been gathered there since the days of the first Ptolemy.

The sword unsheathed against the pagan cult places was sharp but untutored. So it did not discriminate among non-Christian centers of divine service. Nor could those who wielded it, zealots of the faith in Church and street, have been expected to. The Roman government protected synagogues and punished those who damaged them, in line with the policy of extirpating paganism but protecting a degraded Judaism. But the faithful of the Church had their own ideas. The distinction was too refined. Accordingly, the assault against pagan temples spilled over into an ongoing program of attacking synagogue property.

At this same time, moreover, a phenomenon lacking much precedent over the antecedent thousand years came into view: random attacks on Jews by reason of their faith, as distinct from organized struggles among contending forces, Jewish and other armies or mobs. The long-established Roman tradition of toleration of Judaism and of Jews, extending back to the time of Julius Caesar and applying both in law and in custom, now drew to a close. A new fact, at this time lacking all basis in custom and in the policy of state and Church alike, faced Jews: physical insecurity in their own villages and towns. So Jews' synagogues and their homes housed the same thing, which was to be eradicated: "Judaism." A mark of exceptional piety came to consist in violence against Jews' holy places, their property and persons. Coming in the aftermath of the triumph of Christianity, on the one side, and the decisive destruction of the Jews' hope for the rebuilding of the Temple, the hitherto-unimagined war against the Jews, in the last third of the fourth century and the beginning of the fifth, raised once again those questions about the meaning and end of history that Constantine, at the beginning of the age at hand, had forced upon Israel's consciousness.

As to the facts of the war against the synagogue, Avi-Yonah (pp. 218–219) provides the following account.

> The synagogues were the main field of dispute between the church and the Jews. From 388 there begins a period of concentrated mob attacks on Jewish places of worship, usually instigated by zealous Christian preachers. At first the government reacted with vigor. The Christian leaders were ordered to restore the buildings at their own expense. The attacks did not cease. Ten separate edicts had to be published in the years 393–426 which were intended to protect the synagogues and the right of the Jews to pray in them. The unceasing efforts of the ecclesiastical leaders, however, in the end wore down government resistance.
>
> On the 29th September 393 a most energetic order was published by the emperors, directed against all those who would destroy or damage a synagogue under the pretense of furthering Christian faith. The government reaffirmed its position that "it was well known that the Jewish sect is not forbidden by law." Within four years another order had to be reissued, directed to the provincial governors (17th June 397). They were ordered to take care that synagogues should not be molested.
>
> After the death of Arcadius the spirit of this legislation changed. The first law passed by Theodosius II on this subject (29th May 408) was directed against the Purim festivities, which were alleged to include matters offensive to Christianity. Save for such insults to the dominant faith, the Jews were, however, allowed to continue with their ritual as before. In the same year (24th November 408) the government of the Western empire published a law protecting the African church from offences committed by the Donatist sectarians and Jews.
>
> In the meantime the destruction of synagogues continued. In 414 the famous and splendid synagogue of Alexandria was destroyed, in 419 that

of Magina. On the 6th August 420 a new edict was issued, announcing that no innocent Jew was to be molested, and that their synagogues and (private) houses were to be safe from fire and other groundless damage. Even if a Jew was found committing an offence, he should be handed over to the public authorities, and no one should be allowed to lynch him. At the same time the legislation also warned the Jews to refrain from insolence and from insults to the Christian faith, and to trust that the law would protect them. In practice, therefore, this law marks a serious change for the worse in the status of the Jews. We learn from it that Jews were being attacked, and that not only their synagogues but also their private houses were no longer safe. The instigators of these acts used the pretext that the Jews were offending the Christian faith. The legislation pretended to blame the excesses of the mob, but actually he gave them license to carry on, while pretending to be impartial.

Three more years passed, and the situation did not improve. In 423 no less than three laws were passed on this subject. It seems that the Christians now used a simple and effective expedient to prevent the rebuilding of a ruined synagogue. They dedicated it on the spot as a church. The Christian legislators were now in a quandary. The act was clearly illegal, but its result was the creation of a consecrated building, an act which could not be undone under ecclesiastical law. A compromise solution was found in the end: the general prohibition on depriving the Jews of their places of worship was repeated, and no one was to be allowed to burn them. However, if they had been already consecrated as churches, the Jews were to receive another piece of ground of the same size or value as their original property. At the same time the emperor forbade the construction of new synagogues, and ordered that no changes should be made in those already existing. In fact this law gave the mobs both legal justification and what amounted to a reward for their illegal acts. When the Jews asked for this . . . law to be repealed, the emperor replied on the 9th April 423, reaffirming it and adding insult to injury. "It is our duty" so we read in his reply "to diminish the power and the impudence of the abominable Hellenes, Jews and heretics. Therefore we inform the Jews, that we do not agree to fulfil their offensive requests, but order only . . . that in future they should not be persecuted and that their synagogues shall not be seized and burnt." The prohibition of building new synagogues was maintained. Everything already taken from the Jews was lost forever.

This invitation to fresh persecutions fell on fertile ground. Two months later the government had to publish a new edict forbidding "real Christians and those calling themselves thus" from doing violence to Jews and Hellenes who were living peaceably. This time the law was provided with a sanction: the stolen property had to be returned threefold or fourfold. As some governors allowed the mob to do its will, the law menaced them also with the same punishment. In matters of substance, however, the existing laws were maintained: no new synagogues were to be built and the old ones could not be enlarged.

The third *Novella* of Theodosius II (430) summed up all the previous legislation. It laid down definitely that new synagogues were not to be built, and that old ones could be repaired only if they were likely to fall down. Every newly built synagogue was to be turned into a church. Whoever decorated a synagogue which needed no repair was liable to a fine of fifty pounds in gold. The archaeological evidence, however, proves conclusively, that all these prohibitions remained on paper only.

No one can claim that the fourth and final change, vast increase in the Christian population, came about because of the three events I have just now outlined. This change is marked by the growth in Christian communities, from nine known churches in the time of the apostles and one additional one in the second century, eight in the third, and eighteen in the fourth, to fifty-eight in the fifth century (Avi-Yonah, p. 220). Treated as a mission territory, Palestine attracted missionaries from more Christian parts of the Empire, in particular Egypt, for the southwestern part of the country, and Syria, for the northern and eastern ones. A pupil of Antony, Hilarian, took up the work in Gaza, with his disciples working the cities of the south (Avi-Yonah, p. 220). Chrysostom sent monks from Antioch to close pagan temples and found monasteries. While Avi-Yonah points, also, to the immigration of Christian refugees from the West, it is difficult to claim that the formation of a Christian majority included no appreciable number of converted Jews. If Jews did convert in sizable numbers, then we should have to point to the events of the preceding decades as ample validation in their eyes for the Christian interpretation of history. Jews had waited nearly three hundred years from the destruction in 70 to the promise of Julian. Julian, as I said, had had in mind to falsify the prophecies the Gospels had imputed to Jesus. This he stated explicitly. But, as we know, instead of being falsified, Jesus' prophecy had been validated. "No stone had been left on stone" in the Temple, not after 70, not after 361, just as Jesus had said. Instead of a rebuilt temple, the Jews looked out on a world in which now even their synagogues came under threat, and, along with them, their own homes and persons. What could be more ample proof of the truth of the Christians' claim than the worldly triumph of their Church? Resisted for so long, that claim called into question, as in the time of Bar Kokhba, whether it was worth waiting any longer for a messiah that had not come. With followers proclaiming the messiah who had come now possessing the world, the question could hardly be avoided. Accordingly, the Land of Israel having become the Holy Land, the export of its sanctification in the form of the bones of saints and martyrs began. Again an extract by Avi-Yonah (p. 22) provides an ample account:

> While a Christian majority was thus being created in Palestine for the first time in history, its importance grew in Christian eyes for another reason. It became in fact one of the main suppliers of relics of saints. Already in the time of Julian the alleged remains of John the Baptist and of the prophet Elisha were smuggled out to Egypt. In the fifth century the discovery of such relics and their veneration grew apace. Among such relics were not only those of Christian saints but also of heroes of the Old

Testament. Naturally the former Land of Israel enjoyed an almost complete monopoly in this respect.

The upshot is that the changes in the condition of Israel in its land were of a stunning character. The shift was not so much political as religious. A second Israel now came to the land, but with its own maps. The territory could never again be the same. No longer to be seen as mere pagans, who could be kept at arm's length, the Christians in the Holy Land revered the same saints, serendipitously finding the body of Zechariah in 412, that of Rabban Gamaliel and his sons (!) in 415. Here was a situation without precedent, in an age lacking all preparation: a kind of Israel had come to power, claiming kinship to the same saints, access to the same Scriptures, service of the same, sole God, creator of the world and protector of Israel, revering the same place, and even participating in the same history of Israel as Israel itself. If Israel's faith in the coming of the Messiah and the rebuilding of the Temple was now seen to have been tested in 361, then it had failed. If Israel's condition in its own land, now exposed to violence, and the state of Israel's synagogues everywhere, now subjected to everyday threats of destruction, were permitted to give testimony, then Israel's faith in the coming of the Messiah and in God's love and favor for its worship in the synagogues was apt to waver.

Once more I repeat my original caveat. We cannot argue that, because a fair part of the population of the Land of Israel, possibly including Jews, evidently adopted Christianity after the conversion of Constantine, the failure of Julian's plan to build the Temple, and the beginning of the Christian war against synagogue buildings and the start of chronic Jewish insecurity, *therefore* the population that converted did so in the aftermath, and on account, of the cumulative effect of these events. It would a needless error to claim: *post hoc, ergo propter hoc.* My sole observation is that before us is a familiar pattern: (1) messianic hope, (2) postmessianic disillusion, (3) holy book. This pattern had played itself out two hundred years earlier, in the aftermath of the Bar Kokhba War. We recall Justin's Trypho, an imaginary Jew who had gone into exile after Bar Kokhba's war and with whom Justin conducted a disputation. Justin's Trypho found in Christianity the correct interpretation for the pattern of events in the recent past. Had he risen from the dead, that same imaginary Trypho would not have found perplexing the parallel events two centuries later. What now happened had already happened. What things had proved before, they proved once again. Christians were not slow to say so. As I said, the program of settling upon the Holy Land a new landscape of holy places, transforming through piety ordinary bones into relics and stones here and there into the locus of faith, changed the Land of Israel into the Holy Land. So the site of Judaism became the locative version of utopian and now universal Christianity. For two hundred years, matters would remain as they were, until Islam changed everything, and not only in the Land of Israel, as successor faith for most of the Near and Middle East, North Africa, Spain, and southern France (speaking only of the Mediterranean). When that happened, Israel would once more ask urgently after redemption.

The last and most interesting question is also the least accessible of solution: Why did the Talmud of the Land of Israel come into being at just the time that it did, not before, not afterward? To answer that question is not possible. We have no range of well-established choices and alternatives. That is to say, we cannot claim that a given set of conditions generally will result in a certain and predictable response, that faced with a finite range of problems, people will write a given sort of book. It is one thing to notice that the Mishnah came in the aftermath of a messianic explosion and catastrophe, and that, it would appear, our Talmud came into being in sequence with the conversion of Constantine, the amazing plan of Julian, then the destruction of synagogues and the beginnings of a long age of chronic insecurity. It is quite another to allege that, whenever Jews would pass from one frame of mind to another, from despair to hope to debacle, they wrote Talmuds—or seized upon rationality against despair. To take one absurd instance to the contrary, the passage from the hopes of the nineteenth century to the calamities of our own day carried Israel back to its Land, but thus far has yielded no new Talmuds. To be sure, were an unthinkable catastrophe to follow, perhaps the surviving remnant would once again turn deeply inward, finding shelter in a cocoon of reason against an irrational world and fate. But who would want to find out? What would it prove, and for whose edification? Accordingly, it is true, one might wish to speculate that the document was not brought into being at an earlier time, or at a later one, but only at just this time, on account of such-and-so considerations. But, as I just said, when such speculation is completed, we have slight means of testing the answers. We cannot, for example, create, or discover the replication of, those same conditions under which (we posit in our theory) the document was made. So we cannot find out whether work along the same lines was found necessary under similar circumstances.

Not only so, but we cannot even relate the enormous accomplishment of intellectual creativity represented by our Talmud to the large-scale events of the day. We want to study, in the past in Brown's words (italics mine), *"the nexus that links the inner experiences of men to the society around them"* (*Religion,* p. 16). But we see that the Talmud of the Land of Israel does not commonly enter into articulated relationships with the world in which it was made. Beyond the commonplace theory that persecution stimulated people to write down traditions they feared would otherwise perish, there is no interplay. Now that theory may or may not be so. It has been stated a great many times, but proven or even tested not even once. It need not detain us.

But if it is legitimate to speculate that the people who made up the Talmud of the Land of Israel did so because they suffered persecution and feared for the future of what they knew and valued, then it also is taken for granted, even in the fastnesses of the most pious students of the problem, that the document does emerge for a particular reason at a particular circumstance: out of history and not Heaven. From this it should follow that, given those same circumstances, we should expect more Talmuds (or equivalent documents) to be written. But more Talmuds were never written, while the circumstance of persecution proved to be replicated more than a few times even among those very sorts of people who, in the Talmud's day, made the Talmud.

Accordingly, we cannot take for granted that we know the way in which society or circumstance provoked the sort of putting things together represented by the formation of the Talmud's units of discourse around its broken-up Mishnah rules. Indeed, it is difficult even to imagine how the inner world of reason and orderly restraint, represented by the reasoned discourse of the Talmud, can have entered any sort of symbiosis whatsoever with the outer world of chaos and calamity in which the masters and disciples, the judges and apprentices, the clerks and their patriarch did their work. Tiberias, Sepphoris, Caesarea, and Lud—why there? Why then? We cannot answer those questions. We can at best merely point to the dominant traits and events of the age and world in which the people did their work and wonder why there, why then, did they do what they did, that is, make the Talmud as we know it. All we know for sure is that the Talmud's paramount points of insistence constitute a point-by-point program in defiance of the age: certainty over doubt, authority over disintegration, salvation over chaos, above all, hope and confidence in an age of despair.

Part Two

Text

2

The Period at Hand

The Age of Formulation and Redaction

The period to which the Yerushalmi testifies is circa A.D. 350–400 (or 425). People generally assume the Talmud of the Land of Israel came to closure at about 400. Three of the thirty-nine tractates (the Babas, on civil law) were redacted about 350, the rest about 400. Now we know that the units of discourse of which the document is composed were formulated separately from the work of ultimate redaction, though we do not know for how long, or under what circumstances, these units were worked out. We are not apt to claim too much, however, if we maintain that *at the very least,* the Yerushalmi tells us what people were thinking in the last half of the fourth century. Furthermore, since the people who made up the bulk of the document's treatment of the Mishnah surely provide us with an entirely accurate picture of how they saw things, we are likely to be on firm ground indeed in proposing to describe a kind of Judaism fully revealed, amply expressed in the literary evidence, for the five decades from circa 350 to circa 400. To be sure, we do not know whether, and to what extent, the Yerushalmi records viewpoints of the period from the completion of the Mishnah, in circa 200, to the time of the formation and closure of the Yerushalmi itself, circa 350. Accordingly, the Judaism of the Yerushalmi may have taken shape from 200 to 350, but it is a Judaism that surely flourished in the last half of the fourth century.

The Legacy of the Mishnah: The Period of the Inheritance

Nearly every discourse—perhaps 90% of the whole—of the Yerushalmi addresses one main point: the meaning of the Mishnah. For the Yerushalmi, the life of Israel reaches the level of analysis within the integument of the Mishnah. That is to say, the Mishnah is about life, while the Talmud is about the Mishnah. Accordingly, the traits of the Mishnah defined the problematic, of both intellect and politics, confronting the heirs of the Mishnah, the disciples of the final generation of the Mishnah's redaction and formulation onward. They, for their part, set the patterns that followed, treating the Mishnah as Torah, proposing to receive and realize its revelation.

But, I must stress, we do not know how over a long span of time they did their work. We have only the final result, the Talmud itself. It is not (yet) possible to describe the stages by which the rabbis of successive generations in the third and fourth centuries, differentiated by location and school, on the one side, and by the periods in which they flourished, on the other, received and revised the legacy of the Mishnah. The reason is that, on the surface, such evidence as we have, differentiating one authority from another, one period of work from another, one school from another, consists in only one fact. A great many sayings in Yerushalmi are assigned to particular names. If we could demonstrate that what the Talmud assigns to an authority really was said by him, then, on the face of it, we should have ample evidence of the history of the discussions ultimately preserved by the Talmud. For if we knew that Rabbi X really said what he is supposed to have said, then we might assign to him (his day, his school, town, and generation) the opinions he held. These opinions then might be differentiated from the ones belonging to Rabbi Y (at another time, in another school, town, and generation). Knowing what one man or group thought at one time, we might then compare and contrast that corpus of ideas and modes of thought with those presented by a different group of people at another place and time. The upshot would be the history of the reception and realization of the legacy of the Mishnah, both in its parts (individual laws) and as a whole: the formation over two hundred years, in sequence, of rabbinic Judaism upon the foundations of the Mishnah.

Even though, to date, little has been done to write the history of the Mishnaic component of Rabbinic Judaism as preserved in the pages of the Palestinian Talmud, within the stated supposition, such a history in time may surely be recovered and written. Unhappily, we are not now in a position to compose such a history of Talmudic ideas. We cannot yet trace the course of the reception and exegesis of the Mishnah in the circles of sages over the long history of the third and fourth centuries. The reason is that, so far as I can see, we are not presently able, through exercises of falsification and validation, to test the allegation that a given statement was made, either in its exact wording or as to its gist, by a specified sage.

The possibility of proving that a statement in a given name really was made by that person, along with the alternative of demonstrating that another statement in that same name really was not made by him, depends upon the character of extant evidence. If we had a book or a collection of sayings or statements demonstrably belonging to a given authority, independent of the Talmud and its allegations in that authority's name, we would be able to compare what we find in the man's own writing with what we are given as a collective account by the Talmud. But all we know about the named authorities of the Talmud, alas, is what the Talmud tells us. The internal evidence at hand, by itself, is hardly probative of its own assertions.

True, the Talmud itself is quick to point to inconsistencies in opinions assigned to its more important authorities. But consistency testifies as much to the rigorous mind of the framers of the document as it does to the authenticity of the attribution to a given name. It surely is a literary convention; the very character of the Talmud's insistence on consistency in principles assigned to a named figure tells us so. Whether it is more than a convention of juridical thought—for the Talmud is an exercise in legal theory—is not at all to be proved or disproved on the basis of the Talmud's own claims.

If, second, we knew that there was a characteristic mode of formulating ideas, always particular to one authority or school, and never utilized by some other authority or school, we should have a solid, because superficial, criterion for sorting out valid from invalid attributions. But while there are indeed variations in modes of formulating ideas, the main points of discussion are given in terms expressive of conventions of collective speech—how, in the Talmud, people generally are made to say things. Accordingly, the two significant criteria made available by internal evidence—consistency of position or of patterns of distinctive speech—are inadequate to the task. At this time, therefore, it is difficult to trace the unfolding of the reception of the Mishnah among the several generations of authorities. The history of the interpretation of the Mishnah by the Talmudic rabbis may be possible in the future. It cannot be done now.

That means that the history of the Judaism revealed by the Talmud of the Land of Israel to begin with speaks solely of the point—whether a day or a century—at which the Talmud reached closure and completion. As I said above, the Talmud surely provides reliable evidence about the ideas held by the people who concluded the work of framing the Talmud. They wrote down what they thought. I cannot think of a contrary proposition worth analysis. It must follow that we know how the sages of the Holy Land at about A.D. 400 (to use the conventional date) wished to read the Mishnah and view much else as well. We may therefore describe how they received the Mishnah and what they did to it. This same description may, and probably does, encompass an account of what their predecessors (undifferentiated, to be sure), backward to the Mishnah itself, chose to do with the Mishnah. But we cannot show it, so we do not know it.

It is possible, to take one example, that Yohanan, who supposedly died about 280, said what he said in the interpretation of the Mishnah because of certain concerns or currents of his own day. It would then follow that we may attempt to relate to events of the third century the unfolding of the interpretation of the Mishnah by the Talmud. But, I stress, we cannot show it, so we do not know it. We only know how things came out at the end. We are not even certain that the state of the world, of the Jewish corner of the world, or of the sages' corner of the Jewish world, had any material impact at all upon Mishnah interpretation, even at the point at which we do know the work drew to a close. For the law has its own inner logic, autonomous of the facts of history and society. These can have dictated what people said by making available a limited range of choices. We may not assume without further analysis that what people said about the Mishnah took shape in circumstances of the day, rather than in response to tensions within the Mishnah's logic itself. We know for certain only how matters came out at the end. The upshot is obvious. We may relate the reception of the Mishnah in the Talmud to the state of affairs pertaining at the end of the fourth century. But we do not know that the way things were earlier, in the middle of the third or the beginning of the fourth century, had any impact upon the way people interpreted the Mishnah. We have in the end only the final statement, not its intermediate stages. The Judaism to which the Yerushalmi testifies, then, is the state of mind of some sages in the Land of Israel at the end of about two hundred years of study of the Mishnah and of certain other developments.

The Talmud's One Voice

In fact we may adduce striking evidence (1) that the Talmud does speak in particular for the age in which its units of discourse took shape, and (2) that that work was done toward the end of that long period of Mishnah reception that began at the end of the second century and came to an end at the conclusion of the fourth century.

As I shall now explain, the Talmud speaks about the Mishnah in essentially a single voice, about fundamentally few things. Its mode of speech as much as of thought is uniform throughout. Diverse topics produce slight differentiation in modes of analysis. The same sorts of questions phrased in the same rhetoric—a moving, or dialectical, argument, composed of questions and answers—turn out to pertain equally well to every subject and problem. The Yerushalmi's discourse therefore forms a closed system in which people say the same thing about everything. That is a stunning fact, for it clearly defines the choice at hand. Let us first turn to the Talmud's ubiquitous and monotonous voice: Who is telling me these things? Whence the conceptual and rhetorical continuities? Then we shall take up the choices on how to explain the literary facts we have established.

When the Talmud of the Land of Israel speaks about a passage of the Mishnah, it generally takes up a single, not very complex or diverse, program of inquiry. That has already been demonstrated through the taxonomies of volume 35. What we shall now see is that the Talmud also utilizes a single, rather limited repertoire of exegetical initiatives and rhetorical choices for whatever discourse about the Mishnah the framers of the Talmud propose to undertake. Accordingly, as is clear, the Talmud presents us with both a uniformity of discourse and a monotony of tone. The Yerushalmi speaks in a single voice. That voice by definition is collective, not greatly differentiated by traits of individuals. (Individuals in the Yerushalmi, unlike in the Mishnah, do not speak uniformly, but the differences are not marked.) Let me spell this out, because its consequences for the history of the ideas contained within Yerushalmi will prove definitive.

The Yerushalmi identifies no author or collegium of authors. When I say that the Talmud speaks in a single voice, I mean to say it everywhere speaks uniformly, consistently, and predictably. The voice is the voice of a book. The message is one deriving from a community, the collectivity of sages for whom and to whom the book speaks. The document seems, in the main, to intend to provide notes, an abbreviated script which anyone may use to reconstruct and reenact formal discussions of problems: *about this, one says that.* Curt and often arcane, these notes can be translated only with immense bodies of inserted explanation. All of this script of information is public and undifferentiated, not individual and idiosyncratic. We must assume people took for granted that, out of the signs of speech, it would be possible for anyone to reconstruct speech, doing so in accurate and fully conventional ways. So the literary traits of the document presuppose a uniform code of communication: a single voice.

The ubiquitous character of this single and continuous voice of the Talmud argues for one of two points of origin. First, powerful and prevailing conventions may have been formed in the earliest stages of the reception and study of the Mishnah, then carried on thereafter without variation or revision. Or, second, the framing of sayings into uniform constructions of discourse may have been accomplished only toward the end of the period marked by the formation of the Talmud's units of discourse and their conglomeration into the Talmud of the Land of Israel as we know it.

In the former case, we posit that the mode of reasoned analysis of the Mishnah and the repertoire of issues to be addressed to any passage of the Mishnah were defined early on, then persisted for two hundred years. The consequent, conventional mode of speech yielded that nearly total uniformity of discourse characteristic of numerous units of discourse of the Yerushalmi at which the interpretation of a law of the Mishnah is subject to discussion. In the latter case we surmise that a vast corpus of sayings, some by themselves, some parts of larger conglomerates, was inherited at some point toward the end of the two hundred years under discussion. This corpus of miscellanies was then subjected to intense consideration as a whole, shaped and reworded into the single, cogent, and rhetorically consistent Talmudic discourse before us.

As between these two possibilities, the latter seems by far the more likely. The reason is simple. I cannot find among the units of discourse in the Mishnah evidence of differentiation among the generations of names or schools. There is no interest, for instance, in the chronological sequence in which sayings took shape and in which discussions may be supposed to have been carried on. That is to say, the Talmudic unit of discourse approaches the explanation of a passage of the Mishnah without systematic attention to the layers in which ideas were set forth, the schools among which discussion must have been divided, the sequence in which statements about a Mishnah law were made. That fact points to formation at the end, not agglutination in successive layers of intellectual sediment.

Let me spell this out. In a given unit of discourse, the focus, the organizing principle, the generative interest—these are defined solely by the issue at hand. The argument moves from point to point, directed by the inner logic of argument itself. A single plane of discourse is established. All things are leveled out, so that the line of logic runs straight and true. Accordingly, a single conception of the framing and formation of the unit of discourse stands prior to the spelling out of issues. More fundamental still, what people in general wanted was not to create topical anthologies—to put together instances of what this one said about that issue—but to exhibit the logic of that issue, viewed under the aspect of eternity. Under sustained inquiry we always find a theoretical issue, freed of all temporal considerations and the contingencies of politics and circumstance.

Once these elemental literary facts make their full impression on our understanding, everything else falls into place as well. Arguments such as the ones we shall now review did not unfold over a long period of time, as one generation made its points, to be followed by the additions and revisions of another generation, in a process of gradual increment and agglutination running on for two hundred years. That theory of the formation of literature cannot account for the unity, stunning force, and dynamism of the Talmud's dialectical arguments. To the contrary, someone (or small group) at the end determined to reconstruct, so as to expose, the naked logic of a problem. For this purpose, oftentimes, it was found useful to cite sayings or positions in hand from earlier times. But these inherited materials underwent a process of reshaping, and, more aptly, refocusing. Whatever the original words—and we need not doubt that at times we have them—the point of everything in hand was defined and determined by the people who made it all up at the end. The whole shows a plan and program. Theirs are the minds behind the whole. In the nature of things, they did their work at the end, not at the outset. To be sure, the numerous examples we shall now inspect may, as I just said, yield one of two conclusions. We may see them as either the gradual and "natural" increment of a sedimentary process or as the creation of single-minded geniuses of applied logic and sustained analytical inquiry. But there is no intermediate possibility.

One qualification is required. I do not mean to say the principles of chronology were wholly ignored. Rather, they were not determinative of the structure of argument. So I do not suggest that the framers of the Talmud would likely have an early authority argue with a later one about what is assigned only to the later one. That I cannot and do not expect to instantiate. I do not think we shall find such slovenly work in either our Talmud or the other one. Our sages were painstaking and sensible. The point is that no attention ever is devoted *in particular* to the sequence in which various things are said. Everything is worked together into a single, temporally seamless discourse. Thus if a unit of discourse draws upon ideas of authorities of the first half of the third century, such as Simeon b. Laqish and Yohanan, as well as those of figures of the second half of the fourth century, such as Yosé, Jonah, Huna, Zeira, and Yudan, while discourse will be continous, discussion will *always* focus upon the logical point at hand.

It follows that the whole is the work of the one who decided to make up the discussion on the atemporal logic of the point at issue. Otherwise the discussion would be not continuous but disjointed, full of seams and margins, marks of the existence of prior conglomerations of materials that have now been sewn together. What we have are not patchwork quilts, but woven fabric. Along these same lines, we may find discussions in which opinions of Palestinians, such as Yohanan and Simon b. Laqish, will be joined together side by side with opinions of Babylonians, such as Rab and Samuel. The whole, once again, will unfold in a smooth way, so that the issues at hand define the sole focus of discourse. The logic of those issues will be fully exposed. Considerations of the origin of a saying in one country or the other will play no role whatsoever in the rhetoric or literary forms of argument. There will be no possibility of differentiation among opinions on the basis of where, when, by whom, or how they are formulated, only on the basis of what, in fact, is said.

In my view it follows that the whole—the unit of discourse as we know it—was put together at the end. At that point everything was in hand, so available for arrangement in accordance with a principle other than chronology, and in a rhetoric common to all sayings. That other principle will then have determined the arrangement, drawing in its wake resort to a single monotonous voice: "the Talmud." The principle is logical exposition, that is to say, the analysis and dissection of a problem into its conceptual components. The dialectic of argument is framed not by considerations of the chronological sequence in which sayings were said but by attention to the requirements of reasonable exposition of the problem. That is what governs.

In the next section I shall backtrack and provide ample exemplification and instantiation for these statements that, first, the Yerushalmi speaks with a single, fixedly modulated voice; and, second, the Yerushalmi exposes the logic of ideas in a dialectical argument framed without regard to the time and place of the participants. I shall give a repertoire of examples for each proposition. Seen at length, these may prove somewhat tedious. But they also show beyond doubt that the Yerushalmi is like the Mishnah in its fundamental literary traits, therefore also in its history. That is to say, we know that the Mishnah was formulated, in its rigid, patterned language and carefully organized and enumerated groups of formal-substantive cognitive units, in the very processes in which it also was redacted. Otherwise the correspondences between redactional program and formal and patterned mode of articulation of ideas cannot be explained, short of invoking the notion of a literary miracle. The Yerushalmi evidently underwent a process of redaction, in which fixed and final units of discourse (whether as I have delineated them or in some other division) were organized and put together. The probably antecedent work of framing and formulating these units of discourse appears to have gone on at a single period. By this I mean, among a relatively small number of sages working within a uniform set of literary conventions, at roughly the same time, and in approximately the same way. These framers of the various units of tradition may or may not have participated in the work of closure and redaction of the whole. We do not know the answer. But among themselves they cannot have differed very much about the way in which the work was to be carried on. For the end-product, the Talmud, like the Mishnah, is uniform and stylistically coherent, generally consistent in modes of thought and speech, wherever we turn. That accounts for the single voice that leads us through the dialectical and argumentative analysis of the Talmud. That voice is ubiquitous and insistent. Let us now listen to it.

Instances of the Talmud's Monotonous Voice

Discourse Conducted in Complete Anonymity

We begin with a set of instances which illustrate the fundamental traits of discourse. What we see is that the discussion is coherent and harmonious, moving from beginning to what was, in fact, a predetermined end. The voice, "the Talmud," speaks to us throughout, not the diverse voices of real people engaged in a concrete and therefore chaotic argument. As in Plato's dialogues, question and answer—the dialectical argument—constitute conventions through which logic is exposed and tested, not the reports of things people said spontaneously or even after the fact. The controlling voice is monotonous, lacking all points of differentiation of viewpoint, tone, mode of inquiry and thought. That is what I mean to illustrate here. To prove this same proposition incontrovertibly, I should have to cite a vast proportion of the Yerushalmi as a whole. A few instances must suffice.

Y. Niddah 1:3. In the opening passage the language of the Mishnah pericope is subjected to close analysis and clarification. What is important in the three units of discourse before us is that matters are conducted so that a single voice—"the Talmud"—leads us through the problem. Unit II is striking. Clearly, an editor has selected and inserted the passage of Tosefta cited here. We can surmise, by reference to the passage of the Mishnah under discussion, why the passage seemed important. Unit III, likewise, carries on a dialectical argument, from III.A to B to C, without significant variation of tone or style. The reason is that discourse takes place on a single plane, established and defined solely by the logic at hand. The use of question and answer is artifice and does not indicate an actual conversation.

A. *Who is a virgin [among the four women who fall into the category of those for whom the time of first seeing blood suffices, without scruple as to prior contamination by reason of doubt]?*

B. *Any girl who has never in her life produced a drop of [menstrual] blood,*

C. *even though she is married.*

I. A. Thus is the teaching of the Mishnah: *Any girl who has not seen menstrual blood in her life, and even though she is married.*

B. They [thus] spoke of a virgin as to blood[, that is, a girl who had never menstruated], not a virgin as to the hymen.

C. There are cases in which a girl is a virgin as to blood and not a virgin as to the hymen. There are cases in which she is a virgin as to the hymen but is not a virgin as to blood.

D. [A girl is] a virgin as to the hymen when she produced a drop of blood and afterward was married.

E. [She is a] virgin as to blood when she was married and afterward produced a drop of blood.

II. A. It was taught in a Tannaitic saying:

B. **There are three kinds of virgins: a virgin woman, a virgin sycamore, and virgin soil. A virgin woman is any woman who has never been laid. A virgin sycamore is any that has never been chopped down. Virgin soil is any that has never been worked. Rabban Simeon b. Gamaliel says, "It is any in which there is not a single sherd" [T. Sheb. 3:14H, 15].**

III. A. [The law (M. Nid. 1:3B) that a girl who has not produced a drop of blood does not impart retroactive uncleanness even when she does produce a drop] applies even if she was married, even if she became pregnant, even if she gives suck [to her baby], and even if she excretes blood for all seven days for a male or all fourteen days [of clean blood] for a female.

B. And does she have a divining tool in hand [to know whether it will be a male or a female]?

C. When [the child] is male, it is for seven days, and when it is a female, it is for fourteen days [after birth, that the stated rule applies].

Y. Horayot 2:1. Once again we have a sustained discussion, this time on the exegetical foundations of a law of the Mishnah. The voice of the Talmud is undifferentiated; the entire passage concentrates on the substance of matters. A single hand surely stands behind it all, for there is not a single seam or margin. So to give an account of the matter, we must speak in the name of "the Talmud." That is, "the Talmud" wants to know the relationship of an anointed priest to a court, the reciprocal authority of autonomous institutions. Scripture has specified several autonomous persons and institutions or groups that atone with a bullock for erroneous actions committed inadvertently. So the Talmud now raises the interesting question of the rule that applies when one of these autonomous bodies follows instructions given by another. The unit explores this question, first establishing that the anointed priest is equivalent to the community, just as Scripture states, and drawing the consequence of that fact. Then comes the important point that the anointed priest is autonomous of the community. He atones for what he does, but is not subject to atonement by, or in behalf of, others.

A. *[If] an anointed [high] priest made a decision for himself [in violation of any of the commandments of the Torah] doing so inadvertently, and carrying out [his decision] inadvertently,*

B. *he brings a bullock [Lev. 4:3].*

C. *[If] he [made an erroneous decision] inadvertently, and deliberately carried it out.*

D. *deliberately [made an erroneous decision] and inadvertently carried it out,*

E. *he is exempt.*

F. *For [as to A–B] an [erroneous] decision of an anointed [high priest] for himself is tantamount to an [erroneous] decision of a court for the entire community.*

I.   A. ["If any one sins unwittingly in any of the things which the Lord has commanded not to be done and does any one of them, if it is the anointed priest who sins, thus bringing guilt on the people, then let him offer for the sin which he has committed a young bull" (Lev. 4:23–30).] "Anyone. . . ," "If it is the high priest. . . ,"—lo, [the Scripture would seem to imply that] the high priest is tantamount to an individual [and not, vs. M. Hor. 2:1F, to an embodiment of the community and thus not subject to a bullock-offering].

     B. [In this case, Scripture's purpose is to say:] Just as an individual, if he ate [something prohibited] at the instruction of a court is exempt, so this one [subject to court authority], if he ate something at the instruction of the court, is exempt.

     C. Just as an individual, if he ate [something prohibited] without the instruction of a court is liable, so this one, if he ate something not at the instruction of a court, is liable.

D. [To encounter that possible interpretation] Scripture states, "Thus bringing guilt on the people" [meaning] lo, [the high anointed priest's] guilt is tantamount to the guilt of the entire people [just as M. Hor. 2:1F states].

E. Just as the people are not guilty unless they gave instruction [Lev. 4:13], so this one is not guilty unless he gave instruction.

F. There is a Tannaitic tradition that interprets [the matter with reference to] the people [and] the court:

G. Just as [if] the people gave instruction and other people did [what the people] said, [the people] are liable, so this one, [if] he gave [erroneous] instruction and others did [what he said], should be liable.

H. [It is to counter that possible interpretation that] Scripture states, "[If it is the high priest] who sins," [meaning] for the sin that this one himself committed he brings [a bullock], but he does not have to bring a bullock on account of what other people do [inadvertently sinning because of his instruction].

I. There is a Tannaitic tradition that interprets the [matter with reference to] the people [and] the community:

J. Just as, in the case of the people, if others gave erroneous instruction and they [inadvertently] committed a sin, they are liable, so in the case of this one, [if] others gave erroneous instruction and he carried it out [and so sinned], he should be liable.

K. [To counter that possible, wrong interpretation,] Scripture states, "[If it is the high priest] who sins," [meaning] for the sin that this one committed, he brings [a bullock], but he does not have to bring a bullock on account of what other people do [inadvertently sinning because of their instruction].

Y. San. 4:9. We find here a further instance in which the argument is so constructed as to speak to an issue, without regard to the source of sayings or the definition of the voices in conversation. A question is asked, then answered, because the rhetoric creates dialectic, movement from point to point. It is not because an individual speaks with, and interrogates, yet another party. The uniform voice of the Talmud is before us, lacking all distinguishing traits, following a single, rather simple program of rhetorical conventions.

II. A. *And perhaps you might want to claim, "What business is it of ours to convict this man of a capital crime?"* [M. San. 4:9].

B. It is written, "And about sunset a cry went through the army" (1 Kings 22:36).

C. What is this cry?

D. Lo, it is a song, as it is said, "When the wicked perish, there is a song" (Prov. 11:10).

E. But, on the contrary, it also is said, "[That they should praise] as they went out before the army [and say, 'Give thanks unto the Lord, for his mercy endures for ever']" (2 Chron. 20:21).

F. [Omitting the words, "for he is good,"] is to teach you that even the downfall of the wicked is no joy before the Omnipresent.

Y. Makkot 1:5. Here is yet another example in which a sustained conversation on a passage of Scripture, unfolding through questions and answers, conforms to a simple rhetorical program. The voice of the interlocutor is not differentiated from the source of the respondent, for the whole is a single discourse. Not a "real" conversation, but rather an effective presentation of a simple idea is at hand.

I. A. [Scripture refers to the requirement of two or three witnesses to impose the death penalty, Deut. 17:6. Scripture further states, "Only on the evidence of two witnesses or of three witnesses shall a charge be sustained" (Deut. 19:15). The former deals with capital cases, the latter with property cases. Since both refer to two or three witnesses, the duplication is now explained:] Scripture is required to refer to property cases, and also to capital cases.

   B. For if it had referred to property cases and not to capital cases, I might have said, In the case of property cases, which are of lesser weight, three witnesses have the power to prove two to be perjurers, but two may not prove three to be perjurers.

   C. How do I know that that is so even of a hundred?

   D. Scripture states, "Witnesses."

   E. Now if reference had been made to capital cases, and not to property cases, I might have said, In capital cases, which are weightier, two witnesses have the power to prove that three are perjurers but three do not have the power to prove that two are perjurers.

   F. How do I know that that applies even to a hundred?

   G. Scripture says, "Witnesses." [It follows then the Scripture must refer to "two or three" in the context of each matter, since one could not have derived the one from the other.]

All of the units of discourse before us exhibit the same traits. In each instance we see that the conversation is artificial. What is portrayed is not real people but a kind of rhetoric. The presence of questions and answers is a literary convention, not a (pretended) transcription of a conversation. So we may well speak of "the Talmud" and its voice: that is all we have. The absence of differentiation is not the sole striking trait. We observe, also, a well-planned and pointed program of inquiry, however brief, leading to a single purpose for each unit of discourse. While the various units in theme are completely unrelated to one another, in rhetoric and mode of analysis they are essentially uniform: simple questions, simple answers, uncomplex propositions, worked out through reference to authoritative sources of law, essentially an unfolding of information.

Up to this point, we have seen only that the Talmud takes on a persona, becomes a kind of voice. The voice is timeless. On the face of it, the units we have reviewed could have been made up at any time in the period in which the Talmud was taking shape, from 200 to 400. The uniformity of style and cogency of mode of discourse can have served as powerful scholastic-literary conventions, established early, followed slavishly thereafter. The bulk of the units of discourse, however, are not anonymous. They constitute compilations of statements assigned to named authorities. These on the surface testify to specific periods in the two centuries at hand, since the authorities mentioned lived at specific times and places. If, now, we observe the same uniformity of tone and dialectic, we shall address a somewhat more refined problem.

Discourse Involving Named Authorities

The important point in the examples that follow is that while named authorities and sayings assigned to them do occur, the dialectic of argument is conducted outside the contributions of the specified sages. Sages' statements serve the purposes of the anonymous voice, rather than defining and governing the flow of argument. So the anonymous voice, "the Talmud," predominates even when individuals' sayings are utilized. Selecting and arranging whatever was in hand is the work of one hand, one voice.

Y. Abodah Zarah 1:5. What is interesting in this account of the language of the Mishnah is that the framer of the entire discussion takes over and uses what is attributed to Hiyya. The passage requires Hiyya's verson of the Mishnah rule. But Hiyya is not responsible for the formation of the passage. It is "the Talmud" that speaks, drawing upon the information, including the name, of Hiyya. Only the secondary comment in the name of Bun bar Hiyya violates the monotone established by "the Talmud." And at the end that same voice takes over and draws matters to their conclusion, a phenomenon we shall shortly see again. It is not uncommon for later fourth-century names to occur in such a setting.

> A. *These are things [which it is] forbidden to sell to gentiles:*
> B. *(1) fir cones, (2) white figs, (3) and their stalks, (4) frank-incense, and (5) a white cock.*

A. We repeat in the Mishnah-pericope [the version]: *A white cock.*

B. R. Hiyya repeated [for his version of] the Mishnah pericope: "A cock of any sort."

C. The present version of the Mishnah [specifying a white cock] requires also the version of R. Hiyya, and the version of R. Hiyya requires also the [present] version of the Mishnah.

D. [Why both?] If we repeated [the present version of the Mishnah], and we did not repeat the version of R. Hiyya, we should have reached the conclusion that the sages state the rule only in regard to a white cock, but as to any sort of cock other than that, even if this was all by itself [M. A.Z. 1:5D], it is permitted. Thus there was need for the Mishnah version of R. Hiyya.

E. Now if one repeated the version of R. Hiyya, and we did not repeat the version before us in the Mishnah, we should have ruled that the rule applies only in the case of an unspecified cock [requested by the purchaser], but [if the purchaser requested] a white cock, then even if this was all by itself, it would be prohibited [to sell such a cock].

F. Thus there was need for the Mishnah version as it is repeated before us, and there also was need for the Mishnah version as it is repeated by R. Hiyya.

G. Said R. Bun bar Hiyya, "[In Hiyya's view, if a gentile said, 'Who has] a cock to sell?' one may sell him a white cock, [so Hiyya differs from, and does not merely complement, the version of the Mishnah pericope]."

H. [Now if the gentile should say, "Who has] a white cock to sell," we then rule that if the white cock is by itself, it is forbidden, but if it is part of a flock of cocks, it is permitted to sell it to him. [This clearly is the position of the Mishnah pericope, so there is no dispute at all, merely complementary traditions, as argued at D–E.]

Y. Shebuot 3:7. Here is yet another instance, but a more complex and better articulated one, in which topically interesting sayings attributed to two principal authorities, Yohanan and Simeon b. Laqish, provide a pretext for a rather elaborate discussion. The discussion is conducted about what Yohanan and Simeon are supposed to have said. But the rhetoric is such that they are not presented as the active voices. Their views are described. But they, personally and individually, do not express views. Predictably, the language in no way differentiates between Yohanan's and Simeon b. Laqish's manner of speech. Only the substance of what is said tells us how and about what they differ. The reason is obvious. The focus of discourse is the principle at hand, the logic to be analyzed and fully spelled out. The uniform voice of "the Talmud" speaks throughout.

> A. *"I swear that I won't eat this loaf of bread," "I swear that I won't eat it," "I swear that I won't eat it"—*
>
> B. *and he ate it—*
>
> C. *is liable on only one count.*
>
> D. *This is a "rash oath" (Lev. 5:4).*
>
> E. *On account of deliberately [taking a rash oath] one is liable to flogging, and on account of inadvertently [taking a rash oath] he is liable to an offering of variable value.*
>
> I. A. [If someone said], "I swear that I shall eat this loaf of bread today," and the day passed, but then he ate it—
>
> B. R. Yohanan and R. Simeon b. Laqish—both of them say, "He is exempt [from flogging for deliberate failure]."
>
> C. The reason for the position of one authority is not the same as the reason for the ruling of the other.
>
> D. The reason for the ruling of R. Yohanan is on the grounds that the case is one in which there can be no appropriate warning [that what the man is about to do will violate the law, because the warning can come only too late, when the day has already passed].
>
> E. The reason for the ruling, in R. Simeon b. Laqish's view, is that [by not eating] the man is thereby violating a negative rule which does not involve an actual, concrete deed.
>
> F. What is the practical difference between the positions of the two authorities?
>
> G. A case in which he burned the bread and threw it into the sea.
>
> H. If you say that the reason is on the count that the man is not in a position to receive a warning, the man will be exempt [on the same grounds in the present case].
>
> I. But if you say that the reason is that the matter involves a negative commandment in which there is no concrete deed, here we do have a concrete deed [namely, throwing the bread into the sea].

Y. Shebuot 3:9. Here we have a still more striking instance in which the entire focus of discourse is the logic. No rhetorical devices distinguish one party to the argument from the other one. The two speak in rigidly patterned language, so that what is assigned to the one always constitutes a mirror image of what is assigned to the other. That the whole, in fact, merely refers to positions taken by each is clear in the resort to third person and descriptive language, in place of the attributive "said."

A. "I swear that I shall eat this loaf of bread," "I swear that I shall not eat it"—the first statement is a rash oath, and the second is a vain oath [M. Sheb. 3:9A–B].

B. How do they treat such a case [in which a man has taken these contradictory oaths, one of which he must violate]?

C. They instruct him to eat [the loaf].

D. It is better to transgress a vain oath and not to transgress a rash oath.

E. "I swear that I shall not eat this loaf of bread," "I swear that I shall eat it"—the first is rash oath, the second a vain oath.

F. How do they treat such a case?

G. They instruct him not to eat it.

H. It is better to transgress a vain oath by itself, and not to transgress both a vain oath and a rash oath.

I. "I swear that I shall eat this loaf of bread today," "I swear that I shall not eat it today," and he ate it—

J. R. Yohanan said, "He has carried out the first oath and nullified the second."

K. R. Simeon b. Laqish said, "He has nullified the first and not carried out the second."

L. "I swear that I shall not eat this loaf of bread today," "I swear that I shall eat it today," and he ate it—

M. R. Yohanan said, "He has nullified the first oath and carried out the second."

N. R. Simeon b. Laqish said, "He has nullified the first oath and as to the second, they instruct him to carry it out with another loaf of bread."

O. "I swear that I shall eat this loaf today," "I swear that I shall eat it today," and he ate it—

P. R. Yohanan said, "He has carried out both oaths."

Q. And R. Simeon b. Laqish said, "He has carried out the first, and as to the second, they instruct him to carry it out with another loaf of bread."

R. "I swear that I shall not eat this loaf of bread," "I swear that I shall not eat it today," and he ate it—

S. in the view of R. Yohanan, he is liable *on only one count.*

T. In the view of R. Simeon b. Laqish, is he liable on two counts?

U. [No.] Even R. Simeon b. Laqish will concede that he [has repeated himself] because he merely [wishes to] keep himself away from prohibited matters [and that is why he repeated the oath, but only one count is at hand].

Y. San. 5:2. The final example does utilize the attributive, with the implication that we have an effort to represent not merely the gist of an authority's opinion but his exact words. Even if we assume that before us are *ipsissima verba* of Rab and Yohanan, however, we have still to concede the paramount role of "the Talmud" in the formation and unpacking of the argument. For, as we notice, as soon as Rab and Yohanan have spoken, curiously mirroring one another's phrasing and wording, the monotonous voice takes over. At that point, the argument unfolds in a set of questions and answers, the standard dialectic thus predominating once again. The secondary expansion of the matter, beginning at O, then adduces a piece of evidence, followed by an anonymous discourse in which that evidence is absorbed into, and made to serve, the purposes of the analysis as a whole. Once more the fact that each item is balanced by the next is not the important point, though it is striking. What is important is that movement of the argument is defined by "the Talmud," and not by the constituents of discourse given in the names of specific authorities. The mind and voice behind the whole are *not* Rab's and Yohanan's, or, so far as we can see, those of their immediate disciples. The voice is "the Talmud's." "The Talmud" does not tire, as its tertiary explication, testing the views of each and showing the full extent of the position taken by both principal parties, runs on and on. Only at the end, with Mana and Abin, fourth-century figures, do named authorities intervene in such a way as to break the uniform rhetorical pattern established by "the Talmud."

A. There we learned:

B. *He concerning whom two groups of witnesses gave testimony—*

C. *these testify that he took a vow to be a Nazir for two spells,*

D. *and those testify that he took a vow to be Nazir for five spells—*

E. *The House of Shammai say, "The testimony is at variance, and no Naziriteship applies here at all."*

F. *And the House of Hillel say, "In the sum of five are two spells, so let him serve out two spells of Naziriteship"* [*M. Naz. 3:7*].

G. Rab said, "As to a general number [the Houses] are in disagreement [that is, as to whether he has taken the Nazirite vow at all]. But as to a specific number, all parties agree that [the testimony is at variance]. [Following the versions of Y. Yeb. 15:5, Naz. 3:7: the sum of five includes two, as at M. 5:2F.]"

H. R. Yohanan said, "As to spelling out the number of vows there is a difference of opinion, but as to a general number, all parties concur that [within the general principle of five spells of Naziriteship there are two upon which all parties concur]. [The testimony is at variance.]"

I. What is meant by the "general number," and what is meant by "counting out the number of specific vows" [the man is supposed to have taken]? [Examples of each are as follows:]

J. The general number—one party has said, "Two," and one party has said, "Five."

K. Counting out the number of vows one by one is when one said "One, two," and the other said, "Three, four."

L. Rab said, "If the essence of the testimony is contradicted, the testimony is not null."

M. And R. Yohanan said, "If the essence of the testimony is contradicted, the testimony is null."

N. All parties concede, however, [that] if testimony has been contradicted in its nonessentials, the testimony [of the first set of witnesses] is not nullified.

O. The full extent of the position taken by R. Yohanan is seen in the following case:

P. For Ba bar Hiyya in the name of R. Yohanan: "The assumption [that a loan has taken place is] confirmed [by testimony] that one has counted out [coins].

Q. "If this witness says, 'From his pocket did he count out the money,' and that one says, 'From his pouch did he count out the money,'

R. "we have a case in which a testimony is contradicted in its essentials [within the same pair of witnesses, who thus do not agree]. [This testimony is null.]"

S. Here even Rab concedes that the testimony is null.

T. Concerning what do they differ?

U. Concerning a case in which there were two *groups* of witnesses.

V. One states, "From the pocket did he count out the money," and the other says, "From the pouch did he count out the money."

W. Here we have a case in which testimony is contradicted in its essentials. The effect of the testimony [in Yohanan's view] is null.

X. But in the view of Rab, the effect of the testimony is not null.

Y. If one witness says, "Into his vest did he count out the money," and the other says, "Into his wallet,"

Z. in the opinion of all parties, the testimony is contradicted in its nonessentials and therefore the testimony is not nullified. [This testimony is not about the essence of the case.]

AA. If one party says, "With a sword did he kill him," and the other party says, "With a staff did he kill him," we have a case in which testimony has been contradicted in its essentials [just as in a property case, so in a capital one].

BB. Even Rab concedes that the effect of the entire testimony is null.

CC. In what regard did they differ?

DD. In a case in which there were two sets of two witnesses:

EE. One group says, "With a sword . . . ," and the other says, "With a staff . . . "

FF. Here we have a case in which the testimony has been contradicted in its essentials, and the effect of the testimony is null.

GG. But in the view of Rab, the effect of the testimony is not null.

HH. One witness says, "[The murderer] turned toward the north [to flee]," and the other witness says, "He turned toward the south," in the opinion of all parties, the testimony [of one group] has been contradicted in its nonessentials, and the testimony has not been nullified.

II. The full force of Rab's opinion is indicated in the following, which we have learned there:

JJ. [*If one woman says, "He died," and one says, "He was killed," R. Meir says, "Since they contradict one another in details of their testimony, lo, these women may not re-marry."*] *R. Judah and R. Simeon say, "Since this one and that one are in agreement that he is not alive, they may re-marry"* [*M. Yeb. 15:5B–D*].

KK. Now did he not hear that which R. Eleazar said, "R. Judah and R. Simeon concur in the matter of witnesses [that where they contradict one another in essentials, their testimony is null]"?

LL. If so, what is the difference between such contradiction when it comes from witnesses and the same when it comes from co-wives?

MM. They did not treat the statement of a co-wife concerning her fellow wife as of any consequence whatsoever.

NN. Said R. Yohanan, "If R. Eleazar made such a statement, he heard it from me and said it."

OO. The Mishnah pericope is at variance with the position of Rab. *All the same are interrogation and examination in the following regard: When the witnesses contradict one another, their testimony is null* [*M. San. 5:2F*]. [Rab does not deem it invariably null, as we have seen.]

QQ. Said R. Mana, "Rab interprets the Mishnah rule to speak of a case in which one witness contradicts another [but not in which a *set* of witnesses contradicts another such *set* in some minor detail]."

RR. Said R. Abin, "Even if you interpret the passage to speak of contradictions between one set of witnesses and another, still Rab will be able to deal with the matter. For a capital case is subject to a different rule, since it is said, 'Justice, [and only] justice, will you pursue'" (Deut. 16:20). [Thus capital trials are subject to a different set of rules of evidence from those applicable in property cases, of which Rab spoke above at L.]

Since this final example is somewhat protracted, we had best review the point of citing it before we proceed. The issue of the interpretation of the passage of the Mishnah, A–F, is phrased at G–H, the conflict between Rab and Yohanan. We note that the former spent most of his mature years in Babylonia, the latter in the Land of Israel. Accordingly, considerations of geographical or institutional relationship play no role whatsoever. The language of the one is a mirror image of what is given to the other. Then the Talmud takes over, by providing an exegesis of the cited dispute, I–K. This yields a secondary phrasing of the opinions of the two authorities, L, M, with a conclusion at N. Then the position of Yohanan is provided yet a further amplification, O–R. But what results, S, is a revision of our view of Rab's opinion. Consequently, a further exegesis of the dispute is supplied, T–U, spelled out at W–X, then with further amplication still, now at Y–BB. Once more we attempt a further account of the fundamental point at issue between the two masters, CC–HH, and, in the model of the foregoing exercise with Yohanan, Rab's view is carried to its logical extreme, II–JJ. The final part of the passage, tacked on and essentially secondary, allows for some further discussion of Rab's view, with a late authority, Mana, and his contemporary, Abin, QQ–RR, writing a conclusion to the whole. Up to that point, it seems to me clear, what we have is a rather elegant, cogent, highly stylized mode of exposition through argument, with a single form of logic applied time and again.

When I claim that the Talmud's focus of interest is in the logical exposition of the law, here is a good instance of what I mean. The materials are organized so as to facilitate explanations of the law's inner structure and potentiality, not to present a mere repertoire of ideas and opinions of interest for their own sake. The upshot is a sustained argument, not an anthology of relevant sayings. Such a cogent and ongoing argument is more likely the work of a single mind than of a committee, let alone of writers who lived over a period of ten or fifteen decades.

Conclusion

The role of individuals in the passages we have reviewed is unimportant. The paramount voice is that of "the Talmud." The rhetoric of the Talmud may be described very simply: a preference for questions and answers, a willingness then to test the answers and to expand through secondary and tertiary amplification, achieved through further questions and answers. The whole gives the appearance of the script for a conversation to be reconstructed, or an argument of logical possibilities to be reenacted, in one's own mind. In this setting we of course will be struck by the uniformity of the rhetoric, even though we need not make much of the close patterning of language, for example, Rab's and Yohanan's, where it occurs. The voice of "the Talmud," moreover, authoritatively defines the mode of analysis. The inquiry is consistent and predictable; one argument differs from another not in supposition but only in detail. When individuals' positions occur, it is because what they have to say serves the purposes of "the Talmud" and its uniform inquiry. The inquiry is into the logic and the rational potentialities of a passage. To these dimensions of thought, the details of place, time, and even of an individual's philosophy are secondary. All details are turned toward a common core of discourse. This, I maintain, is possible only because the document as a whole takes shape in accord with an overriding program of inquiry and comes to expression in conformity with a single plan of rhetorical expression. To state the proposition simply: it did not just grow, but rather, someone made it up.

Instances of the Predominance of Logic over Chronology

The Talmudic argument is not indifferent to the chronology of authorities. But the sequence in which things may be supposed to have been said—an early third century figure's saying before a later fourth century figure's saying—in no way explains the construction of protracted dialectical arguments. The argument as a whole, its direction and purpose, always governs the selection, formation, and ordering of the parts of the argument and their relationships to one another. The dialectic is determinative. Chronology, if never violated, is always subordinated. Once that fact is clear, it will become further apparent that "arguments"—analytical units of discourse—took shape at the end, with the whole in mind, as part of a plan and a program. That is to say, the components of the argument, even when associated with the names of specific authorities who lived at different times, were not added piece by piece, in order of historical appearance. They were put together whole and complete, all at one time, when the dialectical discourse was made up. By examining a few units of discourse, we shall clearly see the unimportance of the sequence in which people lived, hence of the order in which sayings (presumably) became available.

The upshot is that chronological sequence, while not likely to be ignored, never determines the layout of a unit of discourse. We can never definitively settle the issue of whether a unit of discourse came into being through a long process of accumulation and agglutination, or was shaped at one point—then, at the end of the time in which named authorities flourished—with everything in hand and a particular purpose in mind. But the more likely of the two possibilities is clearly the latter.

Review

Let us begin by reviewing from the present perspective the units of discourse already in hand.

Y. Abodah Zarah 1:5. Hiyya's name is entered only because he is supposed at this point to have assembled (Tosefta's) materials now found in some corpus of supplements to the Mishnah.

Y. Shebuot 3:7. Yohanan and Simeon b. Laqish stand behind the view under discussion. They lived at the same time and were associated with the same, immense "school," the one at Tiberias. Whether or not the pericope emerges from that school, at some point, let us say, at the end of the third century, we do not know. We certainly cannot show it. The main point is that argument focuses upon the logic adduced in behalf of a shared proposition in the name of each authority, respectively. The analysis works over that logic.

Y. Shebuot 3:9. What has just been said applies here as well. It is difficult to find in the language before us a claim that we cite *ipsissima verba.* The gist of the position of each authority is what is at hand. The purposes of the argument as a whole are served, to be sure, through citing individuals, in the right order.

Y. San. 5:2. Rab and Yohanan both are assumed to have flourished in the middle of the third century. Placing their opinions in conflict does not violate chronology. There is a Mana who was a contemporary of Yohanan. The first Abin, a Babylonian, is supposed to have flourished about a half-century later. Perhaps Mana's saying at QQ stood by itself for a while, and Abin's at RR was added later on. But it is also possible that QQ and RR were shaped in response to one another—that is, at the same time, as yet another layer of argument. The flow of argument from Yohanan and Rab to Mana and Abin is smooth and uninterrupted. The addition at PP–RR seems to me a colloquy to be read as a single statement. If that is the case, then the whole is a unity, formed no earlier than its final element. This seems confirmed by the fact that the set at PP–RR is made necessary by the question at OO, and that question is integral to the exposition of Rab's position *in toto.* Accordingly, it would appear that what we have in the names of the latest authorities is an integral part of the secondary expansion of the primary dispute. In that case, part of the plan of the whole, at the very outset, was the inclusion of these final sayings as elements of the amplification of the dispute. If so, the construction will have come into being as whole not much earlier than the early or mid-fourth century. At the same time, we notice that the glosses of the positions of Rab and Yohanan do not reach us in the name of authorities who are assumed to have flourished prior to the times of the principal authorities.

The main point must not be missed: the needs of the analysis of the positions of Rab and Yohanan, with attention, in particular, to the logic behind the view of each and the unfolding of the argument to expose that logic, explain the composition of the whole. So a clear conception of the direction and purpose of inquiry existed prior to the assembly of the parts and governed the layout of arguments and the dialectic of discourse. Let us now consider from the present perspective further instances in which the names of diverse authorities figure.

Logic as the Governing Principle of Construction

Y. Baba Qamma 2:13. In this protracted discussion, we see how one authority cites another, earlier figure, with the result that the question of consistency of the view of the first authority comes under discussion. Simeon b. Laqish's interpretation of the Mishnah passage is compared with a view of Hoshaiah, yet earlier by a generation and so cited by Simeon b. Laqish. A further discussion has Ami, slightly later than Simeon b. Laqish, interpret Simeon's view. Then an opinion of Hoshaiah—hence prior to both Ami and Simeon b. Laqish—comes under discussion. The reason is not that Hoshaiah is represented as conducting a face-to-face argument with Simeon or Ami. Hoshaiah's position is formulated quite separately from theirs. But it intersects in topic and logic. Therefore the framer of the whole found it quite natural to cite Hoshaiah's views. The context is the main thing. Ilfai-Hilfa was a contemporary of Yohanan. His position in the construction hardly has been dictated by that fact. Rather, what he has to say forms a final topic of discussion, in sequence after the view of Rab, who surely came earlier in the third century than Ilfai.

The main point bears repeating. We do not find that the chronology of authorities bears any important relationship to the arrangement of opinions. We also do not find violation of the order in which authorities flourished. The long argument has been laid out in accord with the principles of logical exposition at hand. For that purpose no attention needs to be paid to the sequence in which people may have expressed their views. But people of different centuries are not made to talk to one another.

A. *"How is the tooth deemed an attested danger in regard to eating what is suitable for [eating]"* [M. 1:4C]?

B. *An ox is an attested danger to eat fruit and vegetables.*

C. *[If, however] it ate [a piece of] clothing or utensils, [the owner] pays half the value of the damage it has caused.*

D. *Under what circumstances?*

E. *[When this takes place] in the domain of the injured party.*

F. *But [if it takes place] in the public domain, he is exempt.*

G. *But if it [the ox] derived benefit [from damage done in public domain], the owner pays for the value of what [his ox] has enjoyed.*

I. A. [To what does the statement, M. 2:3D–G, "Under what circumstances?" apply?] R. Simeon b. Laqish said, "It applies to the first clause. [If, in the public domain, a beast ate what it usually eats, the owner pays nothing. But if, even in the pub-

lic domain, it ate clothing or utensils, the owner is liable because people commonly leave things in public domain, and
the owner of the beast has the responsibility to watch out for
such unusual events.]"

B. R. Yohanan said, "It applies to the entire pericope [including the
consumption of unusual items, such as clothing or utensils].
[If someone left clothing or utensils in the public domain, the
owner of the beast is exempt, because it is not common to
leave such things in public domain.]"

C. The opinions imputed to R. Simeon b. Laqish are in conflict.

D. There R. Simeon b. Laqish has said in the name of R. Hoshaiah,
"[If] an ox stood still and ate produce which was stacked in
piles, [the owner] is liable." [Hence the owner of the beast is
liable if the beast eats what it usually eats in the public domain. M. makes no distinction between the beast's doing so
while walking along and while standing still.]

E. And here he has said that [the owner is exempt if the beast eats
produce in the public domain, on the grounds that that is
common].

F. They said, "There he spoke in the name of R. Hoshaiah while
here he speaks in his own name."

II. A. A statement which R. Simeon b. Laqish said: "[If there were two
beasts in the public domain, one walking, one crouched and]
the one which was walking along butted the one which was
crouching, [the owner] is exempt [because the one which was
crouching bore responsibility for changing the normal procedure, and it is not normal for a beast to crouch in public
domain]."

B. A statement which R. Yohanan said: "[If] the one which was
walking along butted the one which was crouching, [the
owner] is liable." [The owner of the crouching beast still may
ask, "Who gave your beast the right to butt mine?"]

C. [And, Yohanan further will maintain,] it is not the end of the
matter that if the one which was walking along butts the one
which was crouching, or the one which was crouching butts
the one which was walking along, [the owner of the aggressor
is liable].

D. But even if the two of them were walking along, and one of those
which was walking along butted the other which was walking
along, [the owner] is liable [on the same grounds, namely,
while both beasts had every right to be where they were,
there is no right for one beast to butt the other].

E. [Dealing with these same matters in behalf of Simeon b. Laqish,]
R. Ami said, "R. Simeon b. Laqish's position applies only to

a case in which a beast which was walking along butted a beast which was crouching, in which case [the owner] is exempt.

F. "But if a beast which was crouching butted one which was walking along, or one which was walking along butted another which was walking along, [the owner in either case] will be liable."

G. R. Hoshaiah taught, "In all cases, [the owner] is exempt."

H. The basis for R. Hoshaiah's position is that liability for injury done by an ox's horn does not apply in public domain anyhow. [Pené Moshe prefers to read: "This is not a case of damages done by an ox's horn in the public domain."]

I. Rab said, "If the beast stood still [in public domain] and ate up produce which was lying in piles—

J. "now they have made a lenient rule in the case of tooth, in which case an ox walking along consumed produce lying in piles [and so] standing [still],

K. "while they have made a more stringent rule in the case of damages done by the horn,

L. "in which a beast which was walking along has butted a beast which was standing still. [That is, the beast which was walking along does not impose liability on its owner for produce eaten by the way. In this regard a more stringent rule applies to damages done by the beast's horn than those done by the beast's tooth, since if the beast walking along butted one lying down, the owner is liable, while, as we saw, in the case of tooth, the owner is exempt. If, to be sure, the beast had stood still and eaten produce, also in the case of damages done by tooth, the owner is liable.]"

M. Ilfai remarked, "If the beast had stood still and eaten the produce which was lying in piles, [the owner] would be liable.

N. "Now they have made a lenient rule in the case of tooth, in that if the beast which was walking along and ate produce which was lying around, the owner is exempt from paying damages.

O. "But a more stringent rule applies in the case of damages done by the horn when a beast which was walking along butted another beast which was walking along, [and the owner in this case would be liable to damages]."

Y.Niddah 1:5. In the present discussion we have a mixture of authorities of the same age, the third century, but in different countries. Samuel, in Babylonia, Rab and Yohanan, in the Land of Israel, dispute about the same thing and take diametrically opposed positions. Then Zeira, later on in the same period, comments on what has gone before. Once more the chronology and

the logic of what is said are harmonious with one another. But the layout of
the discussion as a whole accords with logical principles and how they are
to be expounded. The issue of chronology of authorities is not definitive.
What comes first are the contrary possibilities of the case. What follows will
be the harmonization and contrast of these views. The names are adduced as
signs for authorities behind principles, not as indications about the sequence
in which things actually were said. That is, the introduction of the second
century figures, Meir and Yosé, serves the purpose of linking together positions on one matter, held by Meir and Yosé, with positions on another matter,
held by Samuel and his opposition, a hundred years later. In all, the entire
construction seems to be work of the people who, at the end, gathered
together the various opinions or positions and made of them a single continuous argument. That again is the main point.

A. *In what case did they lay down the ruling, "Sufficient for her
    is her time [of first discovering the drop of menstrual blood,
    so that there is no prior contamination]"?*

B. *In the case of [a virgin's, a pregnant woman's, a nursing
    mother's, or an old woman's] first producing a drop of blood
    [after missing the period in the latter three instances].*

C. *But in the instance of the second [or later] producing of a
    drop of blood, [the blood] imparts uncleanness for the ante-
    cedent period of twenty-four hours [by reason of doubt as to
    when it first occurred].*

D. *But if [the woman] produced the first drop of blood by rea-
    son of constraint [that is, through an abnormal cause], then
    even in the case of the second drop of blood [we invoke the
    rule of] sufficiency of the time [of finding the blood for de-
    marcating the commencement of the woman's contaminating
    power].*

I. A. Samuel said, "This teaching [of A] applies only to a virgin and
       an old woman. But as to a pregnant woman and a nursing
       mother, they assign to her the entire period of her pregnancy
       or the entire period of her nursing [respectively, for the blood
       ceases, and what does flow is inconsequential, so there is no
       retroactive contamination at all]."

   B. Rab and R. Yohanan—both of them say, "All the same are the
       virgin, the old woman, the pregnant woman, and the nursing
       mother [= B]."

   C. Said R. Zeira, "The opinion of Rab and R. Yohanan accords
       with the position of R. Haninah, and all of them differ from
       the position of Samuel."

   D. For R. Eleazar said in the name of R. Haninah, "On one occa-
       sion Rabbi gave instruction in accord with the lenient rulings

of R. Meir and in accord with the lenient rulings of R. Yosé."

E. What was the nature of the case?

F. [If] the fetus was noticeable, and then [the woman] produced a drop of blood—

G. R. Meir says, "She is subject to the rule of the sufficiency of her time [of actually discovering the blood]."

H. R. Yosé says, "She imparts uncleanness retroactively for twenty-four hours."

I. [If] she produced many drops of blood, then missed three periods, and afterward produced a drop of blood,

J. R. Meir says, "She imparts uncleaness retroactively for twenty-four hours."

K. R. Yosé says, "She is subject to the rule of the sufficiency of her time [of actually discovering blood]."

L. Now if you say that they assign to her the entire period of her pregnancy or the entire period of her nursing, what need do I have for the lenient ruling of R. Yosé? The teaching of R. Meir [in such case] produces a still more lenient ruling than does that of R. Yosé. [For so far as Meir is concerned, if we read his view in the light of Samuel's opinion (A), the nursing mother and the pregnant woman enjoy the stated leniency throughout the period of nursing or pregnancy. The issue, then, is that Meir deems this drop of blood (I) as a second one. Yosé regards the cessation of the period as consequential.]

M. Said R. Mana before R. Yosé, "Or perhaps we should assign [Rabbi's ruling] to the case of the milk [dealt with above, in which Meir and Yosé dispute about whether the woman who hands over her son to a wet nurse retains the stated leniency. At issue then is whether the matter depends upon the status of the woman's milk or on the status of the child]."

N. He said to him, "The matter was explicitly stated in regard to the present issue . . . ."

Conclusion

It seems to me likely that the purposes of dialectical argument determined not only which available sayings were selected for inclusion, but also the order and purpose in accordance with which sayings were laid out. Still that is an essentially subjective judgment of an aesthetic character. Its plausibility will become greater when we consider another way in which materials were laid out, one in which the needs of logical analysis of a proposition do *not* predominate. It is to this alternative mode of selection and organization that we now turn.

Stories, Tales, Fables

A biographical or historical tale with a beginning, middle, and end effectively constitutes a complete unit of discourse. This type of unit is as coherent and well put together as the analytical ones that make up the bulk of the Talmud. One instance of this kind of unit of discourse suffices. In later chapters we shall see others.

Y. San. 2:1 = *Y. Hor. 3:1*. In what follows, the story is integral to a legal discussion. We answer a question of law by telling the tale. The tale cannot be grasped out of its legal context. That is, A–B render C comprehensible, and C is the reason for telling the tale of Simeon b. Laqish and Judah the Patriarch. This tale is no composite but the work of a single narrator. I discern no component added later on, let alone made up and inserted whole. Accordingly, the tale must be treated as an item made up at one time, that is, at the end, and not as the result of a protracted process of accretion. When the tale was made up, of course, is something we cannot know on the basis of the contents of the story.

A. R. Simeon b. Laqish said, "A ruler who sinned—they administer lashes to him by the decision of a court of three judges."

B. What is the law as to restoring him to office?

C. Said R. Haggai, "By Moses! If we put him back into office, he will kill us!"

D. R. Judah the Patriarch heard this ruling [of Simeon b. Laqish's] and was outraged. He sent a troop of Goths to arrest R. Simeon b. Laqish. [R. Simeon b. Laqish] fled to the Tower, and some say, it was to Kefar Hittayya.

E. The next day R. Yohanan went up to the meeting house, and R. Judah the Patriarch went up to the meeting house. He said to him, "Why does my master not state a teaching of Torah?"

F. [Yohanan] began to clap with one hand [only].

G. [Judah the Patriarch] said to him, "Now do people clap with only one hand?"

H. He said to him, "No, nor is Ben Laqish here [and just as one cannot clap with one hand only, so I cannot teach Torah if my colleague, Simeon b. Laqish, is absent]."

I. [Judah] said to him, "Then where is he hidden?"

J. He said to him, "In a certain tower."

K. He said to him, "You and I shall go out to greet him tomorrow."

L. R. Yohanan sent word to R. Simeon b. Laqish, "Get a teaching of Torah ready, because the patriarch is coming over to see you."

M. [Simeon b. Laqish] came forth to receive them and said, "The example which you [Judah] set is compared to the paradigm of your Creator. For when the All-Merciful came forth to redeem Israel [from Egypt], he did not send a messenger or an angel, but the Holy One, blessed be He, himself came forth, as it is said, 'For I will pass through the Land of Egypt that night' (Ex. 12:12)—and not only so, but he and his entire retinue.

N. "'What other people on earth is like thy people Israel, whom God went to redeem to be his people' (2 Sam. 7:23). 'Whom God went' (sing.) is not written here, but 'Whom God went' (plural) [-- meaning, he and all his retinue]."

O. [Judah the Patriarch] said to him, "Now why in the world did you see fit to teach this particular statement [that a ruler who sinned is subject to lashes]?"

P. He said to him, "Now did you really think that because I was afraid of you, I should hold back the teaching of the All-Merciful? [And lo, citing 1 Sam. 2:23f.,] R. Samuel b. R. Isaac said, '[Why do you do such things? For I hear of your evil dealings from all the people.] No, my sons, it is no good report [that I hear the people of the Lord spreading abroad]. If a man sins against a man, God will mediate for him; but if a man sins against the Lord, who can intercede for him? But they would not listen to the voice of their father, for it was the will of the Lord to slay them' (1 Sam. 2:23–25). [When] the people of the Lord spread about [an evil report about a man], they remove him [even though he is the patriarch]."

Miscellanies: The Building Blocks of the Units of Discourse

Thus far we have considered how units of discourse exhibit traits of conceptual unity. Discussion is organized in such a way that the analysis and unfolding of logic form the focus of discourse. Everything is arranged so as to make us see the point immediately and to permit us with little difficulty to follow the discussion, protracted though it may be. Accordingly, the striking trait of the numerous units of discourse we have inspected is the dynamic argument, the dialectical discourse, with its vigorous movement from start to finish. But the Talmud of the Land of Israel consists of more kinds of sayings and stories than those put together into the stunningly cogent constructions we have seen. Some material (not much) is left unworked, with sayings not set into some larger framework of dialectical argument at all. And even within the dialectical arguments that constitute the bulk of the Talmud's units of discourse, there are insertions of sayings essentially outside the stream of exposition. The status of these sayings now requires attention.

The sorts of units of discourse we examine constitute a very small proportion of the Talmud of the Land of Israel. I cite this type in order to establish a contrast between what, in general, was done to reshape all data (ideas, sayings, tales, verses of Scripture) into remarkably cogent dialectical arguments, and what was not but rather was left undone. For in the three passages that follow, we see the raw materials for arguments, but no cogent and sustained construction of a unitary character. When we compare the kinds of constructions we have seen with those now to come, we see still more clearly that the former point toward a single act or occasion of conceptualization and construction. The latter then do not. The dominant traits of cogency, coherence, and purposeful argument exhibited in the former, in the contrast become still clearer, hence less a matter of subjective aesthetic judgment.

Indeed, we may say that if the materials set forth in the preceding units constitute units of discourse, those that follow fall into some other literary redactional class entirely. The former proceed in a protracted and uninterrupted argument, from beginning to end. The latter jump from this to that, or, in some instances, exhibit nothing more than a common theme hence, as I said, constituting anthologies, not units of discourse in a strict sense. Since the bulk of our Talmud is made up of units of discourse of the former sort (entire tractates yield not a single example of the latter), the picture of the Talmud as a whole reveals a document in the main composed of well-conceived and carefully executed arguments. The materials at hand may not so readily be located at the period of final formulation. We cannot say for sure how these miscellanies were made up, what materials were used and revised, who preserved and handed them on, and how, in all, the conglomerations took shape. In some instances we have little more than a published card file, unrevised and unreworked. In others we follow a zigzagging discussion, not quite an argument, but also not a mere miscellany.

Y. Abodah Zarah 2:2. This unit is hardly a unity. But even if we assigned a separate Roman numeral to each distinct unit of thought (e.g., A–C = III, D = IV, E = V), we could not explain the redaction of the whole group of units. There is no sustained argument. At best we have a sequence of sayings on a common topic. But even the topic turns out to be diffuse and imprecise. The overall theme is healing on the Sabbath, which requires attention to what is a danger to life. Nothing is done, however, to explore the logic of the theme. Rather, the opening part of the discussion, A–T, is made up of a large number of individual sayings, bits and pieces of information. Then there is a story, U–Y. The reason for the story's inclusion is clear: scurvy is a danger to life. That a skilled editorial hand is at work is seen at X, which explicitly links the story to A, and, further, Y, which links it to an earlier component, I.D (not given here). Then there follow several more stories, Z, AA. These do not find so natural a place in the sequence. DD turns from healing on the Sabbath to healing through resort to idolatrous practices. Then HH, a separate but linked discussion, begins, pursuing the same theme, the issue of healing, now through violation of sexual taboos. The reason I treat the whole as a single unit of discourse is that the same theme, healing in violation of the law so as to save a life (Sabbath law, idolatry law, sexual law), connects the bulk of the materials. But the sayings and stories have not been reworked into a common discourse, let alone into a single connected argument. They are strung out. There is no significant analysis of a problem, such as we have already come to expect, but rather a repertoire of opinions. The editorial principle revealed here is principally an effort at cogent redaction of available materials in final form rather than a revision, into a seamless discussion, of whatever happened to be in hand.

III. A. Associates in the name of R. Ba bar Zabeda: "Any [wound] which is located from the lips and inward do they heal on the Sabbath [since such a wound involves danger to life]."

   B. R. Zeira objected, "Lo we have learned in the Mishnah: *He who is suffering from his teeth [nonetheless, on the Sabbath] may not suck vinegar through them [M. Shab. 14:4]*. Now are not the teeth interior to the lips? [So why is it not permitted to apply healing on the Sabbath?]"

   C. R. Zeira did not rule as has been stated, but R. Zeira in the name of R. Abba bar Zabeda: "Whatever [wound] is located from the throat and inward do they heal on the Sabbath, [since such a wound involves danger to life]."

   D. R. Zeira, R. Ba bar Zutra, R. Haninah in the name of Rabbi: "They raise up the bone of the head on the Sabbath."

   E. R. Hiyya bar Madayya, R. Jonah, R. Zeira, R. Ba bar Zutra, R. Haninah in the name of Rabbi: "They remove swollen glands of the throat on the Sabbath."

   F. R. Abbahu in the name of R. Yohanan: "An eye which became inflamed do they treat on the Sabbath."

   G. There [in Babylonia] they say in the name of R. Yohanan, "[Injuries] to hands and feet are a danger [to life]."

   H. R. Abbahu in the name of R. Yohanan: "Reddening [of a wound] is a danger [to life, and must be treated on the Sabbath]."

   I. Said R. Abin, "They remove the stinger of a scorpion on the Sabbath."

   J. Rab said, "Wine may be placed outside the eyes [on the Sabbath], but may not be placed inside the eyes."

   K. Samuel said this: "It is prohibited to put tasteless spittle into the eye on the Sabbath."

   L. From this case you learn the rule as to treating scabs [of the eye].

M.   Rabbis of Caesarea say this, "[A wound] in the shape of a frog is a danger [to life]."

N.   R. Hezekiah said in the name of rabbis of Caesarea, "A wound from a spider's bite is a danger [to life and should be treated on the Sabbath]."

O.   R. Samuel bar R. Isaac: "A burn is a danger [to life and should be treated on the Sabbath]."

P.   Said R. Jeremiah, "On the Passover they apply to it leavened [food, for healing, even though ordinarily one may not utilize leavened food on Passover]."

Q.   [If such leaven] should be absorbed, it is permitted [on Passover, as stated above].

R.   Said R. Yosé, "The Mishnah itself has made the same point: [*On the Sabbath one may handle] a sewing needle to take out a thorn [M. Shab. 17:2G]*. Now if you do not concur, then you must explain the difference between removing a thorn and removing pus."

S.   As to an eye which grew dim, they asked R. Jeremiah. He said to them, "Lo, R. Ba is before you."

They asked R. Ba and he permitted them [to apply healing in such a case].

[Jeremiah] said to them, "Also I permit [applying healing in such a case]."

T.   R. Abbahu in the name of R. Yohanan: "Scurvy is a danger to life [and may be healed on the Sabbath]."

U.   R. Yohanan had [scurvy], and he was receiving treatment from [the daughter of] Domitian in Tiberias. On Friday he went to her. He said to her, "Do I need to be treated tomorrow [on the Sabbath]?"

She said to him, "No. But if you should need something, put on seeds of date palms (and some say, seeds of Nicolaos dates), split in half and roasted, and pounded together with barley husks and a child's dried excrement, and apply that mixture. But do not reveal to anyone [this potion which I have prescribed for you]."

The next day he went up and expounded [this very pre-scription] in the study house. She heard about it and choked on a bone, (and some say, she converted to Judaism).

V.   From this story you learn three lessons:

W.   (1) You learn that scurvy is a danger [to life and may be treated on Sabbath] [T].

X.   (2) You learn that any wound which is located from the lips and within do they heal on the Sabbath [A].

Y.   (3) You learn that which R. Jacob bar Aha said in the name of

R. Yohanan, "If [a gentile] was an experienced physician, it is permitted [to accept healing from him or her]" [I.D].

Z. R. Joshua b. Levi had colic. R. Haninah and R. Jonathan instructed him to grind cress on the Sabbath and put old wine in it and drink it, so that he not be in danger [as to his life].

AA. [Joshua b. Levi] had a grandson who swallowed [something dangerous]. Someone came along and whispered over him [and the child was healed]. When he [the magician] went out, [Joshua] said to him, "What did you say over him?"

He said to him such and such a word.

He said to him, "What will be [the child's fate]! If he had died but had not heard [these words], it would have been [better] for him."

BB. [But why should the healing have worked?] It was as an error done by a ruler.

CC. R. Jacob in the name of R. Yohanan: "With all sorts of things do they effect healing, except for an idol, fornication, or committing murder [which explains AA]."

DD. R. Pinhas raised the question, "Certainly the law applies when he said to him, 'Bring me leaves from an idol,' and he brought them to him. But if he said to him, 'Bring me leaves,' without further specification, and he brought them from an idol, [what is the rule]?"

EE. Let us infer the answer to the question from this:

FF. R. Aha had chills and fever. [They brought him] a medicinal drink prepared of the phallus of Dionysian revellers. But he would not drink it. They brought it to R. Jonah, and he did drink it. Said R. Mana, "Now if R. Jonah, the patriarch, had known what it was, he would never have drunk it."

GG. Said R. Huna, "That is to say, 'They do not accept healing from something which derives from an act of fornication.'"

HH. The Sabbath has been removed from the category [of that which may not be violated, even at the cost of death, since as we have seen, many sorts of healings may be administered on the Sabbath in order to save life]. But a betrothed girl has not been removed from the category [of that which may not be violated at the cost of death. So one must die but not violate a betrothed girl, just as GG has stated].

II. *The Sabbath has been removed from the category*—is it not as regards accepting healing [on that day], and, similarly, *a betrothed girl has not been removed from the category*—is it not as regards bringing about healing [in order to save a life]? [That surely is the case.] [One may not save a life by violating a betrothed girl, as JJ–VV will now explain.]

JJ.   And it is not the end of the matter that [if the ailing person said to one,] "Bring me a married woman [so that I may have sexual relations with her and so be healed," that one may not do so], but even if [the ailing person said it was only] to hear the voice [of a married woman, one may not permit him to hear the woman's voice].

KK.   This teaching accords with the following:

LL.   In the days of R. Eleazar, a man so loved a woman that he was in danger of dying [from unconsummated desire]. They came and asked R. Eleazar, "What is the law governing her 'passing before him' so that he may live?"

MM.   He answered them, "Let him die, but [let matters not be done] in such a way."

NN.   "What is the law as to his merely hearing her voice, so that he may live?"

OO.   "Let him die, but [let matters not be done] in such a way."

PP.   Now what was the character of this girl [who was to be kept away from the man pining for her]?

QQ.   R. Jacob bar Idi and R. Isaac bar Nahman—one maintained that she was a married woman, and the other maintained that she was unmarried.

RR.   Now so far as the opinion of the one who maintained that she was a married woman, there are no problems. But as to the one who maintained that she was unmarried, [why should she not have married the man]?

SS.   Now, lo, Bar Koha Nigra so loved a woman in the days of R. Eleazar, that he was in danger of dying [from unconsummated desire]. [Read: And R. Eleazar permitted him to marry her.]

TT.   In the former case [LL–OO, we deal] with a married woman, in the latter [SS] with an unmarried woman.

UU.   Now even if you maintain that both cases deal with an unmarried woman [delete: or in both cases we deal with a married woman], interpret the case to apply to one who formed a desire for the woman while she was still married [in which case even after the divorce he may not marry her].

VV.   There are some who would explain [the rabbi's prohibiting the man to marry the unmarried woman] because she was a woman of high station, and she would not have accepted the judgment of [the rabbi to marry the love-stricken suitor], so whatever [the suitor] might do would be done subject to the prohibition of the rabbi. On that account he did not permit [the marriage].

Y. Shebuot 6:4. What follows is somewhat more characteristic of Yerushalmi's miscellanies. We have an argument, but it is not a coherent one. Rather, discourse goes on a zigzag course, each point generating what follows. No point is closely linked to the beginning, definitive of the purpose of the whole. We start with a proof text, then comment on the proof text, then comment on the comment, then comment on that point, finally illustrate the penultimate comment. The whole may be characterized as having been arranged, not redacted. But it also is much more than a mere repertoire of sayings on a common theme. An ongoing discussion, moving with the wind, so to speak, may well show us what a construction looks like in which editorial work was done not at the end but over a long period of time. The contrast to be drawn to the predominant sort of discourse, in which a complete and seamless discussion unfolds, is striking, and that, of course, is the main point of interest.

III.   A.   If the one who imposes the oath does so falsely, in the end the punishment will come forth against him. If the one who takes the oath does so falsely, in the end the punishment will come forth against him.

    B.   What is the Scriptural basis for the view [that the consequence of a false oath falls upon the one who is subject to the oath, and will not pass to his heirs]?

    C.   As it is said, "I will send it forth, says the Lord of Hosts, and it shall enter the house of the thief, and the house of him who swears falsely by my name; and it shall abide in his house and consume it, both timber and stones" (Zech. 5:4).

    D.   Said R. Samuel bar Nahman, "Angels of destruction [alluded to by Zechariah] do not have joints [so they cannot sit or lie down]."

    E.   What is the Scriptural basis for that statement?

    F.   "The Lord said to Satan, 'Whence have you come?' Satan answered the Lord, 'From going to and fro in the earth, and from walking up and down on it'" (Job 1:7). [Thus Satan could not sit or lie down.]

    G.   Yet here: " . . . and it shall *abide* in his house and consume it, both timber and stones"?

    H.   Come and take note that things which fire cannot burn, a false oath can consume.

    I.   R. Yonah said, "This is on account of lying."

    J.   R. Yosé says, "It also is on account of the truth. [Even if someone takes an oath believing that it is truthful, if the oath turns out not to be truthful, he is punished.]"

    K.   Haggai expounded [in accord with a particular case in line] with this statement of R. Yosé:

    L.   A woman went to cut out her dough with her girlfriend. Now in her kerchief two *denars* were tied up. They fell down and were cut into the dough of the girlfriend. Afterward she re-

membered the two *denars*. She went to seek them in the
house of the other woman, but did not find them. She went to
her and said to her, "Give me the two *denars* which fell and
ended up somewhere in your house." The other said, "I
know nothing about it." If [this woman (I)] knows a thing
about them, may she bury her son. And she ended up burying him. When they were coming up from the graveyard, she
heard a voice saying, "If that woman had known where the
two coins were, she would not have buried her son." [She
went and took the oath again:] "If that woman knows where
they were, may she bury her son." Another son of hers did
she bury. When they went to comfort her, they cut upon a
round loaf of bread and found the two *denars* baked inside
the round loaf of bread.

M.   This is the meaning of the saying, "Whatever one is, innocent
       or guilty—do not get involved with an oath."

Y. Abodah Zarah 1:1. The final item shows us how the zigzag line of thought
we have just seen may run on through quite a protracted discussion. We begin
with proof texts for the rule of the Mishnah, then tight analysis of the rule
by reference to other laws on the same subject, B–C. Once we complete the
initial discussion, G, we go on to a secondary matter, continuous with a mere
detail of the foregoing, H–I. J glosses that. K–L and N–U present a stunning
set of contrasts, bearing a light gloss at M. The whole was formulated by
itself and then inserted here because of K's pertinence to I–J, I assume.
V–EE likewise are inserted whole, another set of materials on Jeroboam. FF,
drawing in its wake GG, is tacked on. HH–ZZ complete the Jeroboam
anthology. Here again we see how already closed pieces of material may be
joined together in a single discussion, still failing to yield the tight and
coherent discourse generally characteristic of the Talmud.

I.   A.   R. Hama bar Uqbah derived Scriptural support for all of those
            [statements about the interval of three days during which it is
            prohibited to do business with gentiles prior to a festival of
            theirs], from the following verse: "[Come to Bethel and trans-
            gress; to Gilgal and multiply transgression;] bring your
            sacrifices every morning, your tithes on the third day" (Amos
            4:4).

      B.   Said to him R. Yosé, "If so, then even in the exilic communities
            [the rule should be the same].

      C.   "[Yet it has been taught in a Tannaitic tradition:] **'Nahum the
            Mede says, "One day in the exilic communities [before
            their festival] it is prohibited [to do business with gentiles,
            and not the three days specified by M. A.Z. 1:1, which ap-
            ply only to the Holy Land]"'** [T. A.Z. 1:1A]."

D. Why so?

E. There [in Babylonia] they looked into the matter and found out that [the pagans] prepare their requirements [for celebrating a festival] in only a single day, so they forbade business dealings with them for a single day. But here [in the Holy Land] they looked into the matter and found out that they prepare their requirements [for celebrating a festival] in a full three days, so they forbade business dealings with them for a full three days.

F. How then does R. Yosé interpret the cited verse of Scripture, "Bring your sacrifices every morning (etc.) . . . "?

G. Concerning the reign of Jeroboam does Scripture speak.

H. Once Jeroboam took up the reign over Israel, he began to entice Israel [toward idolatry], saying to them, "Come and let us practice idolatrous worship. Idolatry is permitted."

I. That is the meaning of the following verse of Scripture: "[Because Syria with Ephraim and the son of Remaliah has devised evil against you, saying,] 'Let us go up against Judah and terrify it, and let us conquer it for ourselves and set up the son of Tabeel as king in the midst of it'" (Is. 7:5–6).

J. Said R. Abba, "We have searched through the whole of Scripture and have found no instance in which his name was Tabeel. But [the meaning is] that he does good for those who serve him."

K. The Torah has said, "I chose him [the tribe of Levi] out of all the tribes of Israel to be my priest, to go up to my altar, to burn incense, to wear an ephod before me (1 Sam. 2:28)."

L. And idolatry says, "[He also made houses on high places,] and appointed priests from the fringe-element of the people, [who were not of the Levites] (1 Kings 12:31)."

M. Said Rabbi, "Not from the thorns that were among the people, but from the refuse that was among the people."

N. The Torah has said, "You shall not let the fat of my feast remain until the morning" (Ex. 23:18).

O. But idolatry has said, "Bring your sacrifices every morning" (Amos 4:4).

P. The Torah has said, "[When you offer a sacrifice of peace offerings to the Lord, you shall offer it so that you may be accepted]. It shall be eaten the same day you offer it, or on the morrow; [and anything left over until the third day shall be burned with fire]" (Lev. 19:5–6).

Q. And idolatry has said, " . . . your tithes on the third day" (Amos 4:4).

R. The Torah has said, "You shall not offer the blood of my sacrifice with leavened bread" (Ex. 23:18).

S. And idolatry has said, "Offer a sacrifice of thanksgiving of that which is leavened" (Amos 4:5).

T. The Torah has said, "When you make a vow to the Lord, your God, you shall not be slack to pay for it; [for the Lord your God will surely require it of you, and it would be a sin in you. But if you refrain from vowing, it shall be no sin in you. You shall be careful to perform what has passed your lips, for you have voluntarily vowed to the Lord your God what you have promised with your mouth]" (Deut. 23:21–23).

U. And idolatry has said, "And proclaim freewill offerings, publish them" (Amos 4:5).

V. Said R. Yudan, father of R. Mattenaiah, "The intention of [a verse of] Scripture [such as is cited below] was only to make mention of the evil traits of Israel.

W. "'On the day of our king [when Jeroboam was made king] the princes became sick with the heat of wine; he stretched out his hand with mockers' (Hosea 7:5).

X. "On the day on which Jeroboam began to reign over Israel, all Israel came to him at dusk, saying to him, 'Rise up and make an idol.'

Y. "He said to them, 'It is already dusk. I am partly drunk and partly sober, and the whole people is drunk. But if you want, go and come back in the morning.'

Z. "This is the meaning of the following Scripture, 'For like an oven their hearts burn with intrigue; all night their anger smolders; [in the morning it blazes like a flaming fire]' (Hosea 7:6)."

AA. "'All night their anger smolders.'

BB. "'In the morning it blazes like a flaming fire.'

CC. "In the morning they came to him. Thus did he say to them, 'I know what you want. But I am afraid of your Sanhedrin, lest it come and kill me.'

DD. "They said to him, 'We shall kill them.'

EE. "That is the meaning of the following verse: 'All of them are hot as an oven. And they devour their rulers' (Hos. 7:7)."

FF. [Concurring with this view], R. Levi said, "They slew them. Thus do you read in Scripture [to prove that 'the princes became sick' (HHL means 'the princes killed (HHL)], 'If anyone is found slain (HLL) (Deut. 21:1).'"

GG. Rabbi does not [concur. He maintains that] they removed them from their positions of power [but did not kill them].

HH. "On the day of our king the princes became sick with the heat of wine" (Hosea 7:5)—it was the day on which the princes became sick.

II. What made them sick? It was the heat of the wine, for they were thirsting for wine.

JJ. "He stretched out his hand with the mockers"—

KK. When he would see an honorable man, he would set up against him two mockers, who would say to him, "Now what generation do you think is the most cherished of all generations?"

LL. He would answer them, "It was the generation of the wilderness [which received the Torah]."

MM. They would say to him, "Now did they themselves not worship an idol?"

NN. And he would answer them, "Now do you think that, because they were cherished, they were not punished for their deed?"

OO. And they would say to him, "Shut up! The king wants to do exactly the same thing. Not only so, but [the generation of the wilderness] only made one [calf], while [the king] wants to make two."

PP. "[So the king took counsel and made two calves of gold] and he set up one in Bethel, and the other he put in Dan (1 Kings 12:29)."

QQ. The arrogance of Jeroboam is what condemned him decisively.

RR. Said R. Yosé bar Jacob, "It was at the conclusion of a sabbatical year that Jeroboam began to rule over Israel. That is the meaning of the following verse: '[And Moses commanded them,] At the end of every seven years, at the set time of the year of release, at the feast of booths, when all Israel comes to appear before the Lord your God at the place which he will choose, you shall read this law before all Israel in their hearing' (Deut. 31:10–11).

SS. "[Jeroboam] said, 'I shall be called upon to read [the Torah, as Scripture requires]. If I get up and read first, they will say to me, "The king of the place [in which the gathering takes place, namely, Jerusalem] comes first." And if I read second, it is disrespectful to me. And if I do not read at all, it is a humiliation for me. And, finally, if I let the people go up, they will abandon me and go over to the side of Rehoboam the son of Solomon.'

TT. "That is the meaning of the following verse of Scripture: '[And Jeroboam said in his heart, Now the kingdom will turn back to the house of David;] if this people go up to offer sacrifices in the house of the Lord at Jerusalem, then the heart of this people will turn again to their Lord, to Rehoboam, king of Judah, and they will kill me and return to Rehoboam, King of Judah' (1 Kings 12:27–28).

UU. "What then did he do? 'He made two calves of gold' (1 Kings

12:28), and he inscribed on their heart, ' . . . lest they kill you' [as counsel to his successors].

VV. "He said, 'Let every king who succeeds me look upon them.'"

WW. Said R. Huna, "'[The wicked go astray from the womb, they err from their birth speaking lies. They have venom like the venom of a serpent, like the deaf adder that stops its ear, so that it does not hear the voice of charmers] or of the cunning caster of spells' (Ps. 58:5). Whoever was associated with him [Jeroboam]—he [Jeroboam] cast a spell over him [in the sin of the bull calves]."

XX. Said R. Huna, "[Hearken, O house of the king! For the judgment pertains to you; for you have been a snare at Mizpah, and a net spread upon Tabor.] And they have made deep the pit of Shittim, [but I will chastise all of them]" (Hos. 5:1–2). For [Jeroboam] deepened the sin. He said, "Whoever explains [the meaning of what was been inscribed on the bull calves] I shall kill."

YY. Said R. Abin bar Kahana, "Also in regard to the Sabbaths and the festivals we find the Jeroboam invited them on his own. That is the meaning of the following verse: 'And Jeroboam appointed a feast on the fifteenth day of the eighth month like the feast that was in Judah, and he offered sacrifices upon the altar; [so he did in Bethel, sacrificing to the calves that he had made]' (I Kings 12:32).

ZZ. "Thus he did in Bethel, having sacrifices made in a month which he made up on his own. This is as you read in Scripture, 'In addition to the Sabbaths of the Lord' (Lev. 23:23). [So Jeroboam confused the people by establishing his own calendar for Bethel, keeping the people back from pilgrimages to Jerusalem in such a way.]"

Reading through this long extract, we may readily forget our purpose. It is to see a passage not redacted at the end and with a clear-cut purpose, but rather formed through some process of agglutination or accretion, whether all at once or over a long period of time. It is the contrast to the strikingly cogent discourses we reviewed above—whether in the form of abstract logical analysis or in the guise of a well-told tale—that I wish to draw. How do we claim to distinguish between, first, a story or an analytical discourse formed at the end, with a single purpose in mind, and, second, a protracted sequence of loosely-strung-together sayings, observations, and remarks? The latter may well take shape over a period of time, though of course we cannot estimate how long. But the former cannot have taken shape other than all at once. That is to say, a story or analysis begins in the mind of an author (or group of authors) who knows precisely what he wishes to accomplish, from beginning to end. And the former sort of unit of discourse predominates.

Conclusion

The upshot is that we indeed may speak about "the Talmud," its voice, its purposes, its mode of constructing a view of the Israelite world. The reason is that, when we claim "the Talmud" speaks, we replicate both the main lines of chronology and the literary character of the document. These point toward the formation of the bulk of materials—its units of discourse—in a process lasting (to take a guess) about half a century, prior to the ultimate arrangement of these units of discourse around passages of the Mishnah and the closure and redaction of the whole into the document we now know.

Let me recapitulate the argument that has led to the conclusion just now stated, since this chapter has been rich in illustration and disproportionately parsimonious in explication. My view is that the reader is better served by a repertoire of sources, selected more or less at random, than by an argument amply expressed but separate from all concrete evidence.

The reason, I claim, that we may rely upon the Talmud to testify to the viewpoint of its framers (we assume, a group of sages) at the end point in the Talmud's formation is simple. We rely upon the document as a whole because it speaks, over all, in a uniform voice. It is not merely an encyclopedia of information, but, in general, a sustained, remarkably protracted, uniform inquiry into the logical traits of passages of the Mishnah. Most of the Talmud deals with the exegesis and amplification of the Mishnah's rules. Wherever we turn, that labor of exegesis and amplification, without differentiation in topics or tractates, conforms to a few simple rules in inquiry, repeatedly phrased, implicitly or explicitly, in a few simple rhetorical forms or patterns. The taxonomies worked out in *The Talmud of the Land of Israel,* vol. 35, *Introduction: Taxonomy,* repeatedly demonstrated the uniform character of the document as a whole. They furthermore defined the essentially simple rules defining that overall character.

Now, as I pointed out in the section above on "The Legacy of the Mishnah," the arguments that constitute the exegetical and amplificatory work of the Talmud often contain names of specific authorities. These figures are assumed to have lived not only at the end of the process of the formation of the document, but at the beginning and middle as well. If we could demonstrate that these authorities really said what was attributed to them, we should be able to compose a history of the exegetical process, not merely an account of its end product. We should further hope to relate what people were saying about laws of the Mishnah to the setting in which they did their work. The setting would be susceptible of description in both its social and intellectual dimensions: several periods of history of the Jews of the Land of Israel from

200 to 400, several sequences of intellectual history (modes of thought, manner of framing questions, ongoing issues, and one-time inquiries). Two hundred years is a long time; much can have happened. Relating the text to its context, not merely over two centuries viewed in retrospect, but decade by decade, can only serve to enlighten us and deepen our understanding of the end product. But, alas, until the end—350–400—it turns out that we cannot relate text to context.

We have very good reason to suppose that the text as we have it does speak about the limited context of the period of the actual framing of the text's principal building blocks. The bulk of this chapter has been devoted to the argument and illustration of that proposition. As I said before, the argument is simple. (1) The building blocks—units of discourse—give evidence of having been put together in a moment of deliberation, in accordance with a plan of exposition, and in response to a finite problem of logical analysis. (2) To state matters negatively, the units of discourse in no way appear to have taken shape slowly, over a long period of time, in a process governed by the order in which sayings were framed, now and here, then and there, later and anywhere else (so to speak). Before us is the result of considered redaction, not protracted accretion, mindful construction, not sedimentary accretion. Now having stated the thesis, I could think of no proof for it, other than what seemed the (to me self-evident) character of the texts themselves. That is why I presented numerous examples of the same fundamental aesthetic trait: careful, purposeful redaction, considered formulation. And, as I said at the outset of this chapter, the traits of the bulk of the Talmud of the Land of Israel may be explained in one of only two ways.

One way is this: the very heirs of the Mishnah, in the opening generation, circa A.D. 200–225, agreed upon conventions not merely of speech and rhetorical formulation, but also of thought and modes of analysis. They further imposed these conventions on all subsequent generations, wherever they lived, whenever they did their work. Accordingly, at the outset the decision was made to do the work precisely in the way in which, two hundred years later, the work turns out to have been done.

The alternative view is that, some time late in the formation of diverse materials in reponse to the Mishnah (and to various other considerations), some people got together and made a decision to rework whatever was in hand into a single, stunningly cogent document, the Talmud as we know it in the bulk of its units of discourse. Whether this work took a day or a half-century, it was the work of sages who knew precisely what they wished to do and who did it over and over again. This second view is the one I take, and on the basis of it the remainder of this book unfolds. The consequence is that the Talmud exhibits a viewpoint. It is portrayed in what I have called "the Talmud's one voice." In the next chapter we shall examine what sages propose to say about the Mishnah through that voice: the point of insistence.

In claiming that we deal not only with uniform rhetoric, but with a single cogent viewpoint, we must take full account of the contrary claim of the Talmud's framers themselves. This claim they lay down through the constant citations of sayings in the names of specific authorities. It must follow that differentiation by chronology—the periods in which the several sages cited actually flourished—is possible. To be sure, the original purpose of citing named authorities was not to set forth chronological lines, but to establish the authority behind a given view of the law. But the history of viewpoints should be possible. As I argued earlier, it *would* be possible if we could show, on the basis of evidence external to the Talmud itself, that the Talmud's own claim in attributing statements to specific people is subject to verification or falsification. But all that I can show is a general respect for chronology, not only authority, in the unfolding of discussion. That is, we are not likely to find in our Talmud that an authority of the early third century is made to comment on a statement in the name of a sage of the later fourth century. But the organizing principle of discourse (even in anthologies) never derives from the order in which authorities lived. And that is the main point. The logical requirements of the analysis at hand determine the limits of applied and practical reason framed by the sustained discourses of which the Talmud is composed.

In order further to illustrate the (ultimately unprovable) proposition at hand, I presented a number of units of discourse organized not in accordance with the requirements of cogent and dialectical argument. These units exhibit one of two qualities. (1) They present an anthology of sayings on a single topic, without reworking these sayings into a coherent argument. (2) They present a sequence of related, short-term statements, zigzagging from point to point without evidence of an overall plan or purpose: this, then that. Stories, tales, and fables, by contrast, do exhibit the traits of unity and purpose so striking in the generality of units of discourse devoted to analysis of law. So the point of differentiation is not subject matter—law as against lore. Rather, it is the literary and conceptual history of the unit of discourse at hand. Now it may well be the case that sayings not reworked into the structure of a larger argument really do derive from the authority to whom they are ascribed. But if the discrete opinions at hand then do not provide us with a logical and analytical proposition, they also do not give us much else that is very interesting. They constitute isolated data, lacking all pattern, making no clear point. The fact that Rabbi X held opinion A, while Rabbi Y maintained position Q, is without sense, unless A and Q together say more than they tell us separately. This they do not, as a review of the odd bits of opinion on what constitutes a danger to health will make amply clear.

So in the end we know what the framers of the Talmud want us to know. And when they fail to frame a cogent statement of matters as they see them, we cannot take their place and use more intelligently than they did the detritus they have left to us. The statements that may "truly" speak of a given age before the end time of rhetorical formalization and conceptual completion and closure are incoherent and desiccated. Efforts to make them coherent by organizing them into categories of our own making, as against the categories created by the Talmud's sages, prove little short of ludicrous. So in all, we know what the Talmud's last authorities want us to know. That seems to me a very ample gift of knowledge—not merely of facts—and a generous challenge to our capacities of description, analysis, and interpretation.

3

The Quest for Certainty

The Challenge of the Mishnah

If we want to know what concerns shaped the imagination of the makers of the Talmud, the sages of the later fourth century, we must ask what they said about the Mishnah. For the Mishnah forms the center of their attention, the focus of nearly the whole of the Talmud's inquiry. In describing, then interpreting, the testimony of the Yerushalmi about the formation of Judaism, therefore, we must locate the points of insistence, the recurrent questions, the patterns of thought, which, all together, tell us what, about the Mishnah in particular, confronted the Talmud's sages as issues of urgency. These then are to be generalized beyond the specificities of exegesis of the Mishnah.

To begin at the beginning, the very character of the Talmud tells us the sages' view of the Mishnah, which presented itself to them as constitutive, the text of ultimate concern. That self-evident fact requires specification when we realize that, to others of the same period as well as to Israelites of an earlier time, discussions of law did not invariably yield secondary compositions upon an authoritative code outside of Scripture. To be sure, the legal texts of the Essene library at Qumran are framed as autonomous statements of ordinary rules and procedures, perhaps comparable with the Mishnah. But these then do not elicit secondary expansion and development, the accretion of sustained discourse, such as the Talmud reveals. If, in the Essene community, another text, besides Scripture, was venerated, a tradition or a *torah* beyond that written down by Moses was authoritative, it was not the Manual of Discipline. Rules for an occasion such as those in the Manual of Discipline did not generate elaborate books of explanation and amplification. Books of *ad hoc* rules, so far as we know, were not venerated, and people who knew those rules and could apply them were not on that account alone treated as holy. Israelites could and did write down rules without making the rule book into a focus of intellectual obsession, creating a line-by-line exegesis for a text, the way the Talmud's sages exalted the phrases and words of the Mishnah and so vastly expanded the whole into something larger and deeper than what it originally had been.

Among whatever candidates, whether the Mishnah, the Manual of Discipline, the Elephantine papyri, or even the Holiness Code, the Priestly Code, and the Covenant Code of the Pentateuch, the mosaics of the written Torah, so far as we know, only the Mishnah received a *talmud*. What separated the Mishnah from all other, earlier Israelite law codes must be located in the fact and circumstance of its formation and reception. But we should be carried far afield to speculate on the comparisons in the diverse states of Israelite politics and culture, revealed among the diverse circumstances in which the various codes, or even fragments, of law came to closure and reached a position of authority for the Jewish nation. It suffices to state the simple conclusion that, for the sages of the later fourth century (and for their predecessors as well, we must assume), the Mishnah, beyond Scripture, constituted Israel's single most important piece of writing. It is, at any rate, the document they cite after Scripture.

That fact is not difficult to interpret. The character of the Talmud presents us with the definitive context. The Talmud is a commentary written by philosopher-lawyers, men of extraordinary power to explain and amplify legal words and phrases, to generalize about rules, to theorize about matters of law as about mathematics. The reason that the sages deemed it urgent to do so, and with such extraordinary vigor and energy, must surely be that the document in hand, the Mishnah, was the authoritative code for their courts. The exposition of the laws of the Mishnah demanded their best energies because the Mishnah's laws governed. Studied, therefore, in their circles of disciples, these laws defined both what was to be done and why sages, in particular, were the ones to do it.

We cannot usefully speculate on whether the work of studying and applying in court the laws of the Mishnah merely began in the final quarter of the two centuries at hand. We cannot say whether the sages who made up the Talmud did so because it was just about 350 that they came into their courts and so needed to master the Mishnah's laws in order to apply them in their decisions. At the other extreme, we do not know if, from the very moment of its closure in 200, the Mishnah was entrusted to sages such as those represented in our Talmud, clerks in the administration of the Jewish nation in the Roman system for the Land of Israel. Stories that say so do not settle the question. We know only this: two hundred years after the closure of the Mishnah, the Talmud came forth with its ample testimony to the concerns of philosopher-lawyers, who, in part, devoted their lives to clerkships in the Jewish government, such as it was, of their country. We have no adequate evidence to show just when these sages received the code and so found it necessary, for pressing, everyday reasons, to rework it into what they made of it. That they did receive and rework the Mishnah we know only because we have the Talmud. Whether the work took them a day or two hundred years is what we cannot say for sure.

To state the obvious, the work was done by people who needed to do the work in just the way they did it. From that simple supposition all else follows. Philosophers (if that is what they were) were drawn to this text, rather than some other, because they were also lawyers. These lawyers' profession centered upon an institution lacking analogy in our own world and hence also lacking a suitable name in our language. We call it simply an "institution." The institution was formed by masters with their disciples and subordinated specialists, such as professional memorizers of traditions. The institution in part intersected with the Jewish government of the country and so constituted a court or bureau of some sort. Certain activities of public administration are well represented, as we shall see. So the institution intersected, also, with the political system of the Jewish sector of the Land of Israel and constituted a kind of inchoate municipality. But the institution did not encompass the Jewish government, which comprised other elements. The tales told about this same institution and the fantasies attached to its principal masters testify to yet another trait. The institution formed a center of supernatural power. So whatever we call it, the institution that received the Mishnah and produced the Talmud turns out to have been protean and remarkably productive. It made Judaism. But in saying so, I have moved far ahead of my story.

Let us return to the lawyer-philosophers of the Talmud. We want to know what, in regard to the Mishnah, they wished to know and how they proposed to find it out. Remaining wholly within the limits of the evidence of the Talmud itself, we have to deal with two distinct questions. First, we ask how the sages of the Talmud explained the Mishnah as a whole. Second, we want to know how they dealt with the Mishnah, piece by piece. In answering both questions, we move from the details constituted by units of discourse and their traits and proceed to generalizations made plausible by the accumulation of observations.

The Talmud's Theory of the Mishnah

Since the Mishnah stands forth as the principal authority for the law and theology of Judaism, so far as the Palestinian Talmud portrayed both, one conclusion must follow. The Mishnah constituted the stable foundation for certainty, the basis for authority, legitimating whatever the Talmudic sages did in their work of governance of Israel in its land. The character of the Talmud makes it clear that the Mishnah constituted the foundation and set goal of the Talmud's sages' quest for authority. By this I mean a simple thing. The character of Talmudic discourse tells us sages believed that if they knew precisely what the Mishnah said and meant, they then knew what they were supposed to do, how things were supposed to be. So the proper interpretation of the Mishnah, in relationship to Scripture to be sure, served as the ultimate guarantee of certainty.

We therefore should anticipate a splendid myth of the origin and authority of the Mishnah, on which, for sages, all else rested. Yet, so far as I can see, the Talmud presents no explicit theory of the Mishnah. Implicitly, however, the Talmud's judgment of the Mishnah is self-evident, hardly demanding specification. After Scripture, the Mishnah is the authoritative law code of Israelite life, the center, the focus, the source. From it all else flows. Beyond the Mishnah is only Scripture. At the same time, the very implicit character of the expression of this fundamental judgment is puzzling. While nearly every unit of discourse of the Talmud—90% of the whole, as I have said— pays its tribute to the importance of interpreting a cited law of the Mishnah, seldom does a passage of the Talmud speak of the Mishnah as a whole, let alone of its origin and authority. It is rare to find an allusion to a complete tractate, or even to a chapter as such. Accordingly, if we want to know how the sages of the Talmud explained to themselves the status of the Mishnah as such, we are at a loss to find out. All is implicit, with views of the whole rarely expressed.

To be sure, other contemporary documents describe the Mishnah as "oral Torah," Torah revealed by God to Moses at Mount Sinai and formulated and transmitted through a process of oral formulation and memorization. The myth of the two Torahs, one in writing, the other transmitted orally but now contained in the Mishnah and its continuations in the Talmuds, plays no substantial role in the Yerushalmi's treatment of the Mishnah. That myth finds expression in the Babylonian Talmud. To be sure, it is easier to say what is than what is not, in either one of the Talmuds. But it suffices at this stage to observe that the myth of the two Torahs is not invoked to account for the striking and paramount trait of the Yerushalmi: its consistent interest in the exposition and amplification of the Mishnah's laws. Nowhere are we explicitly told why that exercise is necessary.

Admittedly, the Yerushalmi knows full well the theory that there is a tradition separate from, and in addition to, the written Torah. But this tradition it knows as "the teachings of scribes." The Mishnah is not identified as the collection of those teachings. An ample instantiation of the Yerushalmi's recognition of this other, separate tradition is contained in the following unit of discourse. What is interesting is that, if these discussions take for granted the availability to Israel of authoritative teachings in addition to those of Scripture, they do not then claim those teachings are contained, uniquely or even partially, in the Mishnah in particular. Indeed, the discussion is remarkable in its supposition that extra-Scriptural teachings are associated with the views of "scribes," perhaps legitimately called sages, but not in a book to be venerated, or memorized as a deed of ritual learning.

Y. Abodah Zarah 2:7.III.

A.   Associates in the name of R. Yohanan: "The words of scribes are more beloved than the words of Torah and more cherished than words of Torah: 'Your palate is like the best wine' (Song 7:9)."

B.   Simeon bar Ba in the name of R. Yohanan: "The words of scribes are more beloved than the words of Torah and more cherished than words of Torah: 'For your love is better than wine' (Song 1:2)." . . .

D.   R. Ishmael repeated the following: "The words of Torah are subject to prohibition, and they are subject to remission; they are subject to lenient rulings, and they are subject to strict rulings. But words of scribes all are subject only to strict interpretation, for we have learned there: *He who rules, 'There is no requirement to wear phylacteries,' in order to transgress the teachings of the Torah, is exempt. But if he said, 'There are five partitions in the phylactery, instead of four,' in order to add to what the scribes have taught, he is liable'* [*M. San. 11:3*]."

E.   R. Haninah in the name of R. Idi in the name of R. Tanhum b. R. Hiyya: "More stringent are the words of the elders than the words of the prophets. For it is written, 'Do not preach—thus they preach—one should not preach of such things' (Mic. 2:6). And it is written, '[If a man should go about and utter wind and lies, saying,] "I will preach to you of wine and strong drink," he would be the preacher for this people!' (Mic. 2:11).

F.   "A prophet and an elder—to what are they comparable? To a king who sent two senators of his to a certain province. Concerning one of them he wrote, 'If he does not show you my seal and signet, do not believe him.' But concerning the other one he wrote, 'Even though he does not show you my seal and signet, believe him.' So in the case of the prophet, he has had to write, 'If a prophet arises among you . . . and gives you a sign or a wonder . . . ' (Deut. 13:1). But here [with regard to an elder:] ' . . . according to the instructions which they give you . . . ' (Deut. 17:11) [without a sign or a wonder]."

What is important in the foregoing anthology is the distinction between teachings contained in the Torah and teachings in the name or authority of "scribes." These latter teachings are associated with quite specific details of the law and are indicated in the Mishnah's rule itself. Further, at E we have "elders" as against prophets. What conclusion is to be drawn from this

mixture of word choices referring to a law or tradition in addition to that of
Scripture? The commonplace view, maintained in diverse forms of ancient
Judaism, that Israel had access to a tradition beyond Scripture, clearly was
well-known to the framers of the Yerushalmi. The question of how these
framers viewed the Mishnah, however, is not to be settled by that fact. As
I said, I cannot point to a single passage in which explicit judgment upon the
character and status of the Mishnah as a complete document is laid down.
Nor is the Mishnah treated as a symbol or called "the oral Torah." But there
is ample evidence, once again implicit in what happens to the Mishnah in the
Talmud, to allow a reliable description of how the Talmud's founders view
the Mishnah.

That view may be stated very simply. The Mishnah rarely cites verses of
Scripture in support of its propositions. The Talmud routinely adduces Scriptural bases for the Mishnah's laws. The Mishnah seldom undertakes the
exegesis of verses of Scripture for any purpose. The Talmud consistently
investigates the meaning of verses of Scripture, and does so for a variety of
purposes. Accordingly, the Talmud, subordinate as it is to the Mishnah,
regards the Mishnah as subordinate to, and contingent upon, Scripture. That
is why, in the Talmud's view, the Mishnah requires the support of proof texts
of Scripture. That fact can mean only that, by itself, the Mishnah exercises
no autonomous authority and enjoys no independent standing or norm-
setting status. The task of the framers of the Talmud is not only to explain
Mishnah law but to prove *from Scripture* the facticity of rules of the Mishnah.
Accordingly, so far as the Talmud has a theory about the Mishnah as such,
as distinct from a theory about the exposition, amplification, and application
to the court system of various laws in the Mishnah, it is quite clear. To state
matters negatively (and the absence of articulate statements makes this the
wiser choice), the Mishnah does not enjoy autonomous and uncontingent
authority as part of the one whole Torah of Moses revealed by God at Sinai.
The simple fact that one principal task facing the sages, as I just said, is to
adduce proof texts for the Mishnah's laws, makes this conclusion ineluctable. It follows that, without such texts, those laws lack foundation. We
now turn to the ways in which the Yerushalmi does this work of founding
upon the secure basis of the written Torah the fundamental propositions of the
Mishnah's laws.

Scripture behind Mishnah in the Yerushalmi

Most units of discourse in the Yerushalmi take up the exegesis and
amplification of the Mishnah. Exegesis for the Talmudic sages means many
things, from the close reading of a line and explanation of its word choices
to large-scale, wide-ranging, and encompassing speculation on legal prin-

ciples expressed, among other places, in the passage at hand. Yet two attitudes of mind appear everywhere.

First, the sages rarely, if ever, set out to twist the meaning of a Mishnah passage out of its original shape. Whatever problems they wish to solve, they do not resort in the statement of the Mishnah's rule to deliberately fanciful or capricious readings of what is at hand. Now that is an entirely subjective judgment, since one generation's plain sense is another age's fancy. What it means is (merely) that our sense and their sense of straightforward reading of a passage are the same. By our standards, they were honest men, because they thought like us. That fact is so blatant and ubiquitous as to require no further specification. Since a common heritage of intellectual procedures, a single view of the correct hermeneutics for a sacred text, read with philosophical clarity and honesty, joins us to them, we may reasonably express puzzlement with another paramount aspect of the Talmud's exegetical program.

The Talmud's sages, second, constantly cite verses of Scripture when reading statements of the Mishnah. These they read in their own way. References to specific verses of Scripture are as uncommon in the Mishnah as they are routine in the Talmud. For the framers of the Talmud, certainty for the Mishnah's rules depended upon adducing Scriptural proof texts. The entire system—the laws, courts, power of lawyer-philosophers themselves—thus is seen to rest upon the written revelation of God to Moses at Sinai, and on that alone. What this means for the sages' view of the Mishnah is that the details of the document depended for validity upon details contained within Mosaic revelation, in the written Torah. While, as we saw, some traditions, deemed entirely valid, were attributed to scribes of olden times, these enjoyed a quite separate and explicitly subordinate status from the statements of the written Torah.

The Mishnah, to begin with, was treated only as a collection of rules, each to be faithfully read by itself as a detail. That is why Scriptural proof texts were cited to support one rule after another, without any large-scale thesis about the status of the document containing those discrete rules. Just as the sages of the Talmud read the Mishnah bit by bit, so they adduced evidence from Scripture for its rules, bit by bit. They cannot, then, have considered the proposition that the Mishnah stood alongside the written Torah, as the oral part of "the one whole Torah of Moses our rabbi." If that version of the Torah myth found its way into the Yerushalmi at all, it played no great role in the approach of the Yerushalmi to the question of authority and certainty of the principal document, the Mishnah itself. The Talmud's fragmented vision of the Mishnah accounts for the character of the Yerushalmi's approach, through passages of the Mishnah, to verses of Scripture.

Let us now proceed to review the ways in which the Talmud presents proof texts for allegations of passages of the Mishnah, a sizable repertoire. We begin with the simplest examples, in which a passage of the Mishnah is cited, then linked directly to a verse of Scripture, deemed to constitute self-evident proof for what has been said. The Mishnah's rule is given in italics.

Y. Abodah Zarah 4:4.III.

A. [Citing M. A.Z. 4:4:] *An idol belonging to a gentile is prohibited forthwith,* in line with the following verse of Scripture: "You shall surely destroy [all places where the nations whom you shall dispossess served their gods]" (Deut. 12:2)—forthwith.

B. *And one belonging to an Israelite is prohibited only after it has been worshipped,* in line with the following verse of Scripture: "Cursed be the man who makes a graven or molten image, an abomination to the Lord, a thing made by the hands of a craftsman, and set it up in secret" (Deut. 27:15)—when he has set it up.

C. There are those who reverse the matter:

D. An idol belonging to an Israelite is prohibited forthwith, as it is written, "Cursed be the man who makes a graven or molten image."

E. And one belonging to a gentile is prohibited only after it has been worshipped, as it is written, "You shall surely destroy all the places where the nations whom you shall dispossess served their gods."

F. R. Isaac bar Nahman in the name of Samuel derived that same view [that an idol belonging to a gentile is prohibited only after it has been worshipped] from the following: If one has inherited [the idol] when it [already] is deemed a god, "in fire shall you burn it," and if not: "where the nations whom you shall dispossess . . . their gods." [You shall tear down their altars and dash in pieces their pillars and burn their Asherim with fire . . .] (Deut. 12:2–3).

Y. Abodah Zarah 4:4.IV.

A. [With reference to the following passage of the Mishnah: *A gentile has the power to nullify an idol belonging either to himself or his fellow, but an Israelite has not got the power to nullify an idol belonging to a gentile (Y. A.Z. 4:4)],* R. Yohanan in the name of R. Yannai derived that view from the following verse of Scripture: "You shall not covet the silver or the gold that is on them or take it for yourselves" (Deut. 7:25). "You may not covet and take [that gold], but others may covet [the gold], and then you may take it."

Y. Niddah 2:6.

    A.   *Five [colors of] blood are unclean in a woman.*

II. A.   Whence do we derive evidence that there are five varieties of unclean blood specified by the Torah?

    B.   Said R. Joshua b. Levi: "'And she has uncovered the fountain of her bloods' (Lev. 20:18) [= two], 'And she will be clean from the source of her bloods' [= two], a discharge of blood from her body (Lev. 15:19) [= one, thus five]."

    C.   And lo: "And if a woman has a discharge of blood" (Lev. 15:25)—this blood [too] should be part of that number.

III. A.   And how do we know that there is unclean blood, and there is clean blood[, so not all blood is unclean, but only the five which are listed]?

    B.   R. Hama bar Joseph in the name of R. Hoshaiah: "It is written, If any case arises requiring a decision . . . (Deut. 17:8). Now 'between blood and (W) blood' is not written, but *of one kind of blood from (L) another.*

    C.   "On this basis there is proof that there is blood that is unclean, and blood that is clean."

Y. Horayot 1:6.

    A.   *"[If] the court made an [erroneous] decision, and the entire community [of Israel], or the greater part of the community carried out their decision, they bring a bullock.*

    B.   *"In the case of idolatry (Num. 14:24), they bring a bullock and a goat,"* the words of R. Meir.

    C.   *R. Judah says, "Twelve tribes [individually] bring twelve bullocks.*

    D.   *"And in the case of idolatry, they bring twelve bullocks and twelve goats."*

    E.   *R. Simeon says, "Thirteen bullocks, and in the case of idolatry, thirteen bullocks and thirteen goats:*

    F.   *"a bullock and a goat for each and every tribe, and [in addition] a bullock and a goat for the court."*

III. A.   R. Abun in the name of R. Benjamin bar Levi: "There is a Scripture that supports the position of the one [Judah, Simeon] who says, 'Each tribe is called a congregation.'

    B.   "For it is written, 'A nation and a congregation of nations will come from you' (Gen. 35:11).

    C.   "And yet [at the time that that statement was made], Benjamin had not yet been born. [So the reference to a coming *congregation* applied to a single tribe.]"

Y. Shebuot 1:4.

    A.   *And for that [uncleanness] for which there is no awareness*
           [of uncleanness] either at the beginning or at the end,

    B.   *"the goats offered on festivals and the goats offered on new*
           months effect atonement," the words of R. Judah.

I. A.   R. Eleazar in the name of R. Hoshaiah: "The Scriptural basis for
           the position of R. Judah is as follows: 'Also one male goat
           for a sin offering to the Lord' (Num. 28:15, in context of the
           offerings of the beginnings of the months)—for a sin about
           which only the Lord knows this goat effects atonement."

    B.   I thus have information concerning the goat offered on the be-
           ginning of the new month. How do I know that that same
           rule applies to the goats offered on the occasion of festivals?

    C.   Said R. Zira, "'*Also* a goat . . . '—the use of the word also adds
           to the first matter under discussion [this other one, namely,
           the goats offered on the festivals]."

The preceding instances all follow a single pattern. A statement of the
Mishnah is given, followed by a verse of Scripture regarded as proof of the
antecedent conception. The first instance, Y. A.Z. 4:4, is the most obvious,
since all we have are sentences from the one document, the Mishnah, juxtaposed to sentences from the other, the Scripture. In the next, out of the same
passage, Yohanan-Yannai first cite, then restate the meaning of, a verse. In
the third, at Y. Niddah 2:6, the words of a verse of Scripture are treated one
by one, each yielding a number of types of blood. So the sense of the verse
is less important than its formal character. By contrast, at the next example,
Y. Hor. 1:6, the substance and sense of the verse, not some minor detail,
govern the matter. The same is the case for Hoshaiah's view at Y. Sheb. 1:4,
in contrast to Zira's. In this last instance we see that a mixture of approaches
to the reading of a verse will be accepted, so that the positions of both parties
to a disagreement enjoy the support of a single passage of Scripture. But all
of these instances of the use of Scripture to sustain allegations of a rule of
the Mishnah have in common their simplicity.

    Along the lines of the foregoing, but somewhat more complex, are exam-
ples in which the language of the Mishnah-rule is not cited verbatim, but its
underlying proposition is stated, then provided with a proof text. Here are
instances of this phenomenon.

Y. Sanhedrin 1:1.I.

    A.   And whence shall we produce evidence from Scripture [for the
           factual statement of M. San. 1:1A]?

    B.   "'And these things shall be for a statute and ordinance' (Num.
           35:29).

    C.   "On the basis of this verse I draw the conclusion that [the reference to both statute and ordinance bears this meaning:] careful cross-examination of witnesses is required not only for capital cases but also for property ones.

D. "And then how do we know that property cases require three [and not twenty-three judges, as in the case of capital cases]?

E. "'The owner of the house shall come near to the judges' (Ex. 22:8)—thus encompassing one judge.

F. "'The case of both parties shall come before the judges' (Ex. 22:9)—thus encompassing a second judge.

G. "' . . . he whom the judges shall condemn shall pay . . . ' (Ex. 22:9)—lo, here is yet a third," the words of R. Josiah.

I. But: " . . . to the judge . . . ,"—lo, one judge is required.

J. " . . . whom the judge shall condemn . . . "—lo, two judges.

K. Now a court cannot be made up of an even number of judges, so they add yet a third judge, so that there are three in all on the court."

Yerushalmi Baba Mesia 2:1.

A. *What lost items are [the finder's], and which ones is he liable to proclaim [in the lost-and-found]?*

B. *These lost items are his [the finder's]:*

C. *"[if] he found pieces of fruit scattered about, coins scattered about, small sheaves in the public domain, cakes of figs, baker's loaves, strings of fish, pieces of meat, wool shearings [as they come] from the country [of origin], stalks of flax, or tongues of purple—lo, these are his," [the words of R. Meir].*

I. A. [Since the operative criterion in M. B.M. 2:1 is that, with undistinguished items such as these, the owner takes for granted he will not recover them and so despairs of them, thus giving up his rights of ownership to them, we now ask:] Whence do we know from the Torah the law of the owner's despair [of recovering his property constitutes relinquishing rights of ownership and declaring the property to be ownerless, hence available to whoever finds it]?

B. R. Yohanan in the name of R. Simeon b. Yehosedeq: "'And so you shall do with his ass; so you shall do with his garment; so you shall do with any lost thing of your brother's, which he loses and you find; you may not withhold your help' (Deut. 22:3)—

C. "That which is [perceived as] lost by him and found by you, you are liable to proclaim [as having been found], and that which is not [perceived as] lost by him [because he has given up hope of recovering it anyhow] and found by you, you are not liable to proclaim.

D.   "This then excludes that for which the owner has despaired,
     which is lost to him and to any one."

Yerushalmi Baba Mesia 3:1.
A.   *He who deposits with his fellow a beast or utensils,*
B.   *and they were stolen or lost,*
C.   *[if the bailee] made restitution and was unwilling to take an
     oath—*
D.   *(for they have said, "An unpaid bailee takes an oath and
     thereby carries out his obligation [without paying compensa-
     tion for the loss of the bailment]"—)*
E.   *[if] then the thief was found,*
F.   *[the thief] pays twofold restitution.*
G.   *[If] he had slaughtered or sold the beast, he pays fourfold or
     fivefold restitution.*
H.   *To whom does he pay restitution?*
I.   *To him with whom the bailment was left.*

I.   A.   Whence do you bring evidence [for the proposition of M. B.M.
          3:1H–I that in a case in which the bailee pays compensation,
          he is given the double indemnity which is collected from the
          thief]?
     B.   "[If a man steals an ox or a sheep and kills it or sells it, he shall
          pay five oxen for an ox, and four sheep for a sheep. He shall
          make restitution; if he has nothing, then he shall be sold for
          his theft.] If the stolen beast is found alive in his possession,
          [whether it is an ox or an ass or a sheep, he shall pay dou-
          ble]" (Ex. 22:1–4).
     C.   Now do we not already know [from Ex. 22:7] that if the thief is
          found, he will pay a double-indemnity?
     D.   So why does Scripture state, "He shall pay double"?
     E.   If it does not apply to the matter at hand, then treat it as referring
          to a further matter, [that is, if it does not mean the thief pays
          a double-indemnity to the one from whom he stole, which we
          know from other references, then treat the point of applica-
          tion as that before us. [For the rules governing bailments
          state, "If a man delivers to his neighbor money or goods to
          keep, and it is stolen out of the man's house, then, if the
          thief is found, he shall pay double" (Ex. 22:7).]

What is striking in the preceding instances is the presence of a secondary
layer of reasoning about the implications of a verse of Scripture. The process
of reasoning then derives from the verse a principle not made explicit
therein, and that principle turns out to be precisely what the Mishnah's rule
maintains. Accordingly, the Mishnah's law is shown to be merely a corollary

of the Scripture's, that is, the obverse side of the coin. Or the Scripture's rule is shown to deal only with the case pertinent to the Mishnah's law, rather than to what, on the surface, that biblical law seems to contain.

We proceed to instances in which a disputed point of the Mishnah is linked to a dispute on the interpretation of the pertinent verses of Scripture. What is important is that the dispute in the Mishnah is made to depend upon not principles of law but readings of the same pertinent verses of Scripture. Once again the net effect is to turn the Mishnah into a set of generalizations of what already is explicit in Scripture, a kind of restatement in other language of what is quite familiar—therefore well-founded.

Y. Makkot 2:2.

    A.   *[If] the iron flew from the heft and killed someone,*

    B.   *Rabbi says, "He does not go into exile."*

    C.   *And sages say, "He goes into exile."*

    D.   *[If] it flew from the wood which is being split,*

    E.   *Rabbi says, "He goes into exile."*

    F.   *And sages say, "He does not go into exile."*

I.   A.   What is the Scriptural basis for the position of Rabbi [at M. 2:2D–E]?

    B.   Here it is stated, " . . . [and the head] slips [from the handle and strikes his neighbor so that he dies . . .]" (Deut. 19:5).

    C.   And later on, the same verb root is used: "[. . . for your olives] shall drop off . . . " (Deut. 28:40).

    D.   Just as the verb root used later means, "dropping off," so here it means, "dropping off."

    E.   What is the Scriptural basis for the position of the rabbis [at M. 2:2F]?

    F.   Here the verb root "slipping" is used.

    G.   And later on elsewhere we have the following: " . . . and clears away many nations before you . . ." (Deut. 7:1).

    H.   Just as the verb root, clearing away, refers to an [active] blow there, so here too it speaks of an [active] blow [by an object which strikes something, e.g., the ax, not chips of wood].

Yerushalmi Baba Mesia 3:9.II.

    A.   What is the Scriptural basis for the opinion of the House of Shammai [that one who expresses the intention of making use of a bailment is liable for any damage done to it, as if he had made use of it (M. B.M. 3:9E–F)]?

    B.   "For *every* breach of trust . . ." (Ex. 22:9)—[even one merely in intention].

    C.   And how does the House of Hillel deal with the cited verse, "For every breach of trust"?

D.   One might suppose that the law applies only to the [bailee] himself. [If his slave or his agent does the deed, how do we know that he is liable? Scripture states, "For every breach of trust"—even if it is by a man bailee's agent, he is liable. (PM: Even though the law of agency does not apply to a sin, in this case Scripture has expanded the range of culpability by its statement, "For every breach of trust.")]

Yerushalmi Sanhedrin 9:3.

A.   *He who hits his fellow, whether with a stone or with his fist,*
B.   *and they diagnosed him as likely to die,*
C.   *[but] he got better than he was,*
D.   *and afterward he got worse, and died—*
E.   *he is liable.*
F.   *R. Nehemiah says, "He is exempt,*
G.   *"for there is a basis to the matter [of thinking that he did not die from the original injury]."*

II. A.   What is the Scriptural basis for R. Nehemiah's opinion?
B.   "[When men quarrel and one strikes the other with a stone or with his fist and the man does not die but keeps his bed,] then if the man rises again and walks abroad with his staff, he that struck him shall be clear" (Ex. 21:18–19).
C.   Now would it have entered your mind that this one should be walking about in the marketplace, while the other is put to death on his account? [Obviously not, and so the purpose of Scripture's statement is as follows:] Even though the victim should die after he was originally examined and diagnosed as dying, the other party is exempt [should the man's condition improve in the meantime].
D.   What is the Scriptural basis for rabbi's opinion?
E.   "And the man does not die but keeps his bed"—
F.   Now do we not know that if he "does not die but keeps his bed"—[why does Scripture specify both his not dying and also his going to bed]?
G.   It is to speak of a case in which they did not make prognosis that he would die. [That is, Scripture is to be interpreted to mean, "if he does not die," that is, they did not reach a prognosis that he would die, but that he would not die.
H.   In this case it is written, "Then if the man rises again and walks abroad with his staff, he that struck him shall be clear" (Ex. 21:19).
I.   [This then means that] lo, if he does not get up, the one who struck him is liable.
J.   If then they reached the prognosis that he would die, in such a

case it is written, "Only he shall pay for the loss of his time, and shall have him thoroughly healed" (Ex. 21:19). [That is, if he was not expected to die, the one who hit him nonetheless must pay the costs of his recovery.]

We see that in the first case both parties to the Mishnah's dispute read the same verse. The difference then depends upon their prior disagreement about the meaning of the verse. The same is so in the second dispute, but now at issue is the force of a particular word in the biblical verse. In the third, each party claims that implicit in what the Scripture says is an excluded, self-evident case. Once more, therefore, the same verse is read in opposed ways, resulting in the dispute in the Mishnah. The underlying supposition is that the Mishnah simply restates in general language the results of the exegesis of biblical law.

We consider, finally, instances in which the the Talmud's discussion consists wholly in the analysis of the verses of Scripture deemed to prove the Mishnah's point. The outcome is that we deal not with a mere formality but a protracted, sustained inquiry. That is to say, the discussion of the Talmud transcends the limits of the Mishnah and becomes a well-developed discourse upon *not* the Mishnah's rule but Scripture's sense.

What is important in the next item is the fact that the search for proof texts in Scripture sustains not only propositions of the Mishnah, but also those of the Tosefta as well as those of the Talmud's own sages. This is a stunning fact. It indicates that the search of Scriptures is primary; the source of propositions or texts to be supported by those Scriptures is secondary. There is no limit, indeed, to the purposes for which Scriptural texts will be found relevant.

Y. Sanhedrin 3:8:II.

A. **How do they carry out a judgment?**

B. **The judges seat themselves, and the litigants remain standing before them.**

C. **Whoever brings claim against his fellow is the one who opens the proceedings [T. San. 6:3],**

D. as it said, " . . . Whoever has a complaint, let him go to them [Aaron and Hur, as judges]" (Ex. 24:14).

E. And how do we know that the one who lays claim against his fellow bears the burden of proof?

F. R. Qerispa in the name of R. Hananiah b. Gamaliel: "' . . let him go to them . . . ,' [meaning,] Let him bring his evidence to them."

G. R. Yohanan raised the question, "In the case of a childless sister-in-law, who brings claim against whom?"

H. R. Eleazar replied, "And is it not written, ' . . . then the brother's wife shall go up to the gate to the elders' (Deut. 25:7)?"

I.   R. Yohanan said, "Well did R. Eleazar teach me."

Y. Sanhedrin 10:4:II.

A.   *The party of Korah has no portion in the world to come and will not live in the world to come* [*M. San. 10:4*].

B.   What is the Scriptural basis for this view?

C.   "[So they and all that belonged to them went down alive into Sheol;] and the earth closed over them, and they perished from the midst of the assembly" (Num. 16:33).

D.   *"The earth closed over them"—in this world.*

E.   *"And they perished from the midst of the assembly"—in the world to come* [*M. San. 10:4D–F*].

F.   It was taught: **R. Judah b. Batera says, "[The contrary view] is to be derived from the implication of the following verse:**

G.   **"'I have gone astray like a lost sheep: seek thy servant [and do not forget thy commandments]' (Ps. 119:176).**

H.   **"Just as the lost object which is mentioned later on is the end in going to be searched for, so the lost object which is stated herein is destined to be searched for"** [T. San. 13:9].

I.   Who will pray for them?

J.   R. Samuel bar Nahman said, "Moses will pray for them:

K.   "'Let Reuben live, and not die, [nor let his men be few]' (Deut. 33:6)."

L.   R. Joshua b. Levi said, "Hannah will pray for them."

M.   This is the view of R. Joshua b. Levi, for R. Joshua b. Levi said, "Thus did the party of Korah sink ever downward, until Hannah went and prayed for them and said, 'The Lord kills and brings to life; he brings down to Sheol and raises up' (I Sam. 2:6)."

At Y. San. 3:8, we see, the search for proof texts is provoked equally by citation of a passage of the Tosefta and by an opinion of a rabbi. D, E–F, give an instance of the former, and G–I, the latter. There is no differentiation between the two processes. At Y. San. 10:4 we have a striking sequence of proof texts, serving, one by one, the cited statement of the Mishnah, A–C, then an opinion of a rabbi in the Tosefta, F–H, then the position of a rabbi, J–K, L–M. The process of providing proof texts therefore is central, the nature of the passages requiring the proof texts a matter of indifference.

We began with the interest in showing how the Scripture is made to supply proof texts for propositions of the Mishnah. But we see at the end that the search for appropriate verses of Scripture vastly transcends the purpose of study of the Mishnah, exegesis of its rules, and provision of adequate authority for the document and its laws. In fact, any proposition to be taken seriously, whether one in the Mishnah, in the Tosefta, or in the mouth of a Talmudic sage himself will elicit interest in Scriptural support. So the main thing is that the Scripture is at the center and focus. A verse of Scripture settles all pertinent questions, wherever located, whatever their source. That is the Talmud's position. That is not the Mishnah's position. For the sages of the Talmud, the quest for certainty lay through the Torah of Moses—the written Torah, there alone.

If the sages of the second century, who made the Mishnah as we know it, spoke in their own name and in the name of the logic of their own minds, those who followed, certainly the ones who flourished in the later fourth century, took a quite different view. Reverting to ancient authority like others of the age, they turned back to Scripture, deeming it the sole reliable source of certainty about truth. Unlike their masters in the Mishnah, theirs was a quest for a higher authority than the logic of their own minds. The shift from age to age then is clear. The second-century masters took commonplaces of Scripture, well-known facts, and stated them wholly in their own language and context. Fourth century masters phrased commonplaces of the Mishnah or banalities of worldly wisdom, so far as they could, in the language of Scripture and its context.

But, as we saw at the end, this quest in Scripture for certainty far transcended the interest in supplying the Mishnah's rules with proof texts. On the contrary, the real issue turns out to have been not the Mishnah at all, not even the indication of its diverse sayings one by one. Once the words of a *sage,* not merely a rule of the Mishnah, is made to refer to Scripture for proof, it must follow that, in the natural course of things, a rule of the Mishnah and of the Tosefta will likewise be asked to refer also to Scripture.

In phrasing this as I have, I have turned matters on their head. The fact that the living sage validates his own words through Scripture explains why the sage also validates the words of the ancient sages of the Mishnah and Tosefta through verses of Scripture. It is one undivided phenomenon. The reception of the Mishnah constitutes merely one, though massive, testimony to a prevalent attitude of mind, important for the age, not solely for the Mishnah. The final passage we reviewed turns out, upon reflection, to be the most suggestive of the Judaism for which the Yerushalmi supplies evidence. In the quest for certainty, proof texts for the Mishnah are beside the point. The main point is this: Certainty is in Scripture, which validates teachings of sages present and past, including sages of the Mishnah.

Certainty in the Mishnah: Determining the Text

The challenge of the Mishnah demanded not only a theory of the ultimate authority of the document and its various laws. It also involved a quite separate set of issues, generated by two things. One was the particular way in which the Mishnah had been formulated and handed on. The other was the peculiar character of the Mishnah's discussions.

As to the former, the Mishnah was not published in the usual way, which was to place a single, authoritative text in an archive, so that all questions of wording in copies of the text might be referred to that one correct version. Rather, it was published through processes of oral formulation, transmission through the memories of professional memorizers, who could be relied upon to repeat exactly the words they had learned.

Second, the Mishnah is not a code of laws, in which people are told what to do and not to do. It is a compilation of opinions on laws, in which various views of what people should and should not do are laid out.

These two peculiarities inherent in the document, its form and its character, produced the two most painful points of uncertainty: the exact wording of the text, the correct decision of the law. Accordingly, the Talmud's sages had these tasks when they approached any passage of the Mishnah. First, they needed to sort out the versions of the wording of a saying of the Mishnah. Second, they had to determine the correct law in a case of dispute.

These two matters, no less than the issue of authority, define principal themes of the thought of the Talmud's sages concerning the Mishnah. The principle expressed in both issues is the same: dogmatically rigid honesty, an absolutely critical approach to all allegations of fact. The sages of the Talmud were confronted with a diversity of claims about matters of detail. As I said, because it had been formulated and handed on through memorization and oral transmission, each passage of the Mishnah existed in numerous versions. Diverse possibilities for reading the text permitted a variety of decisions on the practical law. Accordingly, the condition of the Mishnah generated considerable uncertainty. The character of the document, with its incessant din of contradictory opinions, made necessary a predictable and reliable means of settling matters. So the Mishnah had to be turned into a law code. In this section we shall review evidence on the former matter; in the next, on the latter. Both sections provide ample indication about the character of the quest of the Talmud's sages.

We begin with a story that portrays the way in which the professional memorizer was expected to do his work, repeating the sentence many times until he knew it by heart, checking his version of the saying with that of another authority.

Y. Ketubot 11:7.III.

> E.   Said R. Yosé, "Every hour R. Ila would say to me, 'Repeat as your Mishnah passage: "He inherits her estate and he contracts uncleanness [if he is a priest, in burying her despite the general obligation not to do so except in the case of close relatives]."'"

F. And has it not been taught this way: "A [priest] contracts uncleanness in burying his wife if she is a valid wife for him,
and he does not do so if she is not a valid wife for him"?

The care with which traditions had to be formulated and observed is illustrated in the statement of Yosé, who scrupled about accepting what Mana had
said in Samuel's name: "If Joshua, who was so close to Moses, would not
have said thus, will you say so [in a case which the source of a teaching in
Samuel's name is not certain]?" (Y. Nid. 1:3.VII.T). The other party then
retracted.

The possibility for error was unlimited, as the following indicates. We see
first Tosefta's version of the item, then the statement as to the decided law
and why the statement was formulated as it was. What is important here is
the further indication that the way in which the Mishnah was framed governed the transmission of sayings of Talmudic sages as well.

Y. Horayot 3:4.IV.

X. **Who is one's master?**

Y. **It is the one who has taught him wisdom [and not the master
who has taught him a trade].**

Z. **"It is anyone who started him off first," the words of R. Meir.**

AA. **R. Judah says, "It is anyone from whom he has gained the
greater part of his learning."**

BB. **R. Yosé says, "It is anyone who has enlightened his eyes in his
repetition of traditions" [T. Hor. 2:5C–H].**

CC. R. Abbahu came [and taught] in the name of R. Yohanan: "The
law accords with the position of the one who says, 'It is anyone from whom he has gained the greater part of his learning'" [= AA].

DD. Now why did he not simply interpret the Mishnah pericope by
saying, "The law is in accord with R. Judah"?

EE. [Because there are] repeaters of traditions who will get confused
and switch [matters about]).

Whatever the origin of an authoritative formulation of the law, whether the
Mishnah, Tosefta, or a contemporary sage, high standards of accuracy were
imposed, rigorous tests of accuracy applied. For one thing, a sage had to be
personally acquainted, on the basis of his own visual as well as aural knowledge, with the one who handed on a saying he repeated, as in the following.

Y. Qiddushin 1:7.IV.

E. "Many a man proclaims his own loyalty, but a faithful man who
can find?" (Prov. 20:6).

F. This refers to R. Zeira, for R. Zeira said, "We pay no attention to the traditions of R. Sheshet [which he says in the names of those who originally said them], because he is blind [and may err in identifying the voices of the original authority]."

G. And R. Zeira said to R. Yosa, "Do you know Bar Pedaiah, that you cite traditions in his name?"

H. He said to him, "R. Yohanan said them in his name."

I. Said R. Zeira to R. Ba, bar Zabeda, "Does my lord know Rab, that you cite traditions in his name?"

J. He said to him, "R. Ada bar Ahva said them in his name."

The issue is this: Did a sage actually frame a saying? Or was a saying in his name formulated on the basis of something people saw him *do?* This was made explicit. It is possible that a sage had ruled such in a way as to indicate that his opinion might accord with a given version of the law, when in fact his ruling had carried no such intent. The consequent formulation of an opinion in a sage's name on the basis of his deed or decision therefore had to be tested against evidence of the sage's explicit opinion. Along these same lines, as the second story in the next sequence indicates, a person who thought she knew what a sage had said wished actually to hear the opinion in his own words and in his own voice.

Y. Nazir 7:1.IX.

A. What is the law as to a high priest's contracting corpse-uncleanness in order to raise his hands [to bestow the priestly blessing]?

B. Gebilah, brother of R. Ba bar Kohen, said before R. Yosah in the name of R. Aha, "A priest does contract corpse-uncleanness [e.g., by remaining in the synagogue when a corpse is present] in order to raise his hands [and bestow the priestly blessing]."

C. R. Aha [who had been cited] heard this and said, "I never said such a thing."

D. Then he retracted and said, "Or perhaps he did not hear it directly from me. But it is according to that which R. Judah bar Pazzi in the name of R. Eliezer [said], 'Any priest who stands in the synagogue and does not raise his hands [and bestow the priestly blessing] violates an affirmative commandment.' Now he may have concluded that a positive commandment overrides a negative commandment [that is, not contracting corpse-uncleanness], but I never said such a thing. Bring him and I shall inflict a flogging on him."

Y. Besah 4:5.II.

A. The daughter of R. Hiyya the Elder came to do baking in the oven on the festival day.

B. She found a stone in it. She came and asked her father. He said to her, "Let them go and sweep it out."

C. She said to him, "I cannot do so." [In fact, it is prohibited to sweep out the oven, in line with M. Bes. 4:5C.]

D. He said to her, "Then let them level it down [= M. Bes. 4:5D]."

E. In fact she knew the answer, but she wanted to hear it from her father.

What is important in the stories just now reviewed is their emphasis upon the critical reception accorded statements in the names of various authorities. In the first of the two, Aha found himself hearing in his own name a view of the law he did not hold. He forcefully corrected the matter. In the latter the daughter wished to check her knowledge of the law with her father's authority, by having him repeat the law in the established wording.

The fact that a disciple of a sage had not heard what a master said of course was not permitted to prove that the master had not said it. Other sources of information were available and consulted. But, as the following stories indicate, people would be careful, in formulating an official version of a saying, to indicate the mode in which the saying had taken shape.

Y. Megillah 1:1.VII.

A. Nahman, son of R. Samuel bar Nahman: "'[Therefore the Jews of the villages, who live in the open towns, hold the four-teenth day of the month of Adar as a day for] gladness and feasting and holiday making, and a day on which they send choice portions to one another' (Est. 9:19).

B. "[With reference to 'gladness':] On this basis we learn that it is forbidden to mourn [on that day].

C. "'Feasting': On this basis we learn that it is forbidden to fast on that day.

D. "'And holiday making': On this basis we learn that it is forbidden to do labor on that day."

E. Said R. Helbo, "Many times I sat in session before R. Samuel bar Nahman and I never heard this teaching from him."

F. He said to him, "Are you saying that you heard everything that my father ever said?"

Y. Besah 5:1.II.

A. R. Jeremiah in the name of Rab: "[On the Sabbath] they spread out mats on shavings which cover bricks."

B. Said R. Simeon b. R. Yannai, "I did not hear the teaching from father, [but] my sister reported to me in his name [the follow-ing teaching]: 'As to an egg laid on the festival day, they put

a utensil near it so that it will not roll about, but they do not
put a utensil on top of it [for that purpose].'"

C.   And Samuel said, "They put a utensil over it [for that purpose]."

Y. Megillah 3:12.III.

A.   **A translator who stands before [and serves] a sage has not the
right to change what the sage says when he translates it, or
to use synonyms, or to add to what he says, unless [the
sage] was his [the translator's] father or his master [T.
Meg. 3:41].**

B.   R. Pedat was the Amora [repeating his words in a loud voice] for
R. Yosé.

C.   If R. Yosé said something that he had heard from the father of
R. Pedat, he would say, "Thus did my master [Yosé] say in
the name of my father."

D.   As to things which R. Yosé had not heard from [Pedat's] father
[but from R. Eleazar], he would say, "Thus did Rabbi say in
the name of R. Eleazar."

E.   Bar Yashita was the Amora for R. Abbahu. When the latter said
things that he had heard from his father, he would say, "So
did the Rabbi say in the name of father."

F.   As to things that he had not heard from his father he said, "This
did the Rabbi say in the name of R. Hinenah."

G.   When R. Mana taught among the associates things that he had
heard from his father [Jonah] at home, he would say, "Thus
did the Rabbi say in the name of R. Jonah."

H.   When he would say things which he had heard from his father
in the meetinghouse, he would say, "Thus did R. Jonah say."

Y. Taanit 1:2.II.

H.   R. Hezekiah, R. Nahum, R. Ada bar Abimi were in session.
Said R. Nahum to R. Ada bar Abimi, "Is it not reasonable to
suppose that these measurements were stated to indicate when
it is necessary to say a blessing?"

I.   He said to him, "Yes."

J.   Said R. Hezekiah to R. Ada bar Abimi, "Is it not reasonable to
suppose that these measurements serve to indicate when one
may interrupt a fast?"

K.   He said to him, "Yes."

L.   He said to him, "And why, then, did you agree with what he
said?"

M.   He said to him, "I responded in accord with the theory of my
master."

N.   Said R. Mana to R. Hezekiah, "Who is his master?"

O. He said to him, "R. Zeira."

P. He said to him, "Then we shall say the matter as follows: R. Yosé in the name of R. Zeira: 'The measurements were stated to indicate when it is appropriate to interrupt a fast [undertaken for rain, if it should rain on that day].'"

Above all, we see that the process of formulating and transmitting authoritative sayings was wholly within the sages' society, fully subjected to the social controls of consensus and public scrutiny. The emphasis we have just seen on testing and retesting statements in light of all available information, publicly shared and collectively evaluated, is illustrated in the following story. There we see that a disciple was expected to study with another person, then would exercise supervision of reasoning and the traditions of the other. Idiosyncratic and eccentric traditions were dismissed, not trusted. A single individual's testimony to what an authority had said was not apt to be dismissed, but it also was not likely to be granted immediate credence. We deal with a highly collective labor of attaining certainty through consensus. The prejudice against engaging in processes of learning on one's own and by oneself was blatant.

Y. Nedarim 11:1.IV.

P. Judah of Husa hid in a cave for three days to inquire into the reason for the rule that the maintenance of the life of this town takes precedence over the maintenance of the life of another town.

Q. He came to R. Yosé b. Halapta, saying to him, "I hid in a cave for three days to inquire into the reason for the rule that the maintenance of the life of this town takes precedence over the maintenance of the life of another town."

R. He called R. Abba, his son, saying to him, "What is the reason for rule that the maintenance of the life of this town takes precedence over the maintenance of the life of another town?"

S. He recited for him the following verse: "'These cities had each its pasture lands round about it; so it was with all these cities' (Josh. 21:42). [That is, each city was supplied with all its needs.]"

T. He said to him, "What caused your ignorance? It was that you did not study with your fellow [but all by yourself]."

The most striking characteristic of the materials just now reviewed is this: The same certainty sought in the reading of the texts of passages of the Mishnah was a matter of concern also in the formulation and assessment of versions of sayings assigned to sages themselves. Once more we see that the treatment of the Mishnah serves to exemplify a more pervasive trait of mind, one expressed in approaches to the sayings of authorities of the day, not only of times past. We noted that just as the Talmudic sages adduced verses of Scripture to validate a law of the Mishnah, so they pursued the same mode of exegesis in behalf of a legal or theological statement of their own times. Likewise, just as they assumed that the processes of accurate memorization of what had been orally formulated had brought the Mishnah from its point of origin to their own hands, so they took for granted that those same processes would carry forward an accurate account of what they would formulate in their own names for oral transmission. The sole point of differentiation was quite natural. What was given in their own names might originate either in what they said or in what they did, so they were careful to preserve a record of the source of what was given: observation and surmise, or actual formulation of *ipsissima verba*. But the purpose was the same.

Certainty depended upon disciplined, collective processes of framing and handing on reliable sayings. And, as we know, what was deemed reliable was what could be shown to accord with laws originally laid down in Scripture. It follows that what the sages had in hand was an accurate account of what God had expressed as his will for Israel and revealed to Moses at Mount Sinai. While in our texts the Torah myth did not (yet) encompass the Mishnah in particular (let alone the Talmud!), the Torah myth in general assuredly stands behind the disparate procedures and points of concern we have now surveyed: the search for Scriptural proof for contemporary opinion, the scrutiny of the accuracy of transmission, from times of old or from the present day, of what was, to begin with, Torah. What that means is that, once more, the Mishnah in particular was never the issue. It was part of the answer, not of the question. The question came from elsewhere. Those troubled by the question addressed it to the Mishnah, among other things. At issue were the authority of the sage, the accuracy, back to Sinai, of his opinions, the certainty of his standing. The literary expression of this issue should not confuse us as to its origin and point of reference: this was men, not books.

Certainty in the Mishnah: Deciding the Law

A quite distinct type of uncertainty derives from the failure of the Mishnah's text to specify clear and definite instructions on what to do and what not to do. The carefully exemplified principles, expressed through recurrent rules, yield a surface of differences of opinion on matters of detail. Consequently, the Mishnah generates the necessity to formulate principles for sorting out different viewpoints and so deciding what actually is to be done. For lawyer-philosophers, matters of mere speculation cannot have been especially urgent. We may assume that the reticence of the Mishnah's framers to specify solutions to their endless thought problems implicitly expresses their own judgment on this point. Since they did not have to make concrete decisions, and had, indeed, slight power to effect them, they also did not imagine the need to present their ideas as a practical code of law. That guess, at any rate, seems plausible when we consider what the Mishnah's heirs, later on, found it necessary to do. They framed a program of resolving Mishnaic disagreements that had given no significant hint as to the right answer and the ultimate decision. Whatever the reason for the Mishnah's peculiar character as a set of open-ended disputes, the fact is that, in the period and circumstance represented by the Talmud of the Land of Israel, people believed that decisions had to come forth, arguments had to reach solution, doubt had to be resolved.

One may suppose that the Talmudic sages' program of settling disagreements and stating practical law constituted a criticism of the Mishnah framers' policy. When we considered their insistence upon supplying proof texts for propositions deemed by Our Holy Rabbi not to require them, it seemed clear that a criticism of Rabbi's position was intended. But the opposite is made explicit. Disputes left unresolved served a valuable purpose and do not constitute a flaw in Rabbi's Mishnah, so Yannai.

Y. Sanhedrin 4:2.

A.   *In property cases they decide by a majority of one, whether for acquittal or for conviction,*

B.   *While in capital cases they decide by a majority of one for acquittal, but only with a majority of two [judges] for conviction.*

I.   A.   Said R. Yannai, "If the Torah were handed down cut-and-dried [so that there were no possibility for disagreement in reasoning about the law and no need to make up one's mind], there would be no place [for the world] to stand. [We should not know how to decide a case.]"

B.   What is the Scriptural basis for that statement?

C.   "And the Lord spoke to Moses . . . ," [telling him the diverse arguments relevant to each law].

D.   [Moses] said to him, "Lord of the World! Teach me the [practical] law [so that there will be no doubts about it]."

E.   He said to him, "' . . . follow the majority to incline' [the law to a decision, that is, make a decision in the law by a majority of the judges' opinions] (Ex. 23:2).

F.   "[If] those who declare innocent form the majority, declare the accused innocent. [If] those who declare the accused to be guilty, declare him to be guilty."

G.   [This is] so that the Torah may be expounded in forty-nine ways on the side of a decision of uncleanness, and in forty-nine

ways in favor of a decision of cleanness. ["Now if I reveal
the law to you in all its finality, there will be no possibility
for such a range of argument."]

H.   And so it says, "The promises of the Lord are promises that are
pure, silver refined in a furnace on the ground, purified seven
times seven" (Ps. 12:6). [That is why there must be forty-
nine arguments, G.]

I.   And it says, "Rightly do they love you" (Song 1:4). [In argument to work out a right decision, they express their love for
God.]

The importance of determining which authority's opinion should prevail as
law self-evidently derived from the need to judge practical cases. An instance of the Talmud's portrayal of matters follows, in which we see that the
tradition on the governing rule determined how to decide a particular case.
How matters were worked out prior to the statements of Yohanan, C, and
Rab, D, or in courts in which those statements were not available or not
deemed authority, is not clear.

Y. Ketubot 1:10.

A.   *Said R. Yosé, "There was the precedent of a girl who went
down to draw water from the well and was raped.*

B.   *"Ruled R. Yohanan b. Nuri, 'If most of the men of the town
marry off their daughters to the priesthood, lo, she may be
married into the priesthood.'"*

I.   A.   R. Judah in the name of R. Kahana, "The incident took place at
the wagon station of Sepphoris [where the wagons were
parked for the marketplace, that is, in public domain.]"

B.   Both R. Jeremiah, R. Hama bar Uqba say in the name of R.
Hanina in the name of R. Yannai, "R. Joshua concurs in the
case of a woman who was raped [that she is believed if she
says it was by a man who has not invalidated her, by his act
of sexual relations, from marriage into the priesthood]. [His
position, that a licentious woman does not care with whom
she has sexual relations and hence is not believed when she
says it was with a valid man, does not apply in the present
case.]"

C.   R. Abbahu in the name of R. Yohanan: "R. Joshua concurs in
the case of a woman who was raped."

D.   R. Hiyya bar Ashi said in the name of Rab, "The law accords
with the view of R. Yosé, which he stated in the name of R.
Yohanan b. Nuri."

E.   R. Zeira asked before R. Yosa, "How is a case to be judged?"

F. He said to him, "It is in accord with R. Yosé's view, which he stated in the name of R. Yohanan b. Nuri."

Two different kinds of disputes confronted the Talmud's sages. First, they had to work out the decided law when the correct version of the Mishnah's rule was represented by a named authority, on the one side, and an anonymous statement, on the other (or by a named authority as against "sages say"). Here the principle was laid down that the law follows the majority, as against the minority, under nearly all circumstances. When that was not the case, it had to be specified and explained. Accordingly, the goal of resolving disputes was to uncover the consensus of the collegium of sages as a whole. Here are ways in which that paramount principle is expressed.

Y. Taanit 2:13.I.

E. R. Mana raised the question before R. Yudan: "Did not R. Hezekiah, R. Abbahu in the name of R. Eleazar [state]: 'In any case in which Rabbi [Judah the patriarch in the Mishnah] presented the law as subject to dispute, and then afterward he presented it without ascription, the law follows the version given without ascription'?"

F. He said to him, "It is not Rabbi [who taught it without a named authority]. But here we have a different situation. If Rabbi presented a dispute and then he taught the matter without ascription, the law follows the version not bearing the name of an individual authority.

G. "But in the case in which Rabbi, for his part, did not repeat the tradition as a dispute, but others presented it as a dispute, and Rabbi taught the matter without naming an authority, is it not an argument *a fortiori* that the law should follow the view of the anonymous version of the law?"

H. R. Hezekiah, R. Jacob bar Aha, R. Simeon bar Aba in the name of R. Eleazar: "And even if others taught the tradition as subject to dispute, while Rabbi taught it without ascription, the law accords with the version lacking a named authority."

I. In that case, why did [Yohanan] teach the law as it was given in the name of a single individual [rather than in accord with the anonymous version]?

J. R. Samuel bar Jonah in the name of R. Aha: "That which you have said applies to a case in which there is no dispute alongside the anonymous version of the law. But if there is a dispute alongside the anonymous version of the law, it is not in such a case that the law follows the anonymous version of the law."

K. R. Yosé b. R. Bun in the name of R. Aha: "That which you have
    said applies to the case in which there is a dispute of one in-
    dividual with another individual. But in a case in which there
    is an individual as against sages, it is not in such a case that
    the law follows the opinion presented without the name of an
    individual authority, but rather anonymously."

Along these same lines, if we deal with opinions of individuals, one may join
one's opinion with that of an individual and the master who taught that
individual, and do the same on the other side. But if you have an individual
against sages, there is no choice but to follow the sages (Y. Nid. 1:4.IV).
Again, it is said that if, in a given dispute, Eliezer heard the rule from one
authority, while Joshua heard it in the name of two authorities, the law should
follow Joshua. The principle is: "Greater is the probative value of the
tradition stated by the one who had heard from two authorities than that of
the two who had heard it from a single authority. If both were equal, there
can be a dispute" (Y. Nid. 1:2.II, III).

The emphasis upon consensus produced secondary disagreements on
whether, in fact, the law was accepted by all parties, as in the following
instances.

Y. Qiddushin 2:7.II.

B. It was taught: And in the case of all of them in which he has
    designated part of the produce as heave offering of tithe
    [given to the priest] or as second tithe, what he has done is
    valid.
C. R. Eleazar says, "That is so except in the case of the residue of
    meal offerings [from which no such tithes are taken any-
    how]."
D. R. Jeremiah said, "And as to the rest, there is a dispute [between
    Meir and Judah]."
E. R. Yosé raised the question: "What dispute? [It cannot involve
    the residue of meal offerings.] If we deal with R. Meir [of M.
    Qid. 2:7C–D], [who holds that second tithe belongs to the
    Most High, just as does the remnant of meal offerings], sec-
    ond tithe and residue of meal offerings are in the same cate-
    gory, and, consequently, one has done nothing at all. If we
    deal with R. Judah, who maintains that [a priest] may effect
    betrothal with his share [of Holy things], what he has done is
    valid [since he disposes of his own share, as he would of
    Holy Things]."
F. Said R. Mana, "I went to Caesarea and I heard R. Hezekiah in
    session, teaching: *He who betroths a woman with his share*

of Most Holy Things or Lesser Holy Things—she is not betrothed.

G. "R. Eleazar says, 'That statement represents the opinion of all parties.'

H. "R. Yohanan says, 'The matter is subject to dispute.'

I. "And I said to him, 'From whom did you hear this statement?'

J. "He said to me, 'From R. Jeremiah [= D].'

K. "And I said to him, 'That is well, for he heard that which R. Eleazar stated, namely, R. Eleazar said, "It is the view of all parties, while he said it was subject to dispute [= C, D].'"

L. "R. Yosé, who did not hear that statement, raised the question, for he has said, 'What dispute?' If we deal with R. Meir, he holds that second tithe belongs to the Most High, just as does the remnant of the meal offerings, and, consequently, one has done nothing at all; if we deal with R. Judah, who maintains that one may effect betrothal with his share of Holy Things, what he has done is valid."

Y. Yebamot 4:11.VI.

A. Simeon bar Ba said, "A case came before R. Yohanan, and he decided the case in accordance with the view of R. Yosé."

B. R. Eleazar was troubled at this and said, "Do they abandon the decided law stated anonymously [at M. Yeb. 4:11B] and practice the law in accordance with the opinion of an individual?"

C. A version of the law taught by R. Hiyya is given in the name of R. Meir. Now when he heard that a version of the law taught by R. Hiyya is given in the name of R. Meir, [Eleazar] said, "The old man [Yohanan] knows the laws of divorce very well indeed [and the position of Meir, M. Yeb. 4:11A–E, is to scruple as to writs of divorce].

D. [Repeating what we saw above:] Mana raised the question before R. Yudan: "There R. Hezekiah, R. Abbahu in the name of R. Eleazar said, 'In every setting in which Rabbi [taught] the law in the form of a dispute, and then went and repeated it without assigning it to a named authority, the law is in accord with the unascribed version. And yet do you say this [that here, the law follows Yosé? This question repeats that raised above.]"

E. He said to him, "It is not Rabbi. Perhaps was it another authority who stated matters as a dispute in this way?"

F. [He replied,] "Now would this not produce an argument *a fortiori?* If it is a fact that, when Rabbi formulated the Mishnah as a dispute and then went and reformulated it in accordance with a single, anonymous authority, the law follows the single anonymous authority, then if to begin with Rabbi did not formulate the passage as a dispute, but others formulated it as a dispute, while Rabbi for his part formulated the Mishnah without ascription, is it not an argument *a fortiori* that the law should accord with the view of the anonymous law?"

G. R. Hezekiah, R. Jacob bar Aha, R. Simeon bar Abba in the name of R. Eleazar [said], "And even if others formulated the tradition as a dispute, while Rabbi formulated it without named authorities [anonymously, unanimously] the law accords with the unascribed version."

H. In that case why did [Yohanan at VI.A above] decide the case in accord with a single individual's opinion [rather than in accordance with the unascribed version of the law]?

I. R. Samuel bar Inayya in the name of R. Aha: "That which you have said applies when there is no dispute along with the anonymous opinion. But if [as with M. Yeb. 4:11] there are disputing opinions along with the anonymous one, it is not in such a case that the law follows the view of the anonymous authority."

J. R. Yosé b. R. Bun in the name of R. Aha: "That which you say applies in the case in which two individuals dispute. But if you have an individual disputing with sages, it is not in such a case that the authority who is unnamed determines the decided law."

K. R. Yohanan said, "Any passage which Rabbi taught without naming an authority represents the Mishnah teaching of rabbis [in general], unless one's rabbi explicitly states otherwise."

L. Said R. Zeira before R. Yosé, "It is not that R. Simeon b. Laqish differs [from Yohanan], but he maintains that the majority of anonymous pericopes in the Mishnah accord with the view of R. Meir."

M. R. Zeira raised the question before R. Mana, "Which authority is the greater [and therefore to be relied upon], that of the Mishnah, or that of teachings [alongside, that is, external versions of the same matter or one's master's instruction]?"

N. Is this not what R. Eleazar said, that the authority of the Mishnah is greater [than that of any other version of the law]? For when he heard that which R. Hiyya taught in the name of R. Meir, he said, "The old man knows the laws of writs of divorce very well indeed" [C].

O. [That does not necessarily follow. For] we may say that he accepted the teaching [concerning the authority of the Mish-

nah] from the *master* of the Mishnah, when he heard that
which R. Hiyya taught in the name of R. Meir.

In perusing these lengthy extracts, we should not lose sight of our purpose.
It is to observe the way in which the Talmud's rabbis determined the final
decision of law. The Mishnah's characteristics present the problem, but the
language of the document also helps solve it. Disputes among Talmudic
authorities, as at Y. Qid. 2:7G, H, were then circulated on how to settle
disputes of the Mishnah. The principle amply illustrated at Y. Yeb. 4:11 is
that unascribed rulings have the authority of law, as against those bearing the
name of an individual. A named saying is deemed idiosyncratic, an anonymous one, authoritative. That is why Judah the Patriarch's mode of formulation of the Mishnah was understood to provide hints about the decided law,
as at Y. Yeb. 4:11D. As author of the Mishnah, Rabbi's mode of phrasing
matters could be an indication on how to settle confusion. Secondary principles in this same connection, as at I, J, K, are clear as given.

It goes without saying, therefore, that determining the exact state of
affairs—whether an opinion was that of an individual or the anonymous
consensus of the sages—involved sifting and resifting traditions on the
matter. Statements originating in the Tosefta constituted a particularly valuable and authoritative source of information. Here is a striking instance:

Y. Ketubot 8:2.III.

- A.   A case came before R. Ami. He ruled, "Is not Rabban Gamaliel
      an individual [in relationship to the majority]? We may not
      make a decision relying upon his authority."
- B.   A Tannaitic teaching supports [Ami's view and differs from it:]
- C.   **Then our rabbis went and voted [the following rule]:**
- D.   **In the case of property which fell to her before she was mar-
      ried, and then she was married, if she sold or gave it away,
      the transaction is null [T. Ket. 8:1I–J].**
- E.   That supports him: Her act of sale is null.
- F.   That which differs from him is as follows: Our rabbis went and
      instructed and voted—for until they took the vote, they did
      not differ from him. [He was not a minority.]

The second sort of problem presented by the Mishnah's mode of formulating
its ideas involved conflict of opinions of two named authorities. No anonymous rule could then be invoked to settle a question. Here the Talmud's sages
enjoyed the guidance of other rules of thumb of various kinds. First, there
might be a simple statement pertinent to a given case that the law accorded
with Authority A as against Authority B. Or a later vote of sages decided
matters in favor of Authority A. These two possibilities are illustrated by the
following.

Y. Abodah Zarah 5:13.

    A.   *Libation wine that fell into a vat—*

    B.   *the whole of* [*the vat*] *is forbidden for benefit.*

    C.   *Rabban Simeon b. Gamaliel says, "Let the whole of it be sold to a gentile, except for the value of that volume of libation wine that is in it."*

I.   A.   R. Yosé, R. Yohanan in the name of Ben Beterah: "*Libation wine that fell into a vat—let the whole of it be sold to a gentile, except for the value of the libation wine* [*that is in the vat*]."

    B.   R. Samuel bar Nathan in the name of R. Hama: "The law is in accord with the opinion of Rabban Simeon b. Gamaliel."

    C.   Said R. Yosa, "One of the rabbis went out of the meetinghouse. He stated, 'R. Yohanan and R. Simeon b. Laqish differed from one another.

    D.   "'One of them said, 'The law is in accord with the opinion of Rabban Simeon b. Gamaliel,' and one of them said, 'The law is not in accord with the position of Rabban Simeon b. Gamaliel.'"

Y. Niddah 3:1.

    A.   *She who aborts a shapeless object, if there is blood with it, is unclean, and if not, is clean.*

    B.   *R. Judah says, "One way or the other, she is unclean."*

I.   A.   [The position of the sages of A, who make the matter depend on the presence of blood, is because] the rabbis maintain that it is the source [uterus] that produces the shapeless object [so the woman is clean so far as having given birth, but if she produces blood, it is menstrual blood, and she is unclean as a menstruant. When there is no blood, there of course is no reason to declare her unclean].

    B.   R. Judah says, "It is blood that has congealed and been turned into a shapeless object."

    C.   Said R. Yohanan, "R. Judah declares unclean only in a case in which there are four sorts of blood [in the shapeless object]."

    D.   R. Jacob b. Aha, R. Simeon bar Ba in the name of R. Yosé son of Nehorai: "The law is in accord with the opinion of R. Judah."

    E.   R. Eleazar heard [this statement] and said, "I do not accept the authority of that judgment."

    F.   Samuel said, "The law is in accord with the position of R. Judah."

    G.   Said R. Zeirah, "It is not that he stated that the law is in accord with R. Judah, but he noted that rabbis are accustomed to follow the law in accord with R. Judah."

In the following instance, by contrast, special circumstances are invoked to explain why the decided law follows a given authority.

Y. Abodah Zarah 5:11.II.

- F. R. Jeremiah said in the name of R. Simeon b. Laqish, "Who taught that dough made by Samaritans [is prohibited]? It is R. Eliezer."

- G. Said R. Yosé to R. Haninah of Antonia, "I recall that both you and R. Jeremiah in the name of R. Simeon b. Laqish were teaching, 'Who taught that the leaven of Samaritans is prohibited? It is R. Eliezer.'

- H. "But R. Hila in the name of R. Simeon b. Laqish taught, '[The sages] went down [and adopted the prohibition of] leaven belonging to Samaritans, in accord with R. Eliezer.' [So the cited pericope accords with the sages, not solely with Eliezer.]"

- I. And furthermore, one must note the following, which R. Haninah bar R. Abbahu said: "Father had a case. He sent and asked R. Hiyya and R. Ami and R. Asi, and they instructed him to rule in accord with R. Eliezer [that leaven belonging to Samaritans is prohibited immediately after Passover]."

- J. Now what follows from that? Do people give instruction on the basis of the opinion of an individual [as against the sages as a group]? [Obviously not!]

- K. No, it was because [the sages] went down [and adopted the prohibition of] leaven belonging to Samaritans, in accord with the opinion of R. Eliezer.

- L. Said R. Mana before R. Yosé, "Just as you ruled there, 'The law is in accord with the opinion of R. Eliezer,' so you should rule here, 'The law is in accord with R. Eliezer.'"

- M. He said to him, "And [in fact] for the entire law that applies in this case, [the law is in accord with him]."

What we see in these several cases, from Y. Abodah Zarah 5:13 onward, is that, for the Talmudic authorities, settling disputes presented in laws of the Mishnah posed ongoing problems. Accordingly, the Mishnah as a whole, as much as the diverse readings available for the Mishnah's statements, constituted a source of uncertainty. Accordingly, Yohanan and Simeon b. Laqish sustain a disagreement on whose opinion is law at Y. Abodah Zarah 5:13. What is interesting at the next passage is Samuel's general observation, F, applied to the present case also. So we see that the general principle that the law follows Authority X generated the secondary problem of whether or not that was always the case. In the third instance we have yet another secondary item. Here we know that the law follows Eliezer's opinion. The issue then is whether sages as well concur, in which case the specification of Eliezer's name is moot.

A further fixed principle on disputes between Authority A and Authority B served to settle all disputes. For example: R. Ba, son of a priest, asked before R. Yosé, "Do we not rule, 'In a case of dispute between R. Judah and R. Yosé, the law is not in accord with the opinion of R. Yosé'?" This principle, however, is set aside when an authority has explicitly given an exception to it (Y. Nid. 1:4.III).

We move on, once more, to the character of discourse involving the Tosefta and Talmudic sages themselves. Here we see that precisely the same program of resolving disputes by reference to the opinion of the anonymous majority, on the one side, or to *ad hoc* traditions on a given issue or by rule of thumb on a given pattern of authorities, pertained to issues involving Toseftan and other post-Mishnaic authorities' disputes. There was no difference in how the basic procedures were worked out. Whatever rules applied to settling disputes in the Mishnah governed also in disputes among the contemporary sages themselves. In the following instances we see how precisely the same discourse attached to a Mishnah rule is assigned as well to one in the Tosefta.

Y. Ketubot 5:1.VI.

    A.   R. Jacob bar Aha, R. Alexa in the name of Hezekiah: "The law accords with the view of R. Eleazar b. Azariah, who stated, *If she was widowed or divorced at the stage of betrothal, the virgin collects only two hundred zuz and the widow, a maneh. If she was widowed or divorced at the stage of a consummated marriage, she collects the full amount"* [M. Ket. 5:1E, D].

    B.   R. Hananiah said, "The law accords with the view of R. Eleazar b. Azariah."

    C.   Said Abayye, "They said to R. Hananiah, 'Go and shout [outside whatever opinion you like. But] R. Jonah, R. Zeira in the name of R. Jonathan said, 'The law accords with the view of R. Eleazar b. Azariah.' [Yet] R. Yosa bar Zeira in the name of R. Jonathan said, 'The law does not accord with the view of R. Eleazar b. Azariah.' [So we do not in fact know the decision.]"

    D.   Said R. Yosé, "We had a mnemonic. Hezekiah and R. Jonathan both say one thing."

    E.   For it has been taught:

    F.   **He whose son went abroad, and whom they told, "Your son has died,"**

    G.   **and who went and wrote over all his property to someone else as a gift,**

H. and whom they afterward informed that his son was yet alive—

I. his deed of gift remains valid.

J. **R. Simeon b. Menassia says, "His deed of gift is not valid, for if he had known that his son was alive, he would never have made such a gift"** [T. Ket. 4:14E–H].

K. Now R. Jacob bar Aha [= A] said, "The law is in accord with the view of R. Eleazar b. Azariah, and the opinion of R. Eleazar b. Azariah is the same in essence as that of R. Simeon b. Menassia."

L. Now R. Yannai said to R. Hananiah, "Go and shout [outside whatever you want].

M. "But, said R. Yosé bar Zeira in the name of R. Jonathan, 'The law is not in accord with R. Eleazar b. Azariah.'"

N. But in fact the case was to be decided in accord with the view of R. Eleazar b. Azariah.

What is important here is that the Talmud makes no distinction whatever when deciding the law of disputes in the Mishnah and the Tosefta. The same already formed colloquy applied at the outset to the Mishnah's dispute is then held equally applicable (!) to the Tosefta's. What this means, once more, is that the process of thought is the main thing, without regard to the document to which the process applies.

We move to one instance in which the way people settle disputes in the Mishnah's law turns out to be the same as precisely the way in which the Tosefta's disputes are resolved.

Y. Yebamot 7:2.V.

A. R. Hezekiah in the name of R. Abbahu, R. Judah, R. Simeon, and R. Ishmael all said a single thing [specified below].

B. It has been taught: **"Up to what point may a girl exercise the right of refusal? Until she produces two pubic hairs,"** the words of **R. Meir.**

C. **R. Judah says, "Until the black hair is abundant."**

D. **R. Simeon says, "Until the crest of the genitals begins to flatten"** [T. Nid. 6:5].

E. R. Zeorah, R. Hiyya in the name of R. Simeon b. Laqish: "Until the crest of the genitals begins to flatten, and until the black hair is abundant."

F. R. Abbahu, R. Leazar in the name of R. Hoshiah: "The law accords with the view of R. Judah."

G. R. Joshua b. Levi said, "The law is in accord with the view of R. Judah."

H. A case came before R. Yosé. He said, "Go to R. Abbahu, because he has taught us the opinion that the law is in accord with R. Judah. But we have not been instructed that the law is in accord with R. Judah."

I. R. Haninah said, "The law is in accord with R. Judah."

J. R. Yohanan said to the people of Sepphoris, "Do you say in the name of R. Haninah, 'The law is in accord with R. Judah'? But that is not the case."

As we should now expect, the same principles of resolving disagreements and settling the law pertained to disputes among contemporary authorities as well. First, people carefully followed available traditions, memorized with great precision. If a tradition from a disciple's master was in hand, that would govern the decision in his own court. On the other hand, where there was no such tradition, an authority would rely upon a consensus of sages, whether of his own day or otherwise. In the following, striking case, an authority made certain to join to his decision the authority of two others, so as to represent his view as that of a collegium of sages.

Y. Niddah 2:7.VI.

L. R. Haninah was living in Sepphoris, and cases would come before him. Twice cases went forth [from his court]. Now R. Yohanan and R. Simeon b. Laqish were living there, but he did not add them to his court.

M. They said, "That old man is wise, and his knife is sharp."

N. One time he did join them [to his court, asking them to share in deciding a case].

O. They said, "Why does Rabbi [after ignoring us so long] pay attention to us today?"

P. He said to them, "May [something bad] come upon me, if it is not so that every case that I bring forth from my court I judge in accord with a law that I learned from my teacher as a valid law. [This I learned from him] as many times as there are hairs on my head. [In addition I saw my teacher apply these laws] in practice at least three times. And on that account I rely on my own teaching [without your concurrence]. But this particular case did not come before my teacher as a matter of law or practical decision more than twice. On that account I have joined you with me to make the decision."

We see, therefore, that the example of the master was decisive, if the master's tradition on a disputed law had been confirmed both in the wording of the law and in the actual practice of the court. Then the disciple—himself a great authority—was prepared to apply the law without further ado. But otherwise the disciple was prepared to associate with himself other leading authorities, so providing a firm precedent for further judges.

Finally, we see in this last instance, which follows, how both reason and authority joined to settle the matter. When all parties to a dispute were present, it was not so easy to close discussion and reach a final decision merely by appealing to the number of concurring authorities. Persuasion through reasonable argument in the end was all that could settle issues among the actual participants.

Y. Sanhedrin 3:8.IV.

G.　[If] two say, "We saw a single hair on his privy parts," and two say, "We saw a single hair on his belly"—

H.　R. Yosé and R. Hoshaiah bar R. Shimi—one said, "He is unfit [not yet mature]." The other said, "He is fit."

I.　The one who said that he is unfit deems the testimony to be equivalent to that of one who testifies concerning the appearance of only part of the required sign [of maturity]. The one who said he is valid [maintains], "I say that [there were two hairs, but one of them] may have fallen out."

J.　[If] one party says, "I saw two hairs on his privy parts," and one says, "I saw two hairs on his belly,"

K.　R. Ba said, "In the opinion of all parties, he is now valid [fully mature], [since there is sure evidence that there are the requisite two pubic hairs]."

L.　Said R. Haggai, "In the opinion of all parties he is invalid."

M.　R. Yosé says, "The matter is [still] subject to dispute."

N.　Said R. [Yosé] to R. Haggai, "Lo, R. Yudan [my student] ruled in accord with my view of the matter."

O.　He said to him, "Now since I differ from his master, all the more so do I disagree with him!"

P.　Said R. Mana, "R. Haggai's ruling is quite sound. For if we have a bond which bears four seals, and one party gives testimony concerning two of them, while another gives testimony concerning two of them, and someone cavils at the value of the bond, is the bond of any value whatsoever? [Hardly!] For does not each seal require the validation of two witnesses [and two witnesses are as sound as a hundred]? Here too each sign [of maturity] requires the validation of two witnesses [who suffice for all purposes]."

Q.　R. Hinena derived the same facts from the case of [attesting to full use and enjoyment of a property] throughout the years of usucaption [to which testimony must be brought]. [That is, if one wishes to establish the claim of title through usucaption, he must bring evidence that he has held and used the property

for a given number of years.] "Now if one witness testified
that he had enjoyed usucaption for the first, second, and third
years, and one witness testified that he had enjoyed usucaption for the fourth, fifth, and sixth years, is it possible
that such [joined] testimony is worth a thing? [No!] Is it not
so that each year of usucaption must be attested by two witnesses? Here too each sign [of maturity] requires the validation of two witnesses."

The point then is that where tradition provided certainty, that sufficed. When
it did not, then the sages had to appeal to reason and the inner logic of the
law, an unsteady guide indeed in the setting of different views of reason and
logic. It is no wonder, then, that wherever possible the authority of decided
law, established principles and precedents, should be called upon, in preference to making things up fresh for a new day.

The Mishnah and the Talmud's Quest for Certainty

The vast majority of the Talmud's units of discourse take up the exegesis and
amplification of the laws of the Mishnah. But what the framers of discourse
regarded as appropriate procedures of inquiry into the meaning of the statements of the Mishnah in no way differed from what they accepted as valid
practice in analyzing positions taken in other documents besides the Mishnah, on the one side, and in sayings of their own predecessors and contem-
poraries, on the other. The Mishnah appears to be the focus, and it is. But
the Mishnah does not stand at the center of the Talmud's modes of differentiation. That is to say, from the Talmud's view, certainty about what is to
be done depends not upon a correct understanding (merely) of what the
Mishnah's rules require. Certainty derives, in the first instance, from Scripture. Correct transmission of the exact words of the ancient authorities
promises a second source of reliable knowledge. Following the consensus of
the sages and avoiding the idiosyncratic views of an individual, third, governs the practical working out of the moot points of law.

These three criteria, applied to all matters of doubt, not only the Mishnah's exegesis, then promise that resolution to the unresolved issues of the
ancient inheritance. These are, (1) Scripture, as against the mere assertions
of the Mishnah's authorities; (2) well-attested versions of statements, as
against the plethora of possible wordings; (3) harmonious decisions of the
sages as a collegium, as against an endless exploration of the potentialities
of idiosyncratic principles and eccentric opinions. The sages of the Talmud
of the Land of Israel seek certain knowledge about some few, practical
things. They therefore reject—from end to beginning—the chaos of speculation, the plurality of possibilities even as to word choice; above all, the
daring and confidence to address the world in the name, merely, of sagacity.

True, the Talmud preserves the open-ended discourse of sages, not reduced to cut-and-dried positions. But the Talmud makes decisions.

Once more we observe how the elegant classicism of the Mishnah gives way before another set of concerns entirely. To state matters looking backward from the final stance: reasoned speculation is chaotic, a range of choices in phrasing matters is disconcerting, authority resting on little more than human reflection is insufficient. Speculation gave way to practical reason. As I said in the beginning, what people now sought was how to know what they should do. Unlike Mishnaic sages, they no longer cared merely to ratiocinate on abstract principles, always leaving matters in a state of irresolution. As to ourselves, there is no point in our choosing sides, preferring the more speculative second century over the decisive, thus authoritarian, fourth. The issues were not the same. What bound the one time to the other was the Mishnah, a mere accident of continuity. One thing led to another. What separated them, I think, is the gulf between the ancient world and the medieval one, aborning in Judaism as much as in Christendom.

Even as it speaks of its most intimate and particular concerns in its exegesis of small passages of the Mishnah, the Yerushalmi testifies to a world beyond itself. Talmudic sages spoke of the Mishnah and how to find certainty in its uncertain phrasing and mooted principles. But in doing so they testified vividly about themselves and what they had to do. The text therefore directs us to its matrix: Why these particular points of stress? Discourse on the Mishnah, so peculiar to our Talmud (and the other one) carries us to a world altogether beyond the narrow province of the Mishnah and its exegesis.

The reason is clear. If we proposed to describe the kind of Judaism revealed in the pages of the Talmud of the Land of Israel solely out of what is in those pages, as we can and do describe the Judaism of the Mishnah upon the basis of the resources of the Mishnah alone, we should find ourselves at an impasse. Everything we learn, beyond the simple and trivial facts about what some people thought the Mishnah's rules said and meant, points to a system of Judaism—a world view, a way of life, expressed within a distinct social group—of which the Talmud forms a partial expression, not the entire account. That fact becomes especially clear when we realize that everything sages wished to say about, and do with, a law of the Mishnah, they proposed to say and do also in regard to laws they themselves made up. If laws of the Mishnah were held to require proof texts of Scripture, so too were positions on all manner of subjects in the names of Talmudic sages. If the exact text of the Mishnah had to be ascertained and carefully preserved, the same was true for the exact wording of statements by Talmudic authorities. If the disputes about laws presented in the Mishnah had to be resolved in accord with simple, predictable rules, these same rules applied without variation to disputes among the Talmud's masters. The present (the situation of the fourth century, possibly also the third) was to be projected onto the past, whether the case involved the second century's work or the words of God to Moses over a millennium earlier.

Part Three
Matrix

4

The Quest for Authority

From Text to Matrix

While the Talmud of the Land of Israel aims principally at the exegesis and amplification of the laws of the Mishnah, it also points toward a matrix beyond its text. On the one hand, the Talmudic interest in the Mishnah's statements is purposeful. Transcending the Mishnah's facts, it expresses the speculative concerns of philosophical lawyers wholly within the framework of the Mishnah's modes of thought. But these same exegetes—both the ones who are named and the still more influential ones who speak through the Talmud's single voice—speak implicitly within the framework of a larger world view, not exhausted by the Mishnah. So they bring to the Mishnah a program defined outside of the Mishnah and expressing concerns of a segment of society beyond their own immediate circle.

The Talmud's discussions, to begin with, are not limited to the contents of the Mishnah. Discourse encompasses a world of institutions, authorities, and effective power, quite beyond the imagination of the Mishnah's framers. The Talmud's picture of that world, furthermore, essentially ignores the specifications, for these same matters, of the Mishnah's law. To take one striking example, the Mishnah's government for Israel rests upon a high priest and a king, with administrative courts ascending upward to the authority of the Temple mount. The Talmud does not even pretend that such a world exists, knowing in its place a set of small-claims courts and petty bureaus of state, over which rabbis, defined as judges, lawyers, and masters of disciples in the law, preside. At the head of it all is a patriarch, not a priest anointed for the purpose. That example provides an instance of the curious discontinuity between the Mishnah's view of the world and of the society of Israel, on the one side, and that of the Talmud, continuous with the Mishnah and framed as little more than an exegesis of that code, on the other hand.

To present a complete account of the system of Judaism presented by the Yerushalmi, at once continuous with, and different from, that of the Mishnah, however, we should have to move far beyond the limits of our Talmud.

An adequate description of the system of the Judaism presented in part by our Talmud requires attention to a fair number of documents beyond the one at hand. These include at least eleven compilations of biblical exegeses, the Tosefta, the entirety of the Babylonian Talmud, and various other minor tractates, compositions of prayers, and other writings of rabbis in late antiquity. It therefore would not serve to limit the pertinent data for the description and interpretation of the kind of Judaism to which our Talmud points, merely to the Talmud itself. For we should find ourselves attempting to interpret as a whole what in fact is merely a half-completed description of the entire system. Interpretation under such conditions would prove parlous indeed. Accordingly, having described the period and message of which the Talmud is our sole evidence, we have now to describe the period and message of which, as I said, the Talmud constitutes only one piece of evidence. We recall, furthermore, that what we have in hand by no means constitutes an adequate historical picture of how things were. The Talmud of a certainty tells us only how its framers saw things. That vision, furthermore, is to be located only in the age of the Talmud's formulation and closure, that is, roughly the last half of the fourth century.

What we now undertake provides an account of latent, as against manifest, events, long term trends as depicted at a particular time in a singular sort of evidence. The numerous allusions to things that happened in courts, which we survey at length, tell us not only what happened on that one day, in that one court, at which that particular rabbinical judge is supposed to have made his decision. True, such an event may have taken place. But as a mere one-time event it would not be important to our inquiry. We want to know what it tells us about how things were perceived in general, over all, over half a century. At hand is social description of latent history, as against a narrative account of an event of manifest history.

So we glimpse an internal state of mind, not an external event or circumstance. We have solid and sound evidence of how people saw things: that alone. But that suffices.

Whether the shared attitudes and responses of the Talmud's rabbis shaped the course of events we cannot say. In the tales at hand, they scarcely claim to have decided significant happenings outside their own circle. When sages tell a story of an event on a particular occasion, we have no reason to believe the story, except as an account of what the storyteller wished people to believe. But when the Talmud narrates cases and precedents, we fairly assume that the character of these cases and precedents provides solid evidence about the things rabbis thought they could and could not do in their social role as judges, teachers, and holy men. Accordingly, I propose to describe what Bernard Bailyn calls "private history, reflecting interior states of awareness" (p. 22). I further maintain that, when the rabbis of the Talmud tell us about this state of awareness as it pertains to what they said and did in society at large, all the more so in their own estate and circle, they are to be given a respectful hearing indeed. How things were beyond the range of their vision, we simply do not know.

Types of Authority

Rabbis are portrayed by the Talmud of the Land of Israel as exercising authority not only over their own circles, people who agreed with them, but over the Jewish community at large. This authority was practical and involved very specific powers. The first and most important sort of power a rabbi under some circumstances and in some cases maintained he could exercise was to sort out and adjudicate rights to property and personal status affecting property. The rabbi is described as able to take chattels or real estate from one party and to give them into the rightful ownership of some other. The second sort of power rabbis are supposed to have wielded was to tell people what to do, or not to do, in matters not involving property rights. The Talmud alleges that rabbis could tell people outside the circles of their own disciples and estate how to conduct themselves. A rabbi is presented as able to coerce someone to do what that ordinary Jew might otherwise not wish to do, or to prevent him from doing what he wanted. The first kind of authority may be called judicial, the second, moral. But the distinction is ours, not theirs. The Talmud does not distinguish among the various kinds of authority and power of coercion exercised by rabbis. Let us now spell out the character of rabbinical authority.

The Talmud takes for granted that rabbis could define the status of persons in such ways as to affect property and marital rights and standing. It is difficult to imagine a more effective form of social authority. As we shall see, our Talmud treats as settled fact a range of precedents, out of which the character of the law is defined. In those precedents, rabbis declare a woman married or free to marry; permitted a wife of a priest to eat food in the status of heave-offering or prohibited from doing so; enjoying the support of a husband's estate or left without that support; having the right to collect a previously contracted marriage settlement or lacking that right. In all of these ways, as much as in their control of real estate, commercial, and other material and property transactions among Jews, the rabbis held they governed the Jewish community as effective political authorities. Whatever beliefs or values they proposed to instill in the people, or realize in the collective life of the community, they effected not through moral suasion or pretense of magical power. It was not hocus pocus but political power resting on the force of government authority. They could tell people what to do and force them to do it. That is the type of social authority implicit in the Talmud; that is the system of politics attested and assumed in our documents.

The Talmud is remarkably reticent about the basis for rabbis' power over the Jews' political institutions: who bestowed this-worldly legitimacy and supplied the force? To be sure, the systematic provision of biblical proof texts for Mishnaic laws presents an ample myth for the law. Given by God to Moses at Mount Sinai, the law, including the Mishnah's laws, represents the will of Heaven. But with all the faith in the world, on the basis of such an assertion about God's will, the losing party to a litigation over a piece of real estate will surely have surrendered his property to the other side only with the gravest reservations—if at all. He more likely will have complained to some other authority, if he could. Short of direct divine coercion, upon which a legal system cannot be expected to rely, there had to be more reliable means of making the system work. What these were, however, the Talmud hardly tells us. So, for the present purpose, we cannot pretend to know. We only know rabbis held that they could run courts and make decisions for Jews who were not rabbis or disciples.

One thing is clear. Jews did not live in territorial units, ethnically uniform and distinct from areas inhabited by other, equally distinct groups. Every page of the Talmud bespeaks a polyglot and multiform society. Even towns such as Sepphoris and Tiberias, with mainly Jewish populations, are described as sheltering non-Jewish populations, each one with its particular status and rights. What must follow, as I said in the opening chapter, is that the rabbinical courts ruled an ethnic, not a territorial, domain. Cases involving Jews alone would have come to these courts, with other courts doing an equivalent labor for other groups, and provision made (the Talmud hardly hints at its character) for litigation and determination of other juridical questions between members of different ethnic or other political units. The rabbis' courts formed only one detail within a political system encompassing a great world beyond, and supporting the small world within, the frame of rabbinical authority.

But of that larger structure of politics and government the Talmud tells us virtually nothing. We have therefore to conclude that the Talmud's perspective is that of a very low level of bureaucracy. In the larger political system, the rabbis' courts constituted a trivial detail. The courts in their hands, powerful though they were in affecting the lives of ordinary Israelites, took up minor matters, with which the great powers of government and state—out there, way up and beyond—did not care to deal. So before us is the world of power portrayed by ethnarchic clerks, nobodies in the larger scheme of things.

What is striking, among other matters on which our document maintains a puzzling silence, is not only the relationship of the rabbinical courts to the larger political structure upon which the actions of those courts had to depend. Equally striking is the relationship of the rabbis as judges and administrators to other Jewish community judges and administrators who may have carried out the same tasks and exercised the same responsibilities in regard to the Jewish nation of the Land of Israel. While, to be sure, unlike the case of Babylonian rabbinism, we hear no complaints about unqualified judges, people executing decisions not based upon sound knowledge of the law, hence, nonrabbinic Jewish judges at work in the Jewish nation, we hardly may take for granted that the Talmud tells us all of the facts about the Jewish political structure of the Land of Israel. So on what basis was the Mishnah adopted as the sole legitimate law of the Jewish nation in its Land (if indeed all law derived from the Mishnah)? And at what time did the Jewish political agency (the court, administration, school), established by the imperial government to take charge of the Jewish nation, hand over authority to a bureaucracy of clerks made up solely of people trained in the Mishnah? These are pressing questions to which we have no answers at all.

So we come to a puzzling fact. The Talmud before us describes as natural and normal a world in which the Mishnah is the sole law of Israel, and rabbis are the only qualified authorities to govern Israel in accord with the law of the Mishnah. But the Talmud nowhere celebrates the victory of its authorities and the law it presents over competing authorities and law. It hardly suggests competition of any sort between rabbis and others bearing competing qualifications, or exercising authority to govern without rabbinical approval and appointment. Even if we concede that the Talmud's picture accurately portrays the state of affairs of the Talmud's own time—the last half-century of the fourth century—we still do not know when questions of the authority of the Mishnah's law and the power of the Mishnah's masters were settled in just this way. Was it in circa A.D. 200, when the Mishnah was closed and "published"? What system of law, then, did the Mishnah replace, and why did the people who enforced that other system give way? These two questions, like the two in the foregoing paragraph, merely suggest the range of inquiry presently closed to all imaginable initiative. They only adumbrate the dimensions of the realm of sovereign darkness: the political context in which the Talmud speaks, of which we are totally uninformed.

We turn to what we do know, namely, the Talmud's picture of what rabbis (again: ethnarchic clerks) could force people to do because of their political power and position. Here to be emphasized at the outset is the distance from their world to ours. We are used to regarding some questions as secular, others as religious, some as political, others as moral. We realize sages perceived no such distinction. We take for granted that the rabbi as a supernatural figure is to be described in one setting, the rabbi as politician in a second, the rabbi as a judge in a third, the rabbi as a religious teacher in a fourth, the rabbi as a teacher in a fifth, and so on. So we envision the holy man in a cave, politician in the court of the Jewish patriarch, judge in his court in the piazza, preacher in the synagogue pulpit (to continue the stupefying anachronism!), the teacher in the schoolroom. But the rabbi in his time, as his document describes it, was always and everywhere all of these things at once: the same names appear in every role with slight differentiation. Specialization in the arts of the supernatural or the political was unthinkable. So the same rabbi who was believed able to make rain or stop a pestilence also decided how a contract had to be carried out, who was free to marry whom, and which party to a litigation owned a particular plot in a vegetable garden. It is one thing to acknowledge that political figures also have charismatic charm. It is quite another to come to grips with the detailed facts of the integration, in the person of the rabbi, of this world with the world above, the world to come, and all other worlds, principalities, and powers anyone in the age could imagine or conjure.

But for our part, we still have to sort things out, describing one thing at a time, before trying to interpret all things together. The order in which we shall proceed is dictated by our own bias, which it is our task to counteract. Since we speak of a "religion," specifically a kind of Judaism, we must begin with an account of those things that in our own setting we do not normally deem to fall within the framework of a religious world view and way of life. We proceed from the kind of authority we should deem entirely secular to that we should concede to be wholly religious: from the rabbi as judge, local authority and administrator, to the rabbi as moral authority and supernatural figure. True, in the world in which the rabbi encompassed all of these roles, we find a measure of specialization and differentiation within other religious-social groups. The same Christian saint who sat on a pillar was not apt, in general, to be the one who wrote theological books. Jerome worked in a library, not in a cave. The bishop who ran affairs of his Christian nation was unlikely also to write theological works (though some did). Augustine was a bishop, but most bishops were not Augustines. Only after death were the persons—bodies and bones—of the great theologians treated as supernatural. In their lives, hermits and stylites tended to monopolize people's hope for holiness incarnate.

Accordingly, we should imagine, points of specialization and expert knowledge or ability, also, were differentiated within the rabbinic estate. But our Talmud does not allow us to recognize this, giving us only lawyer-magicians, philosopher-politicians. We meet teachers worried about controlling the weather and administering healing to the sick, while also telling Mrs. Cohen she may eat her husband's holy rations for breakfast, and Mr. Levi to support his stepmother, Mr. Isaac to hand over his back lot to his neighbor, the rightful owner, and Mr. Jacob to fulfill his contract. The same names appear in every context in which the exercise of authority is at issue. But to make sense of that authority, as I said, we have to sort out its types, attempt to classify each story in which one party told another party what to do and made his instructions stick. That is the purpose of the next four sections, with their rapid survey of types of rabbinical authority as portrayed by the Talmud of the Land of Israel.

The Rabbi as Judge

The single most striking trait of reports about what rabbis said and did as judges in courts is the practical character of the authority imputed to rabbis.

From the perspective of the later fourth century, as I said, rabbis are viewed as judges able to take property from one party and assign it to some other. That picture is drawn simply, always *en passant*. Litigants are portrayed not solely as disciples of sages but also as ordinary folk. Decisions are carried out not by persuasion or threats of supernatural retaliation but through coercion (though the political basis is not specified). Appeal to a different court, for example, one instituted by the imperial government, never appears as an avenue explored by the losing party. More important, and surely probative, rabbis' complaints against Jews' appeals to gentile courts to my knowledge do not occur. It follows that, in their view, rabbinical judges exercised unchallenged *de jure* power in their courts. Here I think we have to believe the rabbis' picture. Jewish authorities enjoyed certain limited power over the conduct of everyday life, including all manner of material transactions. Upon that simple fact the tales before us stand in agreement. As testimonies to the ongoing state of affairs, they provide solid evidence on how judges themselves saw things at the time the stories came to closure and redaction.

We begin our brief survey of the Talmud's picture of the rabbi as judge with the most striking kind of power, that exercised over title to land. Possession of real estate conferred the status of householder. It represented ownership of true capital, however insubstantial. The power to transfer ownership from one party to some other, or to govern transactions with that same effect, thus represents the single most important testimony to the character of the authority of the rabbi as judge. Courts exercising authority over an ethnic group spread out among other ethnic groups need not have enjoyed jurisdiction over real estate transactions. Indeed, unless both parties to a dispute were Jews, I do not see how the Jewish national or ethnic courts of the Land can have exercised jurisdiction. But the Talmud's authorities believed their courts could settle litigation over the title to land and the sale of land by minors. These reports, the first on a defense against a claim of title by usucaption, the second on the sale of real property by a minor, leave no doubt as to the Talmud's view of the state of affairs.

Y. Baba Batra 3:3.III.

    A.   R. Yosé b. Haninah asked R. Yohanan, "[If the owner of a property] enters a complaint [against the squatter], what is the law as to his having to do so before a court?"

    B.   R. Yosé in the name of R. Yohanan: "[If] one raises a complaint, he does not have to do so before a court."

    C.   There are those who teach [the aforestated matter as follows:]

    D.   R. Yosé b. R. Haninah asked the disciples of R. Yohanan, "[If the owner of a property] raises a complaint [against the squatter], what is the law as to his having to do so before a court?"

E.   R. Hiyya in the name of R. Yohanan: "[If] one raises a complaint, he must do so before a court."

F.   Samuel said, "Even if one has raised a complaint with [the squatter] before the workers, that constitutes a valid act of complaint."

G.   And does one have to enter a complaint for each of the three years [at the outset, or, if the property is held over a long period of years, must the complaint be entered annually even after the first three years' complaints]?

H.   Gidul bar Minyamin had a case [in which he had entered a complaint for the first three years only]. The judges of his case were Hilqiah bar Tobi, R. Huna, and Hiyya bar Rab. Hiyya bar Rab said to them, "Thus did father say: 'Once he has entered a complaint against [the squatter] for the first three years, he does not again have to enter a complaint against him.'"

Y. Baba Batra 9:6.III.

D.   A youth sold his property, and the case came before R. Hiyya bar Joseph and R. Yohanan, [since the relatives claimed that he sold the property as a minor and had no power to do so].

E.   R. Hiyya bar Joseph ruled, "The prevailing supposition is that [the witnesses signed the deed] for a person of mature mind [and the purchaser of the property has the advantage]."

F.   R. Yohanan ruled, "Since [the purchaser] has come to remove property from the family, it is his burden to bring proof [that the youth was of mature capacities when he made the sale of his property]."

The importance of the preceding case reports lies in their offhand tone. In both instances it is taken for granted that rabbis judge cases involving real estate, drawing upon their own legal traditions to settle the issues. We notice no sign that we have court documents in hand, since there is no recurrent formal pattern so indicating. These are reports in the setting of the analysis of legal theory, as indicated by the inquiry to disciples (Yosé to Yohanan's). The theoretical character of the reports is shown, further, in the preservation of two distinct opinions at Y. B.B. 9:6. There are two possible grounds for settling the case, and each is specified. Accordingly, the Talmud's reports are true to its character as a set of notes on discourse about law. But embedded within these reports is the prevailing assumption that actual cases have come to hand.

As I said, if rabbis as judges maintained they could transfer ownership of the prized form of capital, land, we cannot be surprised that they claimed jurisdiction over lesser chattels and transactions in movables. Such issues involving conflicting claims on the terms of a property lease, and appropriate utilization of property subject to neighbors' rights, are portrayed in the next examples. In the former instance, the rabbinical judge is represented as making a decision in light of what was perceived as sound social policy—keeping land ownership out of the hands of gentiles (here, an Aramaean)—and not merely in accordance with the strict requirements of the law. But Jews alone are involved. In other cases, the comfort and convenience of parties to a common courtyard had to be sorted out, again a typically domestic issue.

Y. Baba Mesia 8:9.II.

 A. Now he who rented a house to his fellow and then proposed to sell it [during the rental period, to a third party]—

 B. Said R. Ami, "It was not with the stipulation that the owner should die from hunger [that the agreement was made]." [If the owner needs to sell the house in order to support himself and his family, he has that right.]

 C. Both R. Zira and R. Hela say, "Under all circumstances it is deemed acquired by the new purchaser.

 D. "But the landlord [who has sold the house] says [to the purchaser], 'Let him be, for it is available to the tenant until his lease runs out.'"

 E. A case came before R. Nisi, who did not accept [the position of Zira and Hela].

 F. Why did he differ from them?

 G. They say, The house in question was assigned as a pledge to a certain Roman [Aramaean]. [If the landlord could not sell it right away and so redeem it from the gentile, the house would have fallen into the gentile's ownership.] It was on that account that he ruled in accordance with R. Ami [that the sale must be consummated forthwith].

Y. Baba Batra 2:3.III.

 E. R. Abimi bar Tobi gave instructions to put a dung heap [or: loom] between one wall and another wall.

 F. R. Isaac bar Haqilah gave instruction to a lumber mill to set [the sawing] at a distance of four cubits from the wall of his property.

Y. Baba Batra 2:3.I.

 A. R. Jacob bar Aha drove a pastry seller from one portico to another [that is, forced him to move away].

 B. There was a pastry seller [who] opened [a store] under [the dwelling of] R. Abedomi, brother of R. Yosé. R. Aha passed

by and did not object [to the opening of the store]. [R. Ab-
edomi] said, "Rabbis pass by and do not object [to this
store]!" R. Aha grew angry with him. R. Abedomi, brother
of R. Yosé grew sick. He became yet sicker. R. Yosé came
up to call on him. He said, "I shall go and raise the question
with [Aha]." He went and spoke, and the court [on which
Aha sat] gave instructions to have pity on him and to prepare
burial shrouds for him [as a sign that Aha had made his peace
with the brother].

C. A man sold off his entire courtyard, leaving for himself one
porch only. He would go up and sit there. The case came before R. Jonah b. R. Yosé. They ruled, "You have no right to
go up and sit on the porch and watch [the owner] go in and
come out of his house."

D. A man sold off half of his courtyard. He left for himself one
bread shop [already situated in the courtyard]. The case came
before R. Jonah and R. Yosé. They ruled, "You are the one
who came to him. He never came to you."

E. And so it was taught:

F. **If the stall or the shop was there before the granary, [the
owner of the granary] does not have the power to object
[T. B.B. 1:4G].**

In the first of the three cases, considerations of national policy took precedence over the established law. In the matter of the Aramaean, retrieving
the house and placing it into Israelite ownership was the prime consideration.
Accordingly, the vision of the rabbinical clerk took in a broader landscape
than the plain law alone. In the second, rabbis ruled on the rights of neighbors to be protected from nuisances. In the third, there is a curious mixture
of law and supernatural intervention. The rabbi who was the injured party
complained at the failure of the rabbinical authority to protect his rights. The
latter then grew angry, and the former fell ill and died. It goes without saying
that if the displeasure of the clerk was believed to bring such serious consequences, ordinary folk who believed that was the case would be careful to
avoid angering a rabbi. But in context the authority of the bureaucrat is not
represented as resting upon the state of his emotions. We do not know just
what sanctions came into play, but we have no reason at this point to believe
the disposition of real estate and rights to the disposition of property depended solely on the feelings of the rabbi.

The sale and disposition of real estate did not normally take place in the
context of active speculation in land. Rather, land and houses were transferred as part of gifts, generally as gifts of contemplation of death or with the
transfer of a woman and her dowry, that is, her share in her father's estate,
from father to husband and, in the event of divorce, back to her father's

house. Instances involving gifts of property, including real estate, in contemplation of death, include the following cases decided by rabbinical judges.

Y. Qiddushin 1:5.III.

O. When a certain man was dying, he said, "Let all my property be given to Mr. So-and-so." Then he went and said, "Let it be written over in a deed and given to him." [He then died.]

P. [The problem is whether it was the donor's intention to give the property over only through a deed. But such a deed is invalid if issued after the testator's death. So] R. Eleazar and R. Simeon b. Yaqim brought the case to R. Yohanan.

Q. He ruled, "If he made that statement in order to transfer ownership to him, all concur that the donee has acquired ownership. If he made that statement in order to give him ownership through a deed, all concur that a man does not impart ownership through a deed after death. [What a dying man says is deemed done. Hence if the statement was merely to strengthen the donee's claim on the property, it was valid as soon as it was made. But if the statement was to do the whole transfer by deed, then as soon as the man died, the instructions he gave on drawing up the deed are null.]"

Y. Ketubot 11:1.VII.

A. R. Yudan fled to Noy [where Yosé was domiciled]. A case came before R. Yosé: "A dying man who said, 'Let the bonds of So-and-so [my bonds] be handed over to So-and-so' [what is the law? Has this statement transferred ownership of the bonds?]"

B. He said to him, "A dying man transfers ownership by a mere verbal declaration only of things which are transferred by a healthy person either through a deed or through an act of drawing the object to the recipient.

C. "But these are acquired through drawing or through a deed . . . "

D. **"A boat is acquired through drawing.**

E. **"R. Nathan says, 'A boat and documents are acquired through drawing and through a writ' [T. Qid. 1:7A-B].**

F. "If one wrote a deed but did not draw the object, or drew the object but did not write a deed, he has accomplished nothing -unless he both writes a deed and draws the object."

What is important in the foregoing is that the rabbinical courts clearly took for granted the power to govern the transfer of title to land. The point at issue, the technicalities of the transfer of title in a case of a gift in contemplation of death, was secondary.

We come to yet another sort of gift, namely, a gift of real estate by a father to a son so that he might marry and start his own family. The issue here is whether movables passed with the real estate.

Y. Ketubot 5:1.III.

E. This statement accords with that which R. Hanania said, "He who marries off his son in a house—the son has acquired ownership of the house. And that rule is on condition that it is the first marriage of the son."

F. R. Hoshaiah taught, "He has acquired ownership of the movables, but he has not acquired ownership of the house itself."

G. Now does he differ [from Hanania]?

H. R. Jeremiah in the name of R. Abbahu: "Interpret [Hoshaiah's] statement to speak of a case in which the father's granary was in the house. [Accordingly, the father uses the house and does not intend to give it away.]"

I. R. Hezekiah in the name of of R. Joshua b. Levi, "[That point is self-evident.] It was necessary [to indicate that] even if there were things in the house which had been borrowed from the marketplace, [the son has not acquired ownership of the house]. [Even if used for such a purpose as temporary storage, the house remains in the domain of the father.]"

J. Said R. Abbahu, "If [the father had made it explicit to the son that he was merely] lending him the house for the purpose of the marriage, then the son has not acquired ownership even [of the movables which are in the house]."

K. A case of this sort came before R. Jacob b. R. Bun, and he decided it in accordance with the view of R. Abbahu.

Once more we note that the case report is preserved only in the setting of a discussion of legal theory. Whether the purpose of the report is merely to preserve the fact or to indicate the decided law is unclear. For our purposes it is significant as evidence that rabbis took for granted they could make practical decisions of this kind.

Finally, a woman might exercise the right to own and sell real estate. At the same time, she possessed only limited rights to support from the husband. Accordingly, the husband enjoyed a lien on her property, since she could not sell her real property and then claim to be impoverished and so to require his support. While she held title to her real estate, the property was indentured to the husband. A concrete case follows.

Y. Baba Batra 8:8.II.

HH. A woman deeded her property as a gift to a certain person. She fell into need and sold her property to her husband. R. Hiyya bar Madayya brought the case before R. Yosé [with the following argument]: "Did not R. Yannai say, 'Rabbi concurs that the first may not give over this property under the law of gifts in contemplation of death'? [That is, the woman was in the status of the first of the sequence of recipients. In Rabbi's view, such a person has the right to ownership of the property itself, and, consequently, just as, if the man should sell the property, it is a valid sale, so here too, if the woman disposed of the property, it is valid.]"

II. [Yosé] said to [Hiyya], "R. Yohanan [holds] also that it does not fall into the category of the gift of a healthy person [so the woman cannot dispose of the property in any wise, but must keep it and derive benefit from it throughout her lifetime]. [Consequently, she cannot dispose of it at all through a donation. Her gift of the property was null.]

JJ. "In the case of the woman, since her husband was liable to provide her maintenance, her deed does not fall into the category of the gift in contemplation of death. [During her lifetime she cannot dispose of the property, since it is indentured to the husband. She cannot sell it for her own needs, since the husband provides for her. Hence any disposition of the land falls after death, at which point the heirs take precedence over someone to whom she might have proposed to give or sell the land. The prior transaction was null.]"

Here the legal discussion flows from a case report, but the shift in the character of discourse makes no difference. The right of the rabbinical court to dispose of the issue is taken for granted by the narrator.

Conflicting claims against estates, of course, involved movables and goods as much as real estate. First, old scores might be settled through litigation against an heir's claim to a common estate, as in the first story that follows. Second, since a widow was supported by the estate until she received full payment of the marriage settlement coming to her upon the death of her husband, as a primary lien against the husband's estate, the rights of a widow came into conflict with those of the heirs to the estate. She would want to be supported for as long as possible, thus to postpone receiving payment of her marriage settlement. The heirs would want to be rid of her as soon as possible. Along these same lines, female heirs, seeking a dowry from the estate, and male heirs, seeking division of the estate so that they could gain possession of their property or capital, came into conflict.

Y. Baba Batra 9:3.IV.

C. A man became a scribe [at the expense of the father, who had paid the tuition for his studies]. His brothers wanted to divide

[his salary with him]. The case came before R. Ami. He said,
"Thus do we rule: 'A person who found an object—do his
brothers share it with him?' [Obviously not.]"

D.   A man went out on a mission[for a salary]. His brothers wanted
to divide [his salary] with him. The case came before R.
Ami. He said, "Thus do we rule: 'A man who went out and
made his living as a bandit—do his brothers share [his booty]
with him?'"

E.   R. Horaina, brother of R. Samuel bar Suseretai—his brother
wanted to divide up [what each party was making, that is,
form a common pot of their earnings or profits]. He said to
him, "Alexander, my brother, you know that our father left
us two thousand. [You yourself know what father left us.
There were only two thousand of his. Whatever there is in
addition is what I myself earned when father was alive, and it
is mine, not part of the estate.]"

Y. Baba Batra 9:1.I.

X.   This is in line with the following [which shows that a claim for
settlement of the marriage contract ends the right of support]:

Y.   The widow of R. Shobetai was wasting the assets of the estate
[by spending too much on her own maintenance]. The children came and approached R. Eleazar. He said to them,
"What can we do for you? You are foolish people, [you have
no remedy against her]."

Z.   When they went out, they said, "As to her marriage settlement,
what should we do?"

AA. Someone told them, "Pretend to sell some of the estate's property, and she will come and lay claim for her marriage settlement, on account of which she will lose the claim of support from the estate."

BB. After some days she came and approached R. Eleazar. He said
to her, "May a curse come upon me, if I said a thing to
them."

CC. [He said,] "Now what can I do for you, for it is a blow of
deceivers [Pharisees] which has struck you."

Y. Ketubot 6:6.II.

J.   [What is the law as to collecting dowry for daughters from
indentured property when there is a fixed value assigned to
the dowry? That is, after the father died, the brothers took
the property and mortgaged it. May the daughters collect
their dowry from this mortgaged property, retrieving it for

that purpose from the possession of the purchaser?] Said R. Zeira, "R. Yohanan would not permit collection [under such circumstances]."

K. Who orders collection [of the dowry from the mortgaged property]? R. Haninah [and R. Ilai] do so.

L. R. Yosa was trustee for the estate of orphans, and some of the daughters sought support [for their weddings]. The case came before R. Eleazar and R. Simeon b. Yaqim. Ruled R. Simeon b. Yaqim, "Is it not better that they should be supported from the property of their father, and not from public charity?"

M. Said to him R. Eleazar, "If such a matter should come before our rabbis, though, they would not touch it. Shall we then decide a practical case in this way? [That is, they are not sure of the law.]"

N. Said to R. Yosé, "I shall provide for them, and if the [male] orphans should come and complain, I shall provide for them too [by retrieving from the girls and giving to the boys]."

O. Even so, the heirs knew about the decision and entered no complaint.

P. R. Zeira asked before R. Yosé, "How do they decide a practical case?"

Q. He said to him, "In accordance with the view of R. Haninah [K]."

R. So the case came from court, decided in accord with the view of R. Haninah.

S. [Disagreeing with this position, said] R. Abun in the name of R. Hela: "They regard the property as if it were destroyed [and totally unavailable, and they do not collect from it for the present purpose]."

The rulings of Ami, Y. B.B. 9:3, show the sage as a judge settling family disputes about property. The item involving Horaina is not presented as a court case, but the issue is the same. Accordingly, to the framer of the passage the difference between a case settled by a rabbinical clerk, presumably for outsiders to the rabbinical estate, and one in which rabbis simply gave their opinions, is null. All stories and cases serve the same purpose, which is to expose the potentialities of the law. But the stories about court settlements and decisions indicate a clear-cut statement that rabbis decided such matters as these. In the second item, Y. B.B. 9:1, Eleazar informs the plaintiffs that his court can do nothing for them, because the law is against them. The people found their own remedy. But the clerk's incapacity stemmed from the substance of the law, not the weakness of his court's authority. The final case shows us a similar situation, in which legal theory and practice were treated on a single plane.

While authority over real transactions in real estate, gifts, and testaments is most striking, ordinary folk would more regularly have encountered rabbinical authority in litigating conflicts of movables, especially arising in trade and commerce, as well as in collection of debts and bailments. These kinds of cases, being trivial in value as compared to those entailing transfer of real property, are apt to have been more common. Breach of contract, for example in commercial transactions, came under rabbinical supervision.

Y. Baba Mesia 4:2.II.

    D.   R. Hiyya bar Joseph handed over a *denar* to a salt merchant for salt. The latter party retracted [as salt went up in price]. He said to him, "Do you not know that a scythe will cut into your thigh: *He who exacted punishment from the men of the Generation of the Flood is destined to exact punishment from him who does not keep his word* [M. B.M. 4:2F]."

    E.   A man handed over money for silk. [The seller] retracted. The case came before R. Hiyya bar Joseph and R. Yohanan. R. Hiyya bar Joseph said, "Either give him [silk] of the value of what he has left as a pledge [in advance of the purchase, which was not the entire purchase price], or submit to the curse, 'He who exacted punishment . . . '"

    F.   R. Yohanan ruled, "Either give him all which he has purchased, or accept the curse, 'He who exacted punishment . . . '"

The sanction for breach of contract is a curse, as specified. The power of the rabbi to call down that curse clearly is taken for granted, and the curse is treated as a perfectly routine court procedure. In this instance, therefore, the rabbi's authority depended upon his imputed status as a supernatural figure; this contrasts with the cases in which the clerk's adjudication of a real estate matter in no way involved magical sanctions.

Another kind of breach of contract was generated by the custom of providing credit for workers with a particular shopkeeper, who would give them food and collect from the householder. Such an arrangement for payment in kind was quite legitimate. But it involved conflicting claims on whether or not full value for services rendered had been handed over.

Y. Shebuot 7:5.V.

    C.   [A householder made arrangements] for shoulder bearers with the storekeeper. They came to [court to] collect what he had not given to them.

    D.   The workers' case came to R. Shimi [to collect their salary, since the storekeeper had given them nothing. He ruled,] "If the shoulder bearers had been told by the storekeeper, 'You have already received [your wages from me, and I have paid you,' that would] not have been the end of the matter. For both parties would have been able to collect [from the householder. The storekeeper thus would never have been in a position to lose out, even if the workers had contradicted him. So why should the storekeeper lose out now?].

E.　"But now [that he concedes to you that he has not paid you up to now, since he has accepted the task of paying the workers,] let them collect [from him, for they have no claim against the householder]."

Once more, the ruling on the case is interesting because it spells out two possibilities, each one dependent upon the formulation of the workers' claim and the storekeeper's response.

One form of contract rabbis would not enforce involved usury, defined as "payment for waiting for one's money." The bulk of the stories in hand, however, narrate transactions involving rabbis themselves, so we cannot show that ordinary folk brought suit in this regard, or could do so.

Y. Baba Mesa 5:6.IV.

A.　Abba bar Zamina gave a *denar* to the baker and bought bread from him at the lowest prevailing price throughout the year.

B.　Now Rab did not approve this arrangement [seeing it as payment for waiting for repayment of the money].

C.　R. Hiyya the Elder had some flax. Ass drivers came to buy it from him. He said to them, "I was not thinking of selling now, but rather at the time at which the crop is more abundant [and demand greater]."

D.　They said to him, "Sell it to us now, in accord with the price which you will get if you sell it later when the crop is more abundant."

E.　He came and asked Rabbi.

F.　He said to him, "It is forbidden, [for this looks as if he is being paid for waiting on repayment of funds]."

The prohibition of usury carried in its wake the view that gold and silver were to be treated as commodities. The issue of fluctuations in the value of gold and silver then brought litigation to court, as did the claim that services had been rendered in exchange for a loan and that thus usury had occurred.

Y. Baba Mesia 4:1.I.

F.　The implication of what Rabbi has said is that gold is in the status of a commodity.

G.　We have a Mishnah teaching which states, "Silver is in the status of a commodity."

H.   The daughter of R. Hiyya the Elder lent Rab [golden] *denars*.
     She came and asked her father [how to collect the debt, since
     in the meantime, gold had risen in value *vis-à-vis* silver]. He
     said to her, "Take from him good and substantial *denars* [of
     the same weight as those you lent]."

I.   From the daughter of R. Hiyya, shall we learn [that gold is
     deemed a commodity]? [Perhaps there was some other consid-
     eration which led to Hiyya's advising her as he did.]

J.   Said R. Idi, "Also Abba, father of Samuel, raised the question
     before Rabbi: 'What is the law as to lending [golden] *denars*
     for the return of [the same weight in golden] *denars?*' He
     said to him, 'It is permitted [to do so].'"

K.   Said R. Jacob bar Aha, "Also R. Yohanan and R. Simeon b.
     Laqish both say that it is permitted to lend [golden] *denars*
     for the return of the [same weight in golden] *denars.*"

Y. Baba Mesia 5:1.VI.

A.   *He who lends money to his fellow [should not live in his
     courtyard for free, nor should he rent a place from him for
     less than the prevailing rate, for that is tantamount to usury
     (M. B.M. 5:1M–O)].*

B.   A man lent money to his fellow. The latter let him space in his
     building. Later on the borrower said to the lender, "Pay me
     the rent for my building."

C.   The lender said to him, "Give me back my money. [I had as-
     sumed you would not charge me rent so long as my money
     was in your hands.]"

D.   The case came before R. Ba bar Mina. He ruled, "Now does [the
     lender] get what he had imagined was free [merely because he
     assumed it]? [Obviously not! He was wrong and has no claim
     at all.]"

The two cases concerning the status of precious metals involve sages and
their families. The third one, by contrast, indicates that usury in kind was an
issue before the courts, and that common folk brought such cases. Whether
the courts would enforce the prohibition against usury under ordinary circumstances is not clear, and we do not know that, if they tried to, they had
the jurisdiction. Still, I do not know why the clerks would have been denied
this, given their reports about their other powers.

Rabbinical courts were called upon to settle cases involving collection of
debts. As in the case of breach of contract, their power involved imposition
of frightening oaths, which people tried to avoid. The rabbinical judges
claimed the power to force the collection of outstanding debts, not only from
the debtor himself, but also from the guarantor of the debt. They also

imposed their own reading on bonds of indebtedness in a case in which the writing was unclear. Finally, they assumed full authority to determine the facts of the matter.

Y. Shebuot 6:2.IV.

A. R. Merinus served as a pledge for someone who borrowed money from his daughter-in-law. The case [of the daughter-in-law's claim] came before R. Hama, father of Bar Qappara, and R. Hoshaiah. After confessing in court [that he had served as a pledge for the debt and was obligated to pay it,] he said, "But I already paid it."

B. They asked R. Hiyya the Elder. He went and asked Rabbi. Rabbi replied, "He who by court decision is obligated to pay a debt does not have the power [to claim that he had already paid it]."

Y. Baba Batra 10:1.V.

H. A bill of indebtedness went from R. Huna [who made no decision on how to read it] to R. Shimi, on which the word *ogdoé* [of *ogdoeconta,* eighty] was erased, and *conta* was clear.

I. Said R. Shimi to R. Huna, "Go and see what is the lowest numeral in Greek that *conta* is combined with."

J. He said, "It is *triaconta* [thirty]."

K. When the party had left, he said, "That man intended to make thirty [by the erasure] and lost twenty [the original was fifty *penteconta*]."

Y. Sanhedrin 3:8.IV.

A. R. Abbahu in the name of R. Yohanan: "He who hides his witnesses behind a wall [to entrap another party] has not accomplished anything."

B. It is in line with the following: There was a man who wanted to join a banquet.

C. [The host] said to him, "Will you give me what you owe me?"

D. He said to him, "Yes."

E. After they got up from the banquet, [the unwanted guest] said to him, "I don't owe you anything at all."

F. [The host] said to him, "I have witnesses [that you confessed to the debt]."

G. [The defendant] said to him, "I only said that because I didn't want to ruin your banquet."

H. The case came before R. Ami, who ruled, "This is in line with that which R. Yohanan has stated, 'He who hides his witnesses behind a wall has not accomplished anything.'"

These rather routine reports leave no doubt that rabbis maintained they could order payment of debts. We have no clear evidence on the actual procedures, particularly with reference to the sort of sanctions rabbis could impose if their orders were not obeyed. The first of the three cases involved a rabbi, but the others make clear that ordinary folk, not bound by the disciplines of the rabbinical estate, were under the jurisdiction of the clerks.

From the collection of debts, secured by the rabbinical courts, we turn to the disposition of bailments—goods left with a party for safekeeping and later collection. Here the litigation was generated by the claim either that nothing had been left, that the bailment already had been returned, or that the bailment itself was subject to more than one claim of ownership.

Y. Qiddushin 2:1.II.

I.   Said R. Ba, "A case came before Rab, and he treated an agent as a witness."

J.   Someone deposited his casks of wine in the cellar of his fellow, and the latter later denied the bailment. Said R. Phineas, "The case came before R. Jeremiah, and he treated the depositor's agent as a witness, [the witness being the stevedore who had carried the casks, thus also the depositor's agent in making the bailment], and he required the bailee to take an oath because of the testimony of the stevedore."

Y. Shebuot 7:2.III.

E.   . . . The sharecropper [of land belonging to] Bar Ziza deposited with a certain man a *litra* of gold. Both Bar Ziza and his sharecropper died. The case came before R. Ishmael b. R. Yosé, [since both estates claimed the money]. He said, "Who does not know that whatever belonged to the sharecropper of Bar Ziza in fact belonged to Bar Ziza? Let the property be given to the estate of Bar Ziza."

F.   Bar Ziza's children came [forward]. [Ishmael] ruled, "Let half of the bailment be handed over immediately to the adults, and [the other half be held for the minors and] given to them when they reach maturity." Thereafter R. Ishmael b. R. Yosé died.

G.   The case then came before R. Hiyya. He ruled, "From the fact [that the sharecropper seemed poor] nothing is to be inferred. There are people who do not show off. Let the bailment be handed over to the children of the sharecropper."

H.   The bailee informed Hiyya that half of the bailment already had been handed over to the children of Bar Ziza.

I.   He said to him, "What you have handed over at the instruction of the court has been validly handed over, and what you now hand over at the instruction of the court likewise do you validly hand over."

We come now to stories about cases of torts and damages brought before rabbinical judges. Instances involve damages by chattels, on the one side, and cases involving theft, on the other.

Y. Baba Qamma 2:5.III.

A. A man brought out the goods of his shop on a cow. An ass came by and broke [the goods].

B. The case came before R. Isaac bar Tabelai. He said to him, "He does not owe you a thing, and not only so, but if the ass had been injured, you would become liable to pay compensation for his injury [since the other party had every right to use the public way]."

Y. Baba Qamma 10:3.II.

B. Rab said, "And that rule, that people must know about the theft, applies only to a case in which he brings forth proof that [the one who had originally sold the property] had spent the night with him [so that we do not have to take account of the possibility that he had sold the objects and now announces that they are stolen]."

C. Assi said, "If the one who sold the property claims, 'I purchased it from So-and-so, [who is no longer in town],' he is believed."

D. A case of this kind came before R. Nisa, and he did not accept that statement.

E. Is it because he differs from the position of Assi?

F. No. That particular man is a known liar, and on that account he did not accept his statement.

What is striking is that the authority of the rabbi extended in particular to the claim that property in another's hands in fact had been stolen. There is no indication as to who went out after thieves or how they were punished. What the bureaus of the Jewish regime settled was only the disposition of property subject to conflicting claims.

The rabbinical courts dealt not only with property, but also with threats to sound social policy. For instance, the sale of animals to gentiles was discouraged, whether on grounds that the beasts might serve some idolatrous purpose, that the beasts would be so worked as to violate the Sabbath law, or that the raising of small cattle posed a severe threat to the ecology of the Land. Accordingly, a penalty quite outside normal judicial procedures was imposed in the following instance.

Y. Abodah Zarah 1:6.IV.

   D.   [There is this precedent.] A certain person sold a camel to an
        Aramaean. The case came before R. Simeon b. Laqish, who
        imposed a penalty on him of twice the proceeds, so that [the
        Israelite] would go after the [Aramaean purchaser] and re-
        cover the camel.

   E.   Said R. Yosé b. R. Bun, "[Simeon b. Laqish] imposed the fine
        on the middleman, [and not on the Israelite who had sold the
        beast to the middleman], and they used to insult [the child of
        the middleman], "A son of the Aramaeans' agent!'"

   F.   [In imposing such a fine, even though, in law, the man was
        exempt from such a fine,] R. Simeon b. Laqish was in accord
        with R. Judah.

Torts involving cultic, as against merely material, damage naturally came to
rabbinical courts.

Y. Sanhedrin 1:1.VI.

   A.   A man deliberately rendered a priest [cultically] unclean. The
        case came before R. Isaac, and he ordered the man to provide
        unconsecrated food for the priest to eat [since he could not
        eat cheaper food in the status of heave offering, which he
        normally ate, by reason of his cultic uncleanness].

These two cases have in common the presence of issues of a nonmaterial
character. In the former case, the rabbinical court imposed a heavy fine so
as to discourage a deleterious practice. In the latter the violation of the taboo
affecting the man brought in its wake an additional cost; this had to be
compensated. It is clear that, in their minds, sages bore responsibility for
more than ordinary real estate and commercial transactions. They were
judicial and social authorities.

   In the light of the practical cases reported in the foregoing stories, we may
hardly be surprised to find numerous references to how court procedures
were carried on, rules of receiving evidence, cross-examining witnesses,
changes of venue, appellate procedures, and the like. These are typified in
the following, which require no further comment.

Y. Sanhedrin 3:8.III.

   A.   R. Huna, when he saw witnesses using identical language,
        would undertake a strict examination. And when he did so, it
        turned out that he was right [that there had been a prior re-
        hearsal on what the witnesses were to say].

   B.   R. Huna would ridicule a judge who [began the proceedings,
        e.g., by asking,] "Do you accept the testimony of one wit-

ness?" But [he maintained that the litigants and not the judges] must open the proceedings.

C. R. Huna, when he knew reason to acquit someone in court, but had not fully worked out his reasoning, would open as follows: "Open your mouth for the dumb, for the rights of all who are left desolate; open your mouth, judge righteously . . ." (Prov. 31:9).

Y. Sanhedrin 3:12.II.

A. R. Levi had a case with a litigant in a matter of houses, and they came to court before R. Eleazar.

B. After the trial was over, he brought evidence.

C. [Eleazar] asked R. Yohanan, who said to him, "So long as he brings proof, he may reverse the decision."

D. R. Abemakhis had a litigation with someone concerning millstones, and they came to court before R. Eleazar. After the trial was over, he brought witnesses.

E. [Eleazar again] asked R. Yohanan, who said to him, "Are you still [in doubt] about this matter? So long as he brings proof, he may reverse the decision."

F. Now why was it necessary to cite two cases?

G. In the case of R. Levi, the court decision had not yet been issued, while in the case of R. Abemakhis, the court decision had already been issued, [so these were two quite separate situations].

On determining the location of a court process, we have a story that takes for granted courts governing Jews were located in a number of towns, that the judges were well known, and that people might express strong preferences for trial before one or another authority.

Y. Sanhedrin 3:2:II.

A. Two men had a case in Antioch. One of them said to his fellow, "That which R. Yohanan will rule [in this case] do I accept for myself."

B. R. Yohanan heard and ruled: "He does not have the power to compel his antagonist [to go to Tiberias for the trial]. But [the court in Antioch] will hear the claims of both parties there. Then if there is need, they may write up the particulars of the case and send the case to the rabbis."

C. R. Eleazar said, "This one says, 'In Tiberias,' and that one says, 'In Sepphoris'—they accept the position of the one who said, 'In Tiberias.'"

The notion that Yohanan exercised appellate authority is striking. It indicates that the court system was well organized, subject to a single overall authority, and governed by a unified legal code. The appellate procedures presumably were well established, so that the storyteller could take for granted Yohanan would invoke routine procedures. Eleazar, to be sure, gives preference to Tiberias over Sepphoris, but the distance was not a day's journey, and so the issue of venue was trivial.

The power of the court to summon a litigant or a witness rested upon the capacity to declare a recalcitrant party to be ostracized or excommunicated. This had the effect of removing him from the Jewish community. Since the penalty is taken for granted as effective, we learn that the rabbis behind the tale assumed general support from the Jewish community for their judicial activities.

Y. Moed Qatan 3:1:VII.

    A.   R. Joshua b. Levi summoned a man to his court three times, and the man did not come. He sent him the message, "If it were not the case that in my entire life I have never declared a man to be subject to a *herem* [ostracism], I should have declared you to be in *herem.* "

    B.   For twenty-four reasons they excommunicated a person, and this is one of them.

    C.   "And that if any one did not come within three days, by order of the officials and the elders all his property should be forfeited, and he himself banned from the congregation of the exiles" (Ezra 10:8).

    D.   Said R. Isaac b. R. Eleazar, "There are many more than those twenty-four cases scattered throughout the Mishnah."

As I suggested, for the penalty of ostracism to work, there had to be general compliance with rabbis' authority. Yet the sanction was invoked, in particular, to force compliance with the court's procedures, not obedience to its decisions in a case of conflicting property claims. There a more formidable sanction had to come into play, for the courts could hardly depend for effective authority only upon a common consensus about what, to begin with, was subject to conflict.

If the Jewish nation at large accepted the sovereignty of rabbinical courts in property disputes, the reason may have been the power of the courts not only to persuade or elicit general support, but also to call upon the power of the state to transfer ownership of real and movable property from one party to another. We come now to a kind of jurisdiction which, in the end, had to enjoy not merely passive acquiescence through fear of ostracism but active support of the people at large, namely, determinations of personal status. While the courts might call upon the state to back up their rulings about property, they are not likely to have enjoyed equivalent support in matters to which the government was probably indifferent, such as whether a given woman was betrothed and so not free to marry anyone but the fiancé, on the one side, or whether she was not betrothed and so free to marry anyone of her choice, on the other. Persistent meddling in such affairs can have generated only widespread protest, unless the community at large acquiesced and indeed actively supported the right of the courts to make such decisions. Nonetheless, even behind these evidences of rabbinical authority, based as they are on sanctions of moral authority, as distinct from the imperial government's ultimate threat of force, there still were elements of exchange of property or things of value. Consequently, when we deal with personal status, we take up yet another aspect of the rabbi's power to judge property cases. For rulings in cases involving personal status—whether or not a woman was betrothed or married, a slave was freed, a man was a valid priest—always carried in their wake material considerations. Indeed, even if the courts were set up only to settle questions of personal status in accordance with the law of the Jewish nation, something of slight concern to the government, the courts would have had to enjoy the power to transfer real property and movables from one party to another. We may hardly be surprised, therefore, to find a substantial repertoire about how rabbis decided questions of the status of women, slaves, and similar sorts of persons in a subordinate or otherwise special status.

As we follow the story of a marriage from beginning to end, that is, from betrothal to either divorce or the death of the husband, in sequence we compile reports of cases of how rabbis intervened in judging important cases down the line. At the outset there was the matter of stipulations made in a writ of betrothal and whether or not these had been met by the specified deadline. The first passage states the law, the second, a case involving application of the law.

Y. Gittin 7:6.II.

    A.   Said R. Abbahu in the name of R. Yohanan: "The provisions of a conditional writ of betrothal are as follows:

    B.   "'I, So-and-so, son of Such-and-such, betroth you, Miss So-and-so, daughter of Such-and-such, on the stipulation that I give you such-and-such a sum of money, and that I marry you by such-and-such a date. If that date comes and I have not married you, I shall have no claim whatsoever on you.'"

    C.   What if an untoward event took place [preventing the marriage, not through the fault of the prospective groom]? [Is the writ deemed null?]

    D.   R. Yohanan said, "The accident is as if it did not happen [and the betrothal is null]. [An accident is no excuse.]"

    E.   R. Simeon b. Laqish said, "The accident most certainly did

happen [and we take it into account]. [Since it was through no
fault of the groom that the betrothal did not lead to a marriage, the writ remains valid and may be carried out.]"

F. In the view of R. Simeon b. Laqish, the groom had to carry out
the stipulation. If the day came and he did not marry her,
then, [as the writ says,] "I shall have no claim whatsoever on
you."

G. When R. Yohanan was dying, he gave instructions to his daughters to carry out the law in accordance with the opinion of R.
Simeon b. Laqish, for a court later on may concur with him,
in which case [my] grandchildren will be in the position of
mamzers [since the court will declare the writ to be valid]. [If
the daughters do not then enter into the stipulated marriage,
but marry another party, they will have violated a valid writ
of betrothal, and, with the women deemed betrothed to one
party, should they produce children by another, the children
will be in the status of *mamzers*.]

H. A man paid in advance to a canal barge operator, but the canal
went dry [so the bargeman could not transport the produce to
market]. The case came before R. Nahman bar Jacob. [If the
defendant claims,] "Here is the barge, bring me the canal"
[Nahman accepts the plea].

I. Abba bar Huna in the name of R. Abba [who does not accept the
claim of an untoward accident] held that the farmer hoped
that the canal would dry up, so he could take his money back.

Y. Qiddushin 3:2.III.

A. [If,] once the time came [for the marriage,] the prospective
husband claims, "I have done [what I promised in the writ of
betrothal]," while she claims, "I have not received [what he
promised],"—

B. R. Abun said, "Since he seeks to retrieve the writ of betrothal
from the woman, it is his task to bring proof. [She wishes to
stand by the document, that is to say, the condition has not
been met, so she is not betrothed. All she wants is to nullify
the transaction.]"

C. Then take note of the case in which there is no such document!
[In that case, who brings proof, since he made the condition
orally, and now he does not seek to retrieve a document of
any sort?]

D. Said R. Yosé, "Since he seeks to bar her from marrying anyone
else, it still is his task to bring proof."

E. [What if] they got married during the time specified by the writ
of betrothal? [Is he believed when he says that he has given

her what he specified, at the appropriate time, that is, before
he married her?]

F. Such a case came before R. Abbahu. He ruled, "Go, pay."

G. The husband said to him, "Rabbi, [according to your ruling, I
never met the stipulated condition, and, accordingly,] I have
not even acquired this woman as my wife at all, and yet you
tell me, 'Go, pay'?"

H. Said R. Abbahu, "In my whole life, this is the only man who
ever made a fool of me."

I. [Abbahu] went and ruled, "If [the husband] retracted, he still
must pay, [so he does not have the right to retract] and if the
wife retracted, she must pay."

J. Now is this not precisely his ruling at the outset [prior to the
man's clever argument]?

K. He treated the matter as a court action. [Since he married her, the
stipulation no longer is in effect, but he must carry it out.]

The first case is not conclusive, since the associated litigants are children of
a rabbi. Whether ordinary folk were so meticulous about the law is unclear.
Where the principle at hand is subject to court action with Jews not of the
rabbinical estate, it involves a claim of mitigating circumstances in a breach
of contract. The second case, Abbahu's ruling, by contrast, pertains not to
the status of persons but to the requirement that the husband transfer property
to the woman. In any event the cases are cited only in the setting of the
analysis of legal issues.

The betrothal took effect with the transfer of something of minimal value.
The assessment of the object's value, and even whether or not the object
could be transferred, came to court.

Y. Nedarim 5:5.II.

A. A man consecrated a woman as his betrothed by giving a Torah
scroll to her. R. Shobetai and R. Hasida brought the case to
R. Yosah. He ruled, "She is not betrothed."

Whether or not a betrothal was valid had a broad range of consequences. For
one thing, once a betrothal had taken effect, the groom might then not marry
any of the close kin of the bride.

If, by contrast, it was determined that an unconsummated betrothal was
null, he might do so. The following reports a case of that sort.

Y. Qiddushin 3:2.VI.

A. [The writ is valid only if it represents] the knowledge and consent of the groom, *and* the knowledge and consent of the
bride.

B. If in his opinion it was a conditional writ, but in her opinion it
    was an act of betrothal—

C. R. Haninah said, "It is a writ of betrothal, and its conditions
    must be met."

D. R. Haggai in the name of R. Zeira said, "It is a valid betrothal.
    [That is so despite the fact that the husband insists it was
    merely a stipulation, which has not been met, and he wishes
    to marry a relative of the original girl.]"

E. R. Haninah took up the debate with R. Haggai.

F. R. Hila said to him, "Offer persuasive arguments to Haggai, for
    Haggai is a reasonable person."

G. R. Zeira said, "In the month of Adar I R. Hila died. In
    Adar II a case came before R. Haninah and associates of the
    rabbis, who wanted to retract and rule in accord with Haggai
    [and so to prohibit the groom from marrying close kin of
    the bride, on grounds that the betrothal was completely
    valid]."

H. Said to him R. Samuel bar Imi, "Did not R. Hila tell you quite
    properly to take up the argument with Haggai, because Hag-
    gai is a reasonable person? [Now you yourself retract and rule
    in accord with his view!]"

I. Said R. Haggai, "The Mishnah supports my position: [*He
    who says to a woman, 'I have betrothed you,' and she says,
    'You did not betroth me,'—he is forbidden to marry her close
    kin, but she is permitted to marry his close kin.*] *If she says,
    'You betrothed me,' and he says, 'I did not betroth you,'*

J. "*he is permitted to marry her close kin, and she is forbidden
    to marry his close kin* [M. Qid. 3:10A–E]. [What this means
    is that, with a writ such as is under discussion, we do not
    maintain that the betrothal is valid and complete.]"

We see in the foregoing that the rabbinical ruling was important not because
of the transfer of a pittance from one party to another. Rather, at issue was
whether the parties might marry one another's close kin. If the betrothal was
held valid, they were not permitted to do so. Hence the principal concern was
personal status.

A further issue pertinent to betrothal had to do with the suitability of both
parties to one another. If a man suffered from a physical blemish, a woman
had every right to know that fact in advance and determine whether or not
she wished to proceed with the betrothal. In the Talmud's view a rabbinical
judge had the power to prohibit certain marriages, and to permit others to
take place.

Y. Yebamot 8:2.II.

> E.   Samuel said, "If a man with a single testicle should come before me for a ruling, I should declare him valid [to enter the congregation] . . . "
>
> G.   Said R. Yudan bar Hanin, "But that is on condition that he has the right testicle intact."
>
> H.   A case came before R. Immi. He said to the woman [who wished to marry such a man], "You are permitted to marry him, my daughter, but you should know that you will not have children by him."
>
> I.   R. Zeira praised this decision, because he laid ·the matter out clearly [by hinting that while permitted, she should not marry him].

Y. Ketubot 7:8.

> A.   *A man who suffered blemishes—they do not force him to put her away.*
>
> B.   *Said Rabban Simeon b. Gamaliel, "Under what circumstances? In the case of small blemishes.*
>
> C.   *"But in the case of major blemishes, they do force him to put her away."*
>
> I.   B.   R. Ba bar Kahana in the name of R. Yohanan: "The law is in accord with the position of Rabban Simeon b. Gamaliel.
>
>   C.   A case came before R. Jeremiah in Kopiah, and he forced him to divorce his wife.

The power to break up a marriage against the wishes of one of the parties is not to be taken lightly. The rabbi could relieve the woman, unable herself to institute divorce, of the unwanted life with a repulsive man and permit her to remarry. The ugly husband could do nothing about it. Were the woman to do so on her own, she would be in the status of an adulteress and children of the second union, *mamzerim,* totally outside of the Israelite community. Accordingly, the power portrayed here as lying in the hands of the clerks was enormous. While the law provided for issues arising in the period in which a marriage was in force, for example, rulings on accusations of adultery, in the nature of things a normal marriage would generate no striking issues for the attention of the rabbinical courts. If, therefore, we skip over to cases pertinent to the cessation of a marriage, we may find further indications and instances of the extent, in the view of the Talmud's framers, of rabbinical authority over material and concrete matters.

This then brings us to the other side of a marriage, its dissolution through divorce or death of the husband. We find ample evidence that rabbinical judges supervised every aspect of the transaction. The procedure according to law involved the delivery of the writ of divorce in the presence of two witnesses, at which point the marriage was deemed severed. The issue of suitable testimony to the act of delivery—the effective act of divorce—had therefore to be worked out. One instance of stories representing rabbinical supervision of the delivery of a writ of divorce is the following.

Y. Qiddushin 3:8.V.

E. Simeon bar Ba brought a writ of divorce and gave it to a woman in the presence of a single witness.

F. The case came before R. Yohanan, who ruled, "A single witness is null in a case involving a married woman.

G. "Did not R. Hiyya bar Assi say in the name of R. Assi, 'A single witness's testimony in the case of a married woman is absolutely worthless'?"

If, further, the writ was brought by messengers, they had to testify that they had witnessed the writing and signing of the writ. In the following cases, that requirement was extended to the transfer of such a writ even within the confines of the area around Caesarea.

Y. Gittin 1:1.VII.

A. R. Eleazar objected to rabbis [= M. Gittin 1:1C], "Just as you maintain [M. Gittin 1:1F]: *He who brings a writ of divorce from one province to another overseas has to say, 'In my presence it was written, and in my presence it was signed,'* so I maintain that he who brings a writ from one province to another in the Land of Israel has to say, 'In my presence it was written and in my presence it was signed.' "

B. Said R. Jacob bar Zebedi, "There was a case concerning one who brought a writ of divorce from the harbor of Caesarea [to Caesarea]. The case came before R. Abbahu. He ruled, 'Yes, you have to say, "Before me it was written and before me it was signed."' And yet the harbor of Caesarea is not equivalent to Caesarea. [So Eleazar is right.]"

C. Said R. Abin, "It was the case of a ship which was en route."

If the original agent delivering a writ got sick, a court would appoint a replacement. This transaction, too, was supervised, as we should expect, by other courts, which recognized the authority of one another as part of a single system:

Y. Gittin 3:6.II.

A. What if the second agent also got sick?

B. Said R. Haninah, son of R. Abba, "Such a case in fact hap-

pened, and someone asked and sent to R. Hiyya and to R.
Yosa and to R. Immi, and they instructed him, 'The latter
agent does not have to say, 'In my presence it was written
and in my presence it was signed,' but he merely states, 'I
am the agent of a court' '' [M. Git. 3:6D–E].

Whether or not a slave might serve as the agent to deliver such a writ was
taken up in a court case.

Y. Gittin 2:6.I.

  A. A case came before R. Immi of a slave who had delivered a writ
    of divorce, [and he declared it] valid.

  B. Said to him R. Abba, "And did not R. Hiyya teach: 'A slave who
    brought a writ of divorce—it is invalid'?"

  C. Said R. Assi, "If it were not for R. Ba [= B], we should have
    been ready to permit a married woman to remarry [with an
    invalid writ of divorce]."

The rabbinical courts carried on a long-standing tradition within Israelite law
on the scribal role in preparing writs of divorce. The character of rulings
before us suggests that most fundamental questions had been settled long
before. In any event, these are matters over which clerks surely had complete
control. People assumed they knew what they were doing, and, for its part,
the state cannot have taken much interest in the administration of such
matters among a subordinate community which had long conducted its own
affairs. A minor point such as the following surely fell within sages' power.

Y. Gittin 4:2.V.

  R. [As to the husband's paying the fee,] it is in line with the follow-
    ing: Doshu, brother of Dodu, was divorcing his wife. The
    case came before rabbis, who ruled that she must pay the fee
    of the scribe.

  S. And have we not learned: *The husband pays the fee of the
    scribe?*

  T. R. Ili in the name of Samuel, "We deal [when the husband pays
    the fee] with a case in which the wife forgives the repayment
    of her marriage settlement [in which case the husband enjoys
    the benefit of the writ and must pay the fee for preparing it,
    since he profits]."

The second means of nullifying a marital bond was through a rite of *halisah,*
removing the husband's shoe, under the circumstances of a levirate connection described at Deut. 25:5–10. The Talmud's claim that a rabbinical
judge administered the law in a given case is illustrated in the following.

Y. Yebamot 12:6.V.

    I.   A case came before R. Hiyya bar Wawa, and he said to him, "My son, this woman does not want to be married to you through a levirate marriage, but perform the rite of *halisah* with her, and so remove your connection from her, and then she may be married to you through a normal marriage."

    J.   After he had performed the rite of *halisah* for her, he said to him, "If Moses and Samuel should come, she will not be permitted to you."

    K.   Concerning [Hiyya, the man] recited this verse, "They are skilled in doing evil, but how to do good they know not" (Jer. 4:22).

Here, the rabbi was able to trick the man into severing the levirate connection to the woman with the promise that, afterward, she would marry him. The man's ignorance of the law is taken for granted. In this way the clerk's court was able to prevent a woman from having to marry someone she did not want.

A woman was free of a prior marital connection, finally, when the death of the husband was adequately attested through witnesses. Rabbinical courts were called upon to evaluate the evidence.

Y. Yebamot 15:1.II.

    A.   What is the law as to a single witness's being believed in time of war?

    B.   Let us derive the answer from the following: There was a man in the time of Rabbi, whom they asked, "Where is So-and-so?" He said to them, "He's dead." "Where is So-and-so?" "He too is dead." He said to him, "Are they all dead?" He said to them, "If they were alive, would they not have come back?"

    C.   R. Jeremiah in the name of R. Haninah, "The case came before Rabbi, and he ruled, 'She who has remarried [on the strength of such testimony] has remarried [and need not go forth], but she who has not remarried should not remarry.'"

    D.   R. Aibu bar Nigri: "This was a decision in time of war, and it follows that in time of war, the testimony of a single witness is accepted."

If a marriage was dissolved through divorce or death, the marriage settlement (*ketubah*), established prior to the formation of the union at betrothal, had to be paid off. It constituted a principal lien on the real property of the husband or his estate. The marriage settlement even during the subsistence of a marriage was an asset of the wife. Charges under limited circumstances might be laid against it before it was collected. Thus certain medical expenses might be deducted by the husband from the value of the wife's marriage settlement, under the stated conditions.

Y. Baba Batra 9:4.II.

B. It was taught: **Rabban Simeon b. Gamaliel says, "In the case of any ailment involving medical care at fixed cost—she is healed at the expense of her marriage-settlement. But as to [ongoing] medical care of unlimited cost—lo, that is equivalent to any other aspect of her [everyday] support [and the husband pays] [T. Ket. 4:5I].**

C. This is in line with the following:

D. A relative of R. Simeon bar Wawa had eye trouble. She came before R. Yohanan [to claim support from her husband]. He said to her, "Has your physician set a fixed price for his treatment? If he has set a fixed price, then the cost comes from your dowry. If he has not set a fixed price for the treatment, then your husband must pay for the cost of the treatment."

E. [Yohanan has thus shown the alternatives to the plaintiff, thus hinting to her an appropriate answer. This is poor judicial practice,] for have we not learned, "Do not behave like advocates"?

F. And [note] that which R. Haggai in the name of R. Joshua b. Levi [said], "It is forbidden to reveal one's decision to an individual, [surely he should not have told her what he did]."

G. [In reply] one may say: R. Yohanan knew that she was an honest woman, on which account he told her [what choices lay before him as judge].

H. [Furthermore,] if the woman's husband claimed that the physician had stipulated a fixed fee for his services, and she claimed that the physician had not done so, to which party do we listen? Is it not to the husband [who can stipulate a fixed fee anyhow]?

I. Said R. Matenaiah, "That which you have said [at F] applies to him whom the judgment will not favor. But as to him whom the judgment will favor, one may inform him of the matter."

This case is not probative of the rabbis' authority over Israelites in general, because it speaks only of a highly educated woman, related to a rabbi and clearly familiar with the law. The rabbi's decision, moreover, is subject to suspicion of having favored her illegitimately.

The more common circumstance for litigation involving the marriage settlement arose when the marriage ended through divorce or the death of the husband. At that point the widow had to secure claim on property of the value of the sum owing to her. This had to be real property, not movables:

Y. Qiddushin 1:3.III.

M.   A widow seized a slave girl as payment for her marriage settlement. R. Isaac ruled, "Since she has seized her, she is properly seized [and the action is valid]. [But that is not the case at the outset, and hence, in general, the slave is not equivalent to real estate.]"

N.   R. Immi took the slave away from her, for she thought that the slave belonged to her, and she was not hers [for the collection of her outstanding marriage settlement]. [The slave is in the status of movables, not real estate.]

We recall that once a claim for the collection of a marriage settlement was issued, a widow might no longer claim day-to-day support from her deceased husband's estate. It, therefore, was very much to the widow's advantage not to have her marriage settlement paid off, as the following case indicates.

Y. Ketubot 4:13.I.

D.   When a certain man was dying, he said, "Pay off that man's [my] wife a marriage settlement [and issue a writ of divorce]."

E.   The case came before R. Mana. He said, "Let the words of the dying man be carried out."

F.   Said to him R. Haninah, "And has a man got the right to nullify a stipulation written in the marriage settlement merely by a verbal declaration? [He has deprived her of support as a widow.]"

G.   He said to him, "You said it. How do you know?"

H.   He said to him, "And we do not deal with a case in Galilee, and we proposed to say, 'Galileans had more concern for the honor owing to them than their money.' [The custom outweighs the dying man's statement. The widow retains the right of support from the estate.]"

We come, finally, to instances in which rabbinical courts dealt with questions of personal status of a rather special character, involving, on the lower end of the scale, slaves, and, on the upper, wives of priests. In fact it is our perspective, not that of the Talmud, that encompasses the condition of slaves within the rubric of cases involving personal status. From the perspective of the law, slaves in general are chattels, movable property to be disposed of in an ordinary way. The principle involved in the following case is that, if one loses property, he retains title to it until he despairs of recovering what has been lost. At that point he is deemed to have relinquished title. Exactly that principle, applicable to a cow or a book, pertains to the slave in the following discourse in court.

Y. Gittin 4:4.IV.

N. The slave girl of Rabbah bar Zutra fled. He despaired of recovering her. He came and asked R. Haninah and R. Joshua b. Levi [after getting her back]. He said to him, "He has not got the right to enslave her again."

The conditions in which a person entered slavery were taken into account. It was assumed that when an Israelite sold himself as a slave, it was because he had no choice at all. This was how he would pay his debts or even secure some small means of support. Courts had the power to redeem Jews from slavery through use of communal funds, that is, tax money. Here is one such case.

Y. Gittin 4:9.

A. *He who sells himself and his children to a gentile—*
B. *they do not redeem him, but they do redeem the children after their father's death.*
I. A. The Mishnah [at M. Git. 4:9A–B] speaks of one who repeatedly has sold himself. But if he sold himself for the first time, they do redeem him.
B. But if he sold himself to Lydians [who are cannibals], then even if it was the first time, they do not redeem him.
C. Someone sold himself to Lydians. The case came before R. Abbahu. He ruled, "What shall we do? He did it for a living [having no alternative, and he should be redeemed]."

We come, finally, to the determination of the status of a woman as legitimate wife of a priest. Scripture provides (Lev. 22:10ff.) that the household of a priest may eat the holy things given to the priest as his rations. Nonpriests, by contrast, may not eat such rations. Accordingly, an important property right was involved in deciding whether a woman was validly married to a member of the priestly caste, or whether, indeed, she was permitted to enter into such a marriage. That is why the courts could rule in matters of personal status such as the following.

Y. Nedarim 11:12.I.

E. Soldiers came into a city, and a woman came and said, "Soldiers embraced me and had sexual relations with me." Nonetheless [Hananiah] permitted her to eat food in the status of heave offering [even though she had been raped].

F. The case [of a priest's daughter, not married] came before R. Isaac bar Tabelai, concerning a woman who said, "My [gentile] stableman seduced me." He said to her, "Is not the stableman prohibited?" And he prohibited her from eating food in the status of heave offering.

G. Here [F] you say that he prohibited, and there [E] you say that her permitted [her to eat heave offering].

H. There [where she is not believed at all] she came with the intent of prohibiting herself, and he declared her permitted [not permitting her to get a divorce from her husband]. But here she came to permit herself [to continue to eat heave offering], so he declared her forbidden.

Y. Gittin 9:4.I.

C. A case came before R. Yohanan. It dealt with the wife of a priest [and if the writ of divorce were deemed valid she could not then go back and live with him]. He proposed to rule in accord with R. Yannai [that the writ was invalid]. When he heard that Rab and Samuel differ, when a case came before him involving even a mere Israelite, [he would validate the writ].

The matter of personal status predominates in the foregoing case reports. The clerks are represented as exercising their judgment in a rather shrewd way. The law settled little when common sense might come into play.

In addition to decisions involving material rights, rabbinical courts ruled on the sorts of women priests might or might not marry. This claim to govern the marital affairs of the priestly caste had earlier provoked bitter opposition from the priesthood; in the period represented by the present case, by contrast, rabbinical authority is not represented as confronting any sort of challenge.

Y. Qiddushin 4:4.IV.

P. A priest married the daughter of proselytes. The case came before R. Abbahu, and he had him put down on the flogging chair [to flog the priest] . . .

R. [Bibi] said to him, "Rabbi, do they flog because of violation of a mere custom [which has not got the status of law]?"

S. He said to him, "If so, you will appear as if you have won me over [not to flog him], and I shall let him loose from the flogging post."

T. After the priest got up, he said to him, "Rabbi, since the strap has been released, I too am permitted [to marry such a woman]."

V.   A. R. Jacob bar Idi in the name of R. Joshua b. Levi: "There was a family in the south, about which there were suspicions [as to its status in the priestly genealogy]. Rabbi sent Rominos to examine it. He examined the family, and discovered that its grandmother had converted to Judaism at an age of less than three years and one day, so he declared the family fit for the priesthood."

The purpose of this protracted survey of types of case reports of rabbis acting as judges has now to be briefly restated. The authorities who stood behind the Talmud, in the latter part of the fourth century, preserved a vast number and wide variety of cases in which, so far as they were concerned, rabbinical courts exercised a kind of authority we may regard only as political and bureaucratic. Persons and property of Israel came under their authority. So the Talmud represents its authorities as judges of litigation and administrators of questions of personal status. Decisions are represented, moreover, as precedents, accepted in theorizing about law and uniformly authoritative for courts spread over a considerable territory. Accordingly, rabbinical judges saw themselves as part of a system and a structure, not merely local strong men or popular sages. A fully articulated system of politics and government, staffed by people who knew the Mishnah and how to apply its law to concrete cases and who had the full power to do so, is represented here. Rabbinical judges knew what to do and had full confidence in their authority to do it.

The Rabbi as Local Authority

The Talmud represents the rabbi not only as a part of a national government and bureaucracy, but also as prefect in his own community. The basis of his authority in this second role was partly the same as with his court role. He could effect judgments bearing significant consequences for the disposition of property, for example, in trade and commerce. But other sorts of decisions shade off into less tangible issues, leading us to a view of the rabbi as something other than a solely political figure. The same local authority who could settle litigations and direct the course of commerce also could tell the people the rules of public fasting. He further could give directions for the disposition of synagogue property and the conduct of worship, though his presence is scarcely represented as important in the liturgy of the synagogue.

The principal evidence of the character of the rabbi as a public figure exercising at one and the same time political and religious authority (again, a distinction important now, not then) derives from stories about the rabbi as the figure mediating between Jews and the outside world. In this context the rabbi comes forth as head of the Jewish nation in his locale. This is because of his power to represent the nation in its dealings with other groups, on the one hand, or to direct Jews on how to conduct those transactions, on the other. Whatever the condition of the Jews' government in the country at large (whether, as seems likely, there was a central institution with power over local prefects, for instance), it is in this context that we see the rabbi as the Big Man (in the anthropological sense) of the Jews. But that portrait emerges from the rabbis' own writings. We do not know how others saw them.

We begin our brief survey of how the rabbi is represented as local authority with the ways in which he mediated between Israel and the gentiles of his town. The first, and most important, relationship was with the government. Here the rabbi's power was limited to accommodating the law of the Jews to the demands of the state, so far as that could be done. A striking instance involved the observance of the total cessation of farming, hence, of productive economic activity, every seventh year, that is, the taboo of the Sabbatical Year. If, as was quite natural, the government insisted on the payment of taxes in that year too, then some sort of crop had to be sown. In the following account, Yannai is represented as allowing minimal agricultural labor, along with the rationale for similar sorts of Jewish compromises with the demands of the state.

Y. Sanhedrin 3:5.II.

N.   When the government first became oppressive, R. Yannai gave instructions that the people might plough one time. There was an apostate to idolatry, who transgressed the laws of the Seventh Year. When he saw them throw up the ploughed clods, he said to them, "Oh! that perversion of the law! You have been given permission to plough [in the Sabbatical Year, because of the government's edict], but have you been permitted to throw up the ploughed clods?"

O.   [As to Yannai's permitting the people to plough in the Seventh Year] said R. Jacob bar Zabedi, "I asked before R. Abbahu, 'Did not Zeira and R. Yohanan in the name of R. Yannai say, [or] R. Yohanan in the name of R. Simeon b. Yehosedeq: "They voted in the upper room of the house of Nitzeh in Lud:

P.   "'In regard to the Torah, how do we know that if an idolater should tell an Israelite to transgress any one of all of the religious duties which are stated in the Torah, except for idolatry, fornication, and murder, that he should transgress and not be put to death . . . ?

Q.   "'Now that rule applies to some matter which is done in private.

R.   "'But if it is a matter of public desecration, then even for the most minor religious duty, one should not obey him. [So how could Yannai have permitted the people to plough in the Seventh Year?]'"

S. (For example, there is the case of Papus and Lulianos, his brother, to whom they gave water in a colored glass flask [bearing an idol's name], and they did not accept it from them.)

T. [Yannai] said, "[The case is different here. For] they do not have in mind to force the Jews to commit apostasy [which is not the issue], but solely to pay taxes. [In such a case it is permitted publicly to violate the laws of the Torah.]"

X. R. Yonah and R. Yosé gave instructions to bake bread for Ursinicus on the Sabbath.

Y. Said R. Mani, "I asked before R. Jonah, 'Father, now did not R. Zeira, R. Yohanan in the name of R. Yannai, R. Jeremiah, R. Yohanan in the name of R. Simeon b. Yehosedeq say: 'They voted in the upper room of the house of Nitzeh, etc. [as above, O–R].' [So how can you permit Jews to bake bread in public on the Sabbath?]"

Z. He did not intend to force them to apostasize; he intended only to eat warm bread.

UU. When Perocles came to Sepphoris, R. Mana instructed the bakers to put out [bread] in the marketplace on the Sabbath.

VV. Rabbis of Naveh gave instructions [to the bakers] to bake leavened bread on Passover.

What is important in these stories is the implication, taken for granted throughout, that the rabbi of a locale served as authority not only in municipal court but also in governing relationships with the state. Yet his authority continued to rest solely on his mastery of the law. That is, he could permit actions normally prohibited in the law. He is represented not as negotiating, only as accommodating. Accordingly, so far as the Jewish nation of the Land of Israel was represented in ongoing relationships with the government, some other sort of figure than the rabbi presumably took charge. Furthermore, the unstated supposition is that Israel stands in a subordinated relationship, able to resist only with difficulty, and then at a very high cost. The alternative to submission is assumed to be death. So the domain over which the rabbi presided flourished on the edge of an active volcano.

The commonsensical distinction expressed in the foregoing stories between accommodating the government's legitimate needs, on the one side, and opposing at all costs its intervention into Israelite faith on the other, represented sound social policy. The community remained intact. But it also survived its subjugation. At the same time the rabbinical authorities kept at a distance recognition of the naked power of the gentile. The Romans ruled by law, which Jews would keep. But so far as rabbis conferred legitimacy, the gentile could not rule by force, nor intervene in the Jews' everyday life.

Y. Sheqalim 7:2.VI.

D.   A man went to buy a piece of meat from a butcher, but he did not give him any. He told a Roman, who brought him meat. He said to him, "Did you not take it from him by force?"

E.   He said to him, "And did I not exchange it for a piece of carrion meat?" [Accordingly, the butcher is now deemed unfaithful and may not be patronized.]

F.   R. Jeremiah in the name of R. Haninah: "The case came before Rabbi, who ruled, '[The Roman] does not have the power to prohibit Israelites from patronizing all of the butchershops in Sepphoris [by what he may say about the conduct of the owners]. '"

In the foregoing story we see once again both the power of the rabbis and the limits of that power. In mediating between Israel and the threatening world, the rabbis could control Israel's response, imparting a sense of predictability and governance of their own fate upon which the Jews, for their part, could rely. But what this meant in the present case is that Jews would buy meat from Jewish butchers thrown into suspicion by the Roman's (or: Aramaean's) deed.

When the rabbis could get away with it, on the other hand, they were prepared to prohibit gentile worship and destroy their religious objects. So accommodation was made to what could not be avoided; there never was a question either of accepting gentile rule as legitimate, on the one side, or of extending to gentiles subject to rabbinical-Israelite authority equivalent toleration, on the other.

Y. Abodah Zarah 4:4.IV.

A.   [With reference to the following passage of the Mishnah: *A gentile has the power to nullify an idol belonging either to himself or his fellow, but an Israelite does not have the power to nullify an idol belonging to a gentile,*] R. Yohanan in the name of R. Yannai derived that view from the following verse of Scripture: "You shall not covet the silver or the gold that is on them or take it for yourselves" (Deut. 7:25). "You may not covet and take [that gold], but others may covet [the gold], and then you may take it."

B.   R. Yohanan said to Bar Derosai, "Go, break all the idols that are in the public baths [of Tiberias]," and he went and broke all of them except for one.

C.   And why so?

D.   Said R. Yosa b. R. Bun, "Because a certain Israelite was suspected of going and offering incense on that one[, and an idol worshiped by an Israelite is not subject to nullification at all]. "

As to the local gentiles, they were to be appeased "for the sake of peace." Here too, of course, there would be no question of violating the laws of the Jews. But could one do business on a gentile feast day? Here a local rabbi gives the answer to that question.

Y. Abodah Zarah 1:3.III.

B. The [Israelite] folk of Girda asked R. Ami, "As to the day on which gentiles make a feast, what is the law [about doing business with them]?"

C. He considered permitting it to them on the grounds of maintaining peace [in relationships].

D. Said to him R. Ba, "And did not R. Hiyya teach: 'On the day of a banquet of gentiles it is forbidden [to do business with them]'?"

E. Said R. Ami, "Were it not for R. Ba, we should have ended up permitting their idolatrous practices. So blessed is the Omnipresent who has kept us distant from them!"

Relationships between Jews and gentiles were hardly so formal and distant as these tales suggest. Jews and gentiles lived side by side. It was perfectly natural for daily interaction to lead to mutual hospitality. Accordingly, the issue of Jews' eating what gentiles cooked had to be faced. A subsidiary problem involved wine. The Mishnah's law took for granted that a gentile would flick a drop of wine as a libation every time he opened a keg. That act rendered the rest of the keg forbidden to Israelite consumption or even benefit, for instance, in trade. The prohibition against wine with which gentiles had had physical contact extended to the casks or skins, the cups, wine presses and vats, and any other utensils in which that wine had been contained. These considerations appear in the stories, told in official and communal settings, over eating food deriving from gentiles, on the one side, and utilizing utensils in which gentiles' wine had been kept, on the other. The first group of tales takes up food prepared by gentiles.

Y. Abodah Zarah 2:8.V.

E. A fire [set by a gentile] broke out in a reed thicket and in a date grove, and there were locusts there, which got roasted. The case then came before R. Mana, who prohibited [Israelites from eating the locusts, because they had been roasted by a gentile, even though it was not the gentile's deliberate action that had led to the locusts' being roasted].

Y. Abodah Zarah 2:8.VI.

A. What is the law governing [Israelite consumption of] their [gentiles'] lupines?

B. Rabbi prohibits.

C.   Geniba permits.

D.   Said Rabbi, "I am an elder, and he is an elder. I intend to prohibit them, and he intends to permit them."

E.   R. Mana bar Tanhum went to Tyre and permitted [Israelites to make use of] lupines prepared by [gentiles].

F.   R. Hiyya bar Ba went to Tyre and found that R. Mana bar Tanhum had permitted lupines prepared by [gentiles]. He went to R. Yohanan. [Yohanan] said to him, "What sort of case came to your hand?"

G.   He said to him, "I found that R. Mana bar Tanhum had permitted [Israelites to eat] lupines prepared by [gentiles]."

H.   [Yohanan] said to [Hiyya], "And did you punish him [by declaring him to be excommunicated]?"

I.   He said to him, "He is a great man, for [so wise is he that] he knows how to sweeten [the water of the] Mediterranean sea."

J.   He said to him, "It is not so, my son. He merely knows how to take the measure of the water. For when the water praises God who created it, [the water] turns sweet. [So his knowledge is not so impressive.]"

The first story indicates that a rabbi was consulted about eating food cooked by gentiles' inadvertent action. It does not tell us who brought the question or who accepted the answer; we cannot take for granted that ordinary folk, not disciples of sages, were involved. The second tale, by contrast, suggests the rabbi's ruling was accepted by a wide audience of Jews. But neither is probative; we may assume that the Talmud takes for granted popular adherence to rabbinical rulings in these matters.

We come now to examples of the numerous stories in which rabbis prohibit not only wine with which gentiles have had any sort of contact, but also utensils which have touched such wine in any way, an extremely well-articulated taboo.

Y. Abodah Zarah 5:4.I.

A.   Said R. Samuel, "A gentile with an Israelite was moving jugs of wine from one place to another. The case came before R. Abbahu who declared the wine prohibited."

B.   They say that the case involved open jars of wine.

Y. Abodah Zarah 4:8.IV.

C.   An Aramaean fell into a vat of wine. The case came before R. Huna. He ruled, "They press down on him [so that he may not move about and stir the wine] until they can cause the wine in the vat to flow out."

D. Said R. Haninah, "[But did we not see that] he spread his hand out [in a gesture of making a libation]?"

E. He said, "Bring wicker baskets and strain out the wine that is under his hands [keeping it separate from the rest]."

Y. Abodah Zarah 4:11.III.

B. A gentile—what is the law as to imparting the status of libation wine through an action done in a fit of temper?

C. Let us derive the law from the following:

D. An Aramean had kegs in a storage house, and an Israelite came along and poured wine into them. The Aramean came along and brought his yoke and raised up the jugs in his anger and emptied them into the vat.

E. Now the case came before the rabbis, who ruled, "A gentile does not impart the status of libation wine through an action done in anger."

Y. Abodah Zarah 2:4.III.

Y. A skin of an Aramaean split open, and an Israelite saved [the wine] in his. The case came before rabbis [concerning the further use of the Israelite's skin]. They ruled, "One fills it with water [and leaves it standing therein] for three days of twenty-four hours each."

Z. R. Yosa went to Tyre. He saw them putting pitch into small skins, and Israelites were buying them. He said to them, "Who permitted you to do this?" They went and asked R. Isaac and R. Mani, who declared the practice to be forbidden.

None of these stories presents any surprises. All of them presuppose rabbis' rulings on practical cases involving the taboo against libation wine. None of them suggests that ordinary folk deliberately violated the taboo, and the final entry takes for granted an entire village accepted rabbinical authority in the matter.

The rabbi's authority as representative of the Jewish nation and mediator between that nation and the gentile world in general, and the government in particular, bore heavy symbolic weight. But in shaping the Jewish community to accord with "the Torah," the rabbi's local authority outside the court produced far more significant, concrete results. It is at this point that we see the shading off of the character of the rabbi's decisions, as they dealt less with disposition of persons and property and more with intangible matters of proper conduct and observance of religious taboos. These matters, still, presented public and social issues, in which the rabbi not merely exemplified, but also enforced, law. In the next section we shall see how the rabbi extended his influence solely through expressing his opinion, as distinct from issuing orders as a public official. But, once again we must remind ourselves, the distinction is ours. The texts before us treat as one all sorts of authority.

When it came to other religious taboos, not involving gentiles, the rabbi as local authority found himself constrained to balance practice as he wanted it with the prevailing custom among faithful Israelites. An accepted pattern was given greater weight than the strict law, when it came to declaring open questions. The issues were less pressing than those involved in relationships with the outside world. Hence there was no reason to stir up the local population. At the same time, the stories tell us that villagers were assumed to accord with the position of a given rabbi as against that of some other; people are scarcely represented as wholly outside the law. In the following discourse we see that an Israelite, not represented as a rabbi, consulted a rabbi on a matter of observance of the festival day.

Y. Besah 1:9.I.

J.   Isaac Dihba asked R. Yohanan, "What is the law on crushing spices for wine on a festival day?"

K.   He said to him, "It is permitted to do so, and do bring me some, so I can drink it too."

L.   R. Abbahu in the name of R. Joshua b. Levi declared it permitted.

M.   R. Zeira asked before R. Abbahu, "Will not he who does it properly crush the spices on the preceding day?"

N.   He said to him, "That is so."

O.   The opinions assigned to R. Abbahu are at variance. Here [L] he has said that it is permitted, while there [M–N] he has said that it is forbidden.

P.   But since R. Abbahu knew that R. Zeirah imposed a strict rule, and they [in his locale] in general impose a strict rule, on that account he treated the matter as they do.

The respect for prevailing custom in trivial matters is illustrated in the following.

Y. Taanit 1:6.II.

L.   There were acacia trees in Magdala of the dyers [which had been used in the construction of the ark, so were treated as forbidden by the inhabitants]. They came and asked R. Hanina, associate of the rabbis, whether they might work with that wood.

M. He said to them, "Since your forefathers have been accustomed to treat them as forbidden [for that purpose], do not change the custom of your forefathers."

Another communal religious practice subject to rabbinical authority was the fast for rain. What is important in the following exchange is again the rabbi's deference to the popular will in the matter.

Y. Taanit 3:11.II.

A. In the time of R. Yudan they decreed a fast, and rain fell in the evening. R. Mana went up to see him. He said to him, "Since I am now thirsty, what is the law on my being permitted to drink?"

B. He said to him, "Wait, for the people may decide to complete the fast [through the coming day, and an individual must then observe it too]."

Still, when people asked for the law, they were told it in terms approved by the rabbinical consensus.

Y. Nedarim 8:1.VI.

Q. R. Jacob bar Aha gave instructions to scribes: "If a woman should come and ask you, say to her, 'On all days it is permitted to fast, except for the Sabbath, festival days, the celebrations of the first day of a new month, the intermediate days of the festivals [of Passover and Tabernacles], Hanukkah, and Purim.'"

But the people did not have to obey the rabbis' ruling, and the Talmud is not reticent to note that fact. At issue in the following is conduct in the week following the fast day of the ninth of Ab, commemorating the destruction of the Temple.

Y. Taanit 4:6.IV.

B. [In the case of an ordinary situation, in which the week prior to the ninth of Ab is subjected to these restrictions,) what is the law on the week afterward?

C. R. Yohanan said, "The week afterward is subject to these restrictions as well."

D. R. Simeon b. Laqish said, "The week afterward is released from these restrictions."

E. R. Hiyya bar Ba instructed the people of Sepphoris [that the week afterward is not subject to the restrictions], but they declined to accept his ruling.

F. Said R. Imi to R. Yos}, "And did not the son of the brother of R. Hiyya the Elder [that is, Rab], differ from [Hiyya bar Ba, in this ruling]?"

G. He said to him "There is an explicit statement of a disagreement in the matter."

H. R. Yohanan said, "The week afterward is subject to the same prohibitions."

I. R. Simeon b. Laqish said, "The week afterward is released from these prohibitions."

J. How does R. Simeon b. Laqish deal with [the fact that Rab concurs with Yohanan's view]?

K. He applies that view to the case of the ninth of Ab which coincides with the Sabbath, [and he does not accept the view of R. Aba, above, E,] and he derives no implications from that fact.

L. R. Isaac b. Eleazar, "When the ninth of Ab had ended, he made an announcement, and they opened the barber shops, and whoever wanted went and got a haircut."

These stories as a group take up remarkably trivial matters. What is important is the status imputed by them to the rabbinical clerks. It is a status based upon knowledge of the law. In each instance people listen to the rabbi because they believe he knows what he is talking about. Where they do not, it is because they have their own traditions and do not require his. We need hardly observe, finally, that all of the stories occur in the larger context of theoretical and analytical discussion of the law. The evidence before us suggests that there was no literary form in which stories such as these would conventionally be cast; there was no systematic effort to collect and organize casebooks. Stories and precedents were preserved only for purposes other than the reason that, to begin with, they were told.

A significant rabbinical function, in towns in which rabbis ruled, was to provide support for the poor by collecting and distributing alms. In these stories we see that the Talmud's framers took for granted rabbis carried out this task, expressing in the way they did the work their convictions on relying ultimately on God, on the one side, and on appeasing public opinion, on the other.

Y. Ketubot 6:5.1.

H. There was the case of a girl who came in the time of R. Ammi. He told her [that she could not have money at that time, since] he had to leave money over [for the poor] for the festival.

I. Said to him R. Zeira, "You are causing a loss to her. But let her take what is in the pot. The Master of the festival is yet alive [God, who will provide]."

Y. Sheqalim 5:4.I.

A.   R. Jacob bar Idi and R. Isaac bar Nahman were supervisors [of the communal funds]. They would give R. Hama, father of R. Hoshaiah, a *denar.* He then would divide it among others [who needed it].

B.   R. Zechariah, father-in-law of R. Levi, was subject to public slander. People said that he did not have need but he took [charity anyhow]. After he died, they looked into the matter and found that he would divide up [the funds] among others [in need].

C.   R. Hinena bar Papa would pass out charity funds by night. One time the lord of the spirits met him. He said to him, "Did not Our Rabbi [Moses] teach us, 'You shall not remove your neighbor's landmark' (Deut. 19:14) [meaning, you should not be out by night, over which I rule]?"

D.   He said to him, "Is it not written, 'A gift in secret averts anger; and a bribe in the bosom, strong wrath'?" (Prov. 21:14).

E.   The other stepped back from him and fled.

F.   Said R. Jonah, "'Happy is he who gives to the poor' is not written here, but rather, 'Blessed is he who considers the poor' (Ps. 41:1).

G.   "This refers to one who examines the religious duty of charity, figuring out how to do it properly."

H.   How then did R. Jonah do it?

I.   When he saw a poor person, son of worthy parents, who had lost his property, he would say to him, "Since I heard that you have inherited property from some other source, take some money now and pay me back later on."

J.   When the poor person would take the money, he would say to him, "It is a gift for you."

These stories do not suggest that the clerk in particular engaged in systematic support of the poor. They are random and individual, bearing slight implication of an ongoing and institutional role. Once again, we are not certain that the clerks in particular did this work to the exclusion of other sorts of Jewish authorities. While rabbis clearly served as supervisors of communal funds, we have no reason to suppose that all supervisors of communal funds were rabbis. Accordingly, the rabbis appear as a kind of caste or estate, but not as the company of everyone involved in the government of the Jewish nation.

Rabbinical authority is represented as extending not only to public observances. Rabbis also instructed individuals on the way to carry out personal rites of a nonprivate character, such as burials. At issue here are decisions on reburial of the deceased; when the rites of mourning, following burial, actually come into effect; and the applicability of rites of mourning to a priest in doubt as to his relationship to the deceased. In all of these instances as in many others, private conduct was deemed subject to public authority, and the rabbi is represented as the source of rulings on them.

Y. Moed Qatan 3:5.XII.

> S. Gamaliel of Quntiah was buried by the people of Kursai in their place. After three days they reconsidered the matter [and wished to bury him in his own town]. They came and asked R. Simeon.
>
> T. R. Simeon said to them in the name of R. Joshua b. Levi, "Since you did not give thought to moving him once the burial had taken place, the rites of mourning are counted from the time at which the original grave was sealed."
>
> U. Jeshua, brother of Dorai, had a case. He came and asked R. Abbahu. He said to him, "The rites of mourning commence once the second grave has been sealed."
>
> V. Said to him R. Jacob bar Aha, "I was with you when you asked that question to R. Abodema of Haifa, who said, 'It is when the first grave has been sealed.'"

Y. Yebamot 11:7.II.

> C. R. Asian bar Yequm had a case. He asked R. Yosa [about how to decide concerning a priest's mourning the death of a child who was subject to doubt]. He said to him, "You do not have [to undertake the rites of mourning in such a case]."

The matter of recognition of legitimate parentage affected a broader range of issues than that in the preceding instances. If the child was conceived in a union of a man and woman not permitted by Jewish law to marry, then the status of the child for diverse purposes had to be determined. For example, in the following story, the issue is whether or not the son of a gentile woman and a Jewish man was deemed an Israelite and so might be circumcised on the eighth day after birth, even on the Sabbath day. If the child was a Jew, then the rite of circumcision was to take place, though this rite required actions otherwise forbidden on the Sabbath day. The question was brought to a Jewish judge, not called a rabbi. Accordingly, someone took for granted the Jewish authority had a right to make such a decision. But the consensus of the sages stood contrary to the authority's ruling. Here we see the parameters of rabbinical authority in the community at large. Where individuals were involved rabbis had a say. Where the community at large possessed a tradition, rabbis generally went along with common custom, especially if it made little difference. Over their own functionaries the rabbinical authorities exercised substantial control.

Y. Yebamot 2:6.III.

M.   Jacob of Kephar Naborayya went to Tyre. They came and asked him, "What is the law as to circumcising the son of an Aramaean woman [and a Jewish man] on the Sabbath?"

N.   He considered permitting them, on the basis of the following verse: "[And on the first day of the second month, they assembled the whole congregation together] who registered themselves by families, by father's houses, [according to the number or names from twenty years old and upward, head by head]" [Num. 1:18]. [Hence the child follows the status of the father.]

O.   R. Haggai heard and said, "Go and bring him to me, so that he may be flogged."

P.   He said to him "On what basis do you flog me?"

Q.   He said to him, "It is on the basis of the following verse of Scripture: 'Therefore let us make a covenant with our God [to put away all these wives and their children, according to the counsel of my lord and of those who tremble at the commandment of our God; and let it be done according to the law]' [Ezra 10:3]."

R.   He said to him, "On the basis of a mere tradition [and not of a verse of the Torah itself] are you going to have me flogged?"

S.   He said to him, "' . . . and let it be done according to the law' (Ezra 10:3)."

T.   He said to him, "And on the basis of what verse of Scripture?"

U.   He said to him, "It is in line with that which R. Yohanan said in the name of R. Simeon b. Yohai, 'It is written, You shall not make marriages with them, [giving your daughters to their sons or taking their daughters for your sons]' [Deut. 7:3]. And it is written, 'For they would turn away your sons from following me, [to serve other gods; then the anger of the Lord would be kindled against you, and he would destroy you quickly]' [Deut. 7:4]. Your son from an Israelite is called your son, and your son from a gentile woman is not called your son, but *her* son.'"

V.   He said to him, "Lay on your flogging, for it will be good to receive [since I have it coming]."

The story need not represent a practical case, since the inquiry concerns abstract law, not a concrete decision. But it makes little difference, for the main point is that rabbinical authorities, hearing such an opinion or decision, took prompt action to correct the error and punish the one who made it. Accordingly, the Talmud takes for granted that the rabbinical group could discipline people who undertook rulings in areas on which "the Torah" had opinions. That the kind of law at hand indeed produced practical precedents is indicated in what now follows.

If there was doubt that the child had in fact been born on the Sabbath day, in consequence of which it was not certain that the circumcision had to take place on the next Sabbath, rabbis ruled in the matter. The sort of evidence they would accept is indicated in the following.

Y. Yoma 3:1.II.

G.   R. Imi permitted carrying on the evidence of the midwife [that the child had been born on the Sabbath, and hence the rite of circumcision might be prepared and carried out on that day].

H.   R. Mattenayyah permitted carrying on the basis of the evidence of the lamplighters [that it was night when the baby was born].

I.   R. Ami permitted carrying on the evidence of women, who testified that [when the child was born] the sun was yet light in the village of Susita.

As communal authority the rabbi quite naturally attended to the disposition of synagogue property, owned as it was by the Jewish nation of any given town. These stories tell us how the Talmud's authorities portrayed the character and limits of their authority over synagogue buildings.

Y. Megillah 3:1.II.

A.   People from Beisan asked R. Immi, "What is the law on buying stones from one synagogue for building another synagogue?"

B.   He said, "It is forbidden."

C.   Said R. Helbo, "R. Immi declared that it is forbidden, only because of the anguish [that will affect the people of the former synagogue, when it is torn down]."

D.   R. Gurion said, "The people of Magdela asked R. Simeon b. Laqish, 'What is the law on purchasing stones from one town to build up another town?'

E.   "He said to them, 'It is forbidden.'"

F.   R. Immi gave instructions, "Even [purchasing stones from] the eastern [part of a town for building up] the western [part of the town] is forbidden . . . "

Y. Abodah Zarah 3:3.II.

    D.   In the days of R. Yohanan [Israelites] began to paint on the walls, and [the sages] did not stop them.

In the foregoing instances the rabbi is portrayed in a familiar role, namely, as clerk in charge of disposition of property. Since he was a principal authority in Jewry, he surely could tell people how to dispose of communal, holy property, such as synagogue buildings.

    Rabbis' interests extended, further, from the disposition and decoration of the buildings to the conduct of the rites.

Y. Berakhot 4:1 [English: T. Zahavy].

And even concerning this he [Yohanan] had no cause to dispute: For Rabbi instructed Abedan his spokesman to announce to the congregation, "Whoever wishes to pray the evening prayer may do so even while it is still daytime." R. Hiyya bar Wawa instructed his spokesman to announce to the congregation, "Whoever wishes to pray the evening prayer may do so even while it is still daytime." [We presume this also permits one to recite the evening prayer for the termination of the Sabbath, on the Sabbath day itself.]

Y. Megillah 4:8.

    A.   *A priest who has blemishes on his hands should not raise his hands in the priestly benediction.*

II.   A.   It has been taught: **But if he was well known in his town, lo, he is permitted [to bless the congregation, despite his blemishes] [T. Meg. 3:29D].**

    B.   R. Naptali had crooked fingers. He came and asked R. Mana. He said to him, "Since you are well known in your town, it is permitted."

    C.   R. Huna would remove someone with a downy beard [from pronouncing the priestly benediction].

Y. Yoma 7:1:IV.

    K.   R. Yosé gave instructions to Bar Ulla, the preceptor of the synagogue of the Babylonians [in his town], "On the day on which you bring out only one Torah, roll it up behind the veil [so as not to bother the community by keeping people waiting]. If it is a day on which you bring out two Scrolls, you should take out one and put it back [and then take out the other]."

I need hardly add that, in the performance of the rites themselves, the rabbi had no special role or privilege. Any qualified male Jew could carry out any of the synagogue procedures, excluding only the priestly blessing.

As local authorities, rabbis would find themselves consulted as often as they took the initiative and intervened. In the former of the two stories that follow, people asked a rabbi how to deal with a water tank from which a snake might have drunk and thus have poisoned the water. In the second, a question on the law allowed a rabbi to register disapproval of illicit behavior over which, it is clear, he had no control, but which, he now maintained, Heaven had punished. In these two stories we see the sort of everyday action a rabbi might, and might not, take. In the former we have a decision affecting public health and welfare, in the latter, one in which, after the fact, the rabbi imposed his, and thus Heaven's, authority in the end.

Y. Abodah Zarah 2:3.I.

> T.   The water tank of Bar Netizah was left uncovered. He asked R. Bar bar Mamal [whether or not he might still make use of the contents]. He said to him, "If [someone] was going in and coming out, it is permitted [on grounds that a person would frighten away a snake]."

Y. Abodah Zarah 2:3.I.

> CC.   A butcher in Sepphoris fed Israelites carrion and *terefah* meat. One time at the eve of the Day of Atonement toward dusk he drank a great deal of wine and got drunk. He climbed up to the roof of his house and fell down and died. Dogs began licking at his blood.
>
> DD.   They came and asked R. Haninah, "What is the law as to carrying in his corpse [out of the public domain] on account of [the dogs]?"
>
> EE.   He said to them, "It is written, 'You shall be men consecrated to me; therefore you shall not eat any flesh that is torn by beasts in the field; you shall cast it to the dogs' (Ex. 22:31). This man stole from the dogs and fed Israelites carrion and *terefah* meat. Leave him be. [The dogs] are eating what belongs to them anyhow."

The stories we have reviewed tell us how the framers of the Talmud wished to portray their own practical position as local authority. They represent the governed as meekly accepting the rulings of the rabbinical governor. Only the subterranean theme that local practice and opinion must come into consideration suggests that rabbinical authority depended, in the end, upon the acquiescence and acceptance of others. Without an explicit account of the workings of the community the foregoing picture remains lifeless—and misleading. Accordingly, we conclude our survey with a story of how local Big Men disposed of the rabbinical Big Man. There can be no doubt that the rabbi was perceived, and saw himself, as an outsider, someone who came from somewhere else to exercise power, a prefect from on high. Whatever his backing from the patriarch and from Heaven, whatever his qualifications as master of Torah teachings and Torah power, in the end the rabbi had to secure acceptance based on solid achievement in relating to the local folk, on the one side, and in winning their respect, on the other. The point of the story comes at IV.Eff., but the details of the opening part are essential for understanding what follows.

Y. Yebamot 12:6.III.

    A.   There [in Babylonia, where they prepare a writ of *halisah*], they state in the writ, "She appeared before us and removed his shoe from his right foot and spit before us with spittle which could be seen on the ground [M. Yeb. 12:6H], and she stated, 'So shall it be done to the man who does not build up his brother's house.'"

IV.   A.   Said R. Abbahu, "Once the spittle has come out of her mouth, even if the wind picked it and carried it away, the rite is valid."

    B.   If she spit blood—

    C.   R. Ba in the name of R. Judah, R. Zeriqan introduced the statement [in the name of] R. Jeremiah in the name of Abba bar Abba, R. Zeira introduced the matter in the name of Samuel: "If there is any remnant of spittle [in it], it is valid."

    D.   A woman without hands—how does she remove the shoe? With her teeth.

    E.   The people of Simonia came before Rabbi. They said to him, "We want you to give us a man to serve as preacher, judge, reader, teacher, and to do all the things we need." He gave them Levi bar Sisi.

    F.   They set up a great stage and seated him on it. They came and asked him, "A woman without arms—with what does she remove the shoe?" And he did not answer.

    G.   If she spit blood . . . ?

    H.   And he did not answer.

    I.   They said, "Perhaps he is not a master of the law. Let us ask him something about lore." They came and asked him, "What is the meaning of the following verse, as it is written, 'But I will tell you what is inscribed in the book, in truth' (Daniel 10:21). If it is truth, why is it described as inscribed? And if it is inscribed, why is it described as truth?"

    J.   He did not answer them.

    K.   They came back to Rabbi and said to him, "Is this a mason of your masons' guild [a pupil of your school]?"

L.   He said to them, "By your lives! I gave you someone who is as good as I am."

M.   He sent and summoned him and asked him. He said to him, "If the woman spit blood, what is the law?"

N.   He answered him, "If there is a drop of spittle in it, it is valid."

O.   A woman without arms—how does she remove the shoe?"

P.   He said to him, "She removes the shoe with her teeth."

Q.   He said to him, "What is the meaning of the following verse, as it is written, 'But I will tell you what is inscribed in the book, in truth' (Daniel 2:10). If it is truth, why is it described as inscribed, and if it is inscribed, why is it described as truth?"

R.   He said to him, "Before a decree is sealed, it is described as inscribed. Once it is sealed, it is described as truth."

S.   He said to him, "And why did you not answer the people when they asked you these same questions?"

T.   He said to him, "They made a great stage and seated me on it, and my heart melted."

U.   He recited concerning him the following verse of Scripture: "'If you have been foolish, exalting yourself, or if you have been devising evil, put your hand on your mouth' (Prov. 30:32).

V.   "What caused you to make a fool of yourself in regard to teachings of Torah? It was because you exalted yourself through them."

While the moral of the story is directed to the disciple of a sage, who is warned not to take pride in the high position to which his learning may bring him, the setting of the story is important in the present context. It tells us the Talmud's framers took for granted that important Jewish authorities, not rabbis, in the end could dispose of a rabbi's claim to make decisions.

Here once more we see how the rabbi is marginal to the Jewish nation in its local life. On the one side, he is on the frontiers of Heaven, bringing down to the nation the teachings of Heaven. On the other, he is an outsider to the community, meant to provide for their needs, but also serving at their pleasure. His standing depends upon what he knows. But it also depends upon the acceptance of those to whom he teaches and governs. So the position of the rabbi as a clerk and a bureaucrat turns out, in a story such as this one, to be far less secure and established than the earlier accounts suggested. Harmonizing together the Talmud's diverse pictures of the authority of the rabbi is hardly necessary; presumably each comes from its own setting and is accurate to that setting. Yet on balance we do gain a coherent picture of how rabbis in general understood the Jewish nation over whom they claimed to rule, and how, in particular, they saw themselves within that nation. The fact that the stories portraying that vision also contain dissonant details, pointing toward a quite different reality from the one imagined by the story-tellers, is hardly surprising.

The Rabbi as Moral Authority

Up to now we have seen how the Talmud portrays rabbis' power over the estates and possessions of the Jews, including communal property and behavior. Rabbis· furthermore made decisions or gave opinions in a domain quite distinct from that of property or of property joined to determination of personal status. These decisions influenced personal behavior in private, rather than coercing it in public. They were meant to establish rules for good public order and decent behavior. Whether rabbis enjoyed the power to force people to behave in the way they wanted is not at issue. Here we see what they thought they could do. So far as the issues at hand related not to property and public policy but to individual conduct, in general it was moral, rather than civil and political, authority that rabbis claimed to exercise. In the present rubric we take up two quite distinct matters: first, releasing vows, second, dealing with affairs of the heart. They belong together because neither can be regarded as tangible, except for the person involved. In the main, social consequences were slight. Yet the intervention of the rabbi was critical in the former instance and consequential in the latter as well.

The notion that sages remit vows was hardly the invention of the rabbis of the Talmud of the Land of Israel: the Mishnah's law is fully developed in this regard. What is important is only that, within its account of the public conduct of rabbis, the Talmud provides ample evidence that rabbis found grounds for the absolution of vows and told people about them. Instances of the matter are in the following stories. Only the final one is striking, in its application of the distinction between a vow, subject to remission, and an oath, not to be released.

Y. Nedarim 9:7.I.

> B.   A woman took a vow against her daughter. She came to R. Yohanan. He said to her, "If you had known that your daughter would have a bad name because of you, would you have taken a vow?"
>
> C.   She said to him, "No," and he released her from the vow.

Y. Nedarim 9:1.IV.

> Q.   R. Simeon did not find grounds for releasing his vow, until one of the sages of Galilee came to him. (There are those who say it was R. Simeon b. Eleazar.) He took him from here and put him there, took him from here and put him there, until he put him into the sun to examine his garments.

R. They said to him, "If you had known that the elder would do this
    to you, would you have taken such a vow?"

S. He said to him, "No." Then he released the vow.

Y. Nedarim 9:1.V.

C. R. Mana took an oath and went up to R. Shammai. He said to
    him, "If you had known that people would become distant
    from you, because you are a constant vow-taker, would you
    have taken such a vow?" He said to him "No." And he re-
    leased him from the vow.

Y. Nedarim 5:4.IV.

F. A certain person vowed not to make a profit. He came before R.
    Yudan bar Shalom. He said to him, "From what did you take
    an oath?"

G. He said to him, "That I would not make a profit."

H. R. Yudan said to him, "Now do people take such an oath as this?
    Perhaps the vow concerned merely not playing dice."

I. The man said, "That is indeed the case. Blessed be He who has
    chosen the Torah and the sages who have said that it is neces-
    sary to specify what is covered by the vow."

Y. Nedarim 11:1.II.

H. Someone came to have a vow released by R. Yosé. The latter
    wrapped himself in his cloak and sat down. He said to him,
    "What sort of oath did you take?"

I. He said to him, "By the Divinity of Israel! She may not come
    into my house [referring to my wife]!"

J. He said to him, "By the Divinity of Israel, she indeed may not
    come into your house [because this is an oath, not a vow, and
    a sage cannot release an oath]."

These tales were told to exemplify not the power of the rabbis but precedents
illustrating proper grounds for absolution of vows. Once more, the power of
the rabbi to do his will rested upon his knowledge of the law. That is the
constant subtheme of all stories at hand. At the same time, we now observe,
the basis of the rabbi's moral authority lay in his reputation for saintliness,
not a love for learning. The following story provides an insight into the ideal
for the sages fostered by the Talmud.

Y. Sotah 1:4.II.

A. R. Zabedeh, son-in-law of R. Levi, would tell the following
    story.

B. R. Meir would teach a lesson in the synagogue of Hammata every Sabbath night. There was a woman who would come regularly to hear him. One time the lesson lasted longer than usual.

C. She went home and found that the light had gone out. Her husband said to her, "Where have you been?"

D. She replied to him, "I was listening to the lesson."

E. He said to her, "May God do such-and-so and even more, if this woman enters my house before she goes and spits in the face of that sage who gave the lesson."

F. R. Meir perceived with the help of the Holy Spirit [what had happened] and he pretended to have a pain in his eye.

G. He said, "Any woman who knows how to recite a charm over an eye—let her come and heal mine."

H. The woman's neighbors said to her, "Lo, your time to go back home has come. Pretend to be a charmer and go and spit in R. Meir's eye."

I. She came to him. He said to her, "Do you know how to heal a sore eye through making a charm?"

J. She became frightened and said to him, "No."

K. He said to her, "Do they not spit into it seven times, and it is good for it?"

L. After she had spit in his eye, he said to her, "Go and tell your husband that you did it one time."

M. She said to him, "And lo, I spit seven times!"

N. R. Meir's disciples said to him, "Rabbi, in such a disgraceful way do they treat the Torah [which is yours]? If you had told us about the incident with the husband, would we not have brought him and flogged him at the stock, until he was reconciled with his wife?"

O. He said to them, "And should the honor owing to Meir be tantamount to the honor owing to Meir's creator?

P. "Now if the Holy Name, which is written in a state of sanctification, the Scripture has said is to be blotted out with water so as to bring peace between a man and his wife, should not the honor owing to Meir be dealt with in the same way!"

Clearly, the issue of this tale transcends the matter of releasing or fulfilling vows. It is once more part of the genre of tales meant to remind disciples not to be arrogant. At the same time, the sense of relation and proportion between saintliness and learning, conveyed by the storyteller, contrasts with the generality of precedents we have seen. Since our interest is focused rather narrowly upon the view of the world of Israel conveyed by our Talmud, we note only that rabbis held, in their view, diverse means for resolving the problem of vows.

Areas in which rabbis might intervene, even without authority narrowly based on law, included two: first, marrying off children; and second, dealing with illicit sexual relations in cases in which the law gave them no standing. In both categories we find stories expressing the limitations of rabbinical power. The father in the first story does not concur that he should get a wife for his son. The actors in the second and third ones pay slight heed to the rabbinical intervenors.

Y. Qiddushin 1:7.I.

> N.   Bar Tarimah came to R. Imi. He said to him, "Persuade father to get me a wife."
>
> O.   He went and tried to persuade him, but the father was not agreeable [to the project].

Y. Sanhedrin 6:3.III.

> F.   A certain saintly man was walking along the way, and he saw two men having sexual relations with a female dog. They said, "We know that he is a saintly man, and he will go and testify against us and our master, David, will put us to death.
>
> G.   "But let us move first and give testimony against him."
>
> H.   They testified against him and he was tried and condemned to death.
>
> I.   That is the meaning of that which David said, "Deliver my soul from the sword, my life from the power of the dog! (Ps. 22:20)."
>
> J.   "From the sword"—from the sword of Uriah.
>
> K.   "From a dog"—from the dog of the holy man.
>
> L.   R. Judah b. Pazzi went to go up to the schoolhouse, and he saw two men having sexual relations with one another. They said to him, "Rabbi, please take note that you are one and we are two, [so your testimony against us will be null in any event]."

Y. Abodah Zarah 2:2.III.

> LL.   In the days of R. Eleazar, a man so loved a woman that he came in danger of dying [from unconsummated desire]. They came and asked R. Eleazar, "What is the law governing her 'passing before him' so that he may live?"
>
> MM.   He answered them, "Let him die but [let matters not be done] in such a way."

NN. "What is the law as to his merely hearing her voice, so that he may live?"

OO. "Let him die, but [let matters not be done] in such a way."

PP. Now what was the character of this girl [who was to be kept away from the man pining for her]?

QQ. R. Jacob bar Idi and R. Isaac bar Nahman—one maintained that she was a married woman, and the other maintained that she was unmarried.

RR. Now so far as the opinion of the one who maintained that she was a married woman, there are no problems. But as to the one who maintained that she was unmarried[, why should she not have married the man]?

SS. Now, lo, Bar Koha Nigra so loved a woman in the days of R. Eleazar, that he was in danger of dying [from unconsummated desire]. [Read: and R. Eleazar permitted him to marry her.]

We see in the following that, as moral authority, rabbis claimed slight capacity to intervene. They had their own views, but they kept them to themselves.

Y. Qiddushin 4:1.VIII.

A. Said R. Yohanan, "As to any family in which some invalidity has been submerged, they do not check too carefully about it."

B. Said R. Simeon b. Laqish, "The Mishnah itself has made the same point": *The family of Beth Seripa was in the land beyond Jordan, and Ben Zion removed it afar by force, and yet another family was there, and Ben Zion brought it near by force* [M. Ed. 8:7].

C. "But sages did not seek to reveal who they were.

D. "But sages hand over the information to their sons and disciples two times every seven years."

E. Said R. Yohanan, "By the Temple service! I know who they are, but what should we do? For the great men of the generation are mixed up with them."

F. Said R. Joshua b. Levi, "Pashhur ben Immer had five thousand slaves and all of them were mixed up with the high priesthood, and they account for arrogance among the priesthood."

G. Said R. Eliezer, "The principal designation of the priests' usurpation is indicated in the following verse: '[Yet let no one contend, and let none accuse,] for with you is my contention, O priest'" (Hos. 4:4).

In these several stories we see how rabbis perceived the limits of their power and authority. When it came to actual sexual practice, they could do virtually nothing. By contrast, when it came to licit relationships, involving public recognition, as in the case of permitting a given marriage, they had a good deal to say. In the final story, moreover, we see that rabbis were constrained by other kinds of powerful Jews and had to keep their peace. A picture of how the rabbis saw the world around them then emerges, in which the rabbi could order some things to be done, persuade or influence people to do certain other things, and, finally, had to keep his mouth shut in the face of other Jewish authorities.

The Rabbi as Supernatural Authority

The rabbi stood on the intersecting borders of several domains: political and private, communal and individual. He served as both legal and moral authority, decisor and exemplar, judge and clerk, administrator and governor, but also holy man and supernatural figure. It is this final aspect of the rabbi as public authority that we take up when we turn to stories about how the rabbi as a public official was expected to, and did, perform certain supernatural or magical deeds. These stories place the rabbi at the border between heaven and earth, as much as he stood at the frontier between Israel and the nations: wholly liminal, entirely exemplary, at one and the same time. What is important here is the representation of the rabbi as *public* authority deemed to exercise *supernatural* power. These tales are separate from views of the rabbi as a supernatural figure in general, which we shall review below. In the present setting, the wonder-working rabbi as a civic figure, in particular, comes to the fore. His task was to use his supernatural power in pretty much the same context and for the same purpose as he used his political-judicial and legal power and learning, on the one side, and his local influence and moral authority, on the other. Once again we remind ourselves, the distinctions are ours, not those of the Talmud, which sees all of these forms of public authority as undifferentiated and of equal consequence.

In the following stories, the responsibility of the rabbis to stop fires is taken for granted. What is striking is that, in the tales, they exercise that responsibility equally through this-worldly and otherworldly means: in the first story, by getting gentiles to do the work; in the second, by using Heaven through calling down rain; in the third, by some sort of merit (not made specific); and in the fourth, by a rabbi spreading out a cloak, which drove the flames away.

Y. Nedarim 4:9.I.

> C.   In R. Ami's time there was a fire in town [on the Sabbath]. R. Ami sent out a proclamation in the marketplace of the Aramaeans, saying, "Whoever does the work will not lose out by it." [Ami could not ask the people to do the work, be-

cause of the restrictions of the Sabbath on the employees of Israelites. Accordingly, he solved the problem in the way proposed in the present context.] . . .

G. There was a case in which a fire broke out in the courtyard of Yos} b. Simai in Shihin, and the soldiers of the camp of Sepphoris came down to put it out. But he did not let them do so.

H. He said to him, "Let the tax collector come and collect what is owing to him."

I. Forthwith clouds gathered, and rain came and put the fire out. After the Sabbath he sent a *sela* to every soldier, and to their commander he sent fifty *denars*.

J. Said R. Hanina, "It was not necessary to do so."

K. There was a Samaritan who was R. Jonah's neighbor. A fire broke out in the neighborhood of R. Jonah. The Samaritan came and wanted to put it out, but R. Jonah did not let him do so.

L. [The Samaritan] said to him, "Will it be on your responsibility if it burns up my property?"

M. [Jonah] said to him, "Yes." And the whole area was saved.

N. R. Jonah of Kefar Ammi spread out his cloak over the grain, and the flames fled from it.

These several stories show that the sage was seen as bearing responsibility to put out fires, and a mixture of legal subterfuge, supernatural intervention, and sagacity is conveyed in the set of tales. When we call the rabbi a supernatural authority, what we mean, then, is to indicate that he was a communal official who, on occasion, was believed to invoke more than this-worldly power to carry out his civil duties.

In the following story the sage as public official protects the town from a siege and violence.

Y. Taanit 3:8.II.

A. As to Levi ben Sisi: troops came to his town. He took a scroll of the Torah and went up to the roof and said, "Lord of the ages! If a single word of this scroll of the Light has been nullified [in our town], let them come up against us, and if not, let them go their way."

B. Forthwith people went looking for the troops but did not find them [because they had gone their way].

C. A disciple of his did the same thing, and his hand withered, but the troops went their way.

D. A disciple of his disciple did the same thing. His hand did not wither, but they also did not go their way.

E.   This illustrates the following apothegm: "You can't insult an
      idiot, and dead skin doesn't feel the scalpel."

The story is told to make its point, but, once more, it serves to convey a
glimpse into the imagination, not merely the morality, of the storyteller and
the Talmud's framers. The power of the sage to ward off the siege was based
upon his saintliness, which consisted in his obedience to the Torah and the
peoples' obedience to him. So whatever public authority the rabbi exercised
is credited, in the end, to his accurate knowledge and sincerity in living up
to his own teachings, on the one side, and the peoples' willingness to accept
his instructions, on the other.

Earlier we noted that rabbis made rules on public fasting. For their part,
they possessed sufficient merit so that, if they personally fasted, they were
supposed to be able to bring rain. Yet another area in which supernatural, as
distinct from this-worldly, authority came to the fore was in preventing
epidemics. The first story provides a routine instance of rainmaking; the
second, of bringing rain and stopping a pestilence, by two themes being
joined together.

Y. Taanit 3:4.V.

A.   R. Aha carried out thirteen fasts, and it did not rain. When he
      went out, a Samaritan met him. [The Samaritan] said to him
      [to make fun of him], "Rabbi, take off our cloak, because it
      is going to rain."

B.   He said to him, "By the life of that man [you]! Heaven will do
      a miracle, and this year will prosper, but that man will not
      live to see it."

C.   Heaven did a miracle, and the year prospered, and that Samar-
      itan died.

D.   And everybody said, "Come and see the fruit [the man's corpse]
      [lying in the] sun."

Y. Taanit 3:4.I.

A.   There was a pestilence in Sepphoris, but it did not come into the
      neighborhood in which R. Haninah was living. And the Sep-
      phoreans said, "How is it possible that that elder lives among
      you, he and his entire neighborhood, in peace, while the
      town goes to ruin?"

B.   [Haninah] went in and said before them, "There was only a
      single Zimri in his generation, but on his account, twenty-
      four thousand people died. And in our time, how many Zi-
      mris are there in our generation? And yet you are raising a
      clamor!"

C. One time they had to call a fast, but it did not rain. R. Joshua carried out a fast in the South, and it rained. The Sepphoreans said, "R. Joshua b. Levi brings down rain for the people in the South, but R. Haninah holds back rain for us in Sepphoris."

D. They found it necessary to declare a second time of fasting, and sent and summoned R. Joshua b. Levi. [Haninah] said to him, "Let my lord go forth with us to fast." The two of them went out to fast, but it did not rain.

E. He went in and preached to them as follows: "It was not R. Joshua b. Levi who brought down rain for the people of the South, nor was it R. Haninah who held back rain from the people of Sepphoris. But as to the Southerners, their hearts are open, and when they listen to a teaching of Light [Torah] they submit [to accept it], while as to the Sepphoreans, their hearts are hard, and when they hear a teaching of Light, they do not submit [or accept it]."

F. When he went in, he looked up and saw that the [cloudless] air was pure. He said, "Is this how it still is? [Is there no change in the weather?]" Forthwith, it rained. He took a vow for himself that he would never do the same thing again. He said, "How shall I say to the creditor [God] not to collect what is owing to him."

The tale about Joshua and Haninah is most striking, because it presents a thoroughly rationalistic picture of the supernatural framework at hand. True, God could do miracles. But if the people caused their own disasters by not listening to rabbis' Torah teachings, they could hardly expect God always to forgo imposing the sanction for disobedience, which was holding back rain. Accordingly, there were reliable laws by which one could deal with the supernatural world which kept those laws too. The particular power of the rabbi was in knowing the law. The storyteller took for granted, to be sure, that in the end the clerk could bring rain in a pinch.

Rabbinical Authority in Context:
In the Service of the Patriarch

The Talmud's account of rabbis' exercise of authority over the life of Israel leaves the impression that, in the main, rabbis formed an autonomous government, a collegium of sages. They not only learned the same law, namely, the Mishnah, with its associated traditions. They also saw themselves as subordinate to the same great authorities of the law, both of times past and of their own day. Accordingly, time and again the picture emerges of a well-organized Jewish government, working not only locally but throughout the Land of Israel, unified in perspective and policy throughout the Israelite sectors of the Land. In consequence we have a view of an effective national government, staffed by the rabbinical estate. The one thing we do not know is the political basis for that government. The reason is, as we have seen, that the rabbinical stories of how sages exercised authority over the property and persons of Jews omit all reference to the foundation of that authority. They take for granted it was knowledge of the law—that alone. In context of legal theory, that assumption is blatant. We, for our part, have to infer on the basis of quite separate kinds of tales, a different account of the larger political context in which the rabbinical judges did their work.

The key to that context lies in stories in which rabbis acknowledged the authority of someone clearly on the margins of their own estate, a figure both rabbinical and other. If there was a political figure in charge of the Jewish community wholly outside the rabbinical estate, he will have appeared in our sources, I am inclined to think, in a guise not much different from that of the Roman overlord or the gentile. One wholly within the rabbinical group by definition will not have provided occasion to speak of such a figure. He will have been no different from any other important rabbi. What is therefore critical is the picture of someone marginal, who as a superior or super-intendent figure both gave orders to rabbis, on the one side, and also under-stood and participated in the rabbinical system of law and learning, on the other. Such stories, we remind ourselves, may or may not reflect the state of affairs at the time of, or prior to, the formation of the Talmud. Accordingly, what I now seek to describe is how sages viewed the larger context for their political power at the time of the Talmud's formation.

The description derives from tales about various figures normally bearing both the rabbinical honorific and the further title, patriarch (*nasi*). Tales about these figures take for granted that the patriarch exercised authority over other rabbis, but that he was essentially one with the other rabbis. Some of the patriarchal tales, moreover, place the patriarch into close relationship with Romans of the highest rank, including the emperor. On the basis of these tales, we notice, the Talmud posits the existence, in addition to the rabbinical bureaucrats, of a patriarch who hired them, used their services for the administration of the local affairs of the Jewish nation in the Land of Israel, and validated their decisions, even while maintaining his autonomy from, and superiority over, the clerks who made those decisions. So in the Tal-mud's view the context of rabbinical authority found definition in a figure at the margins of both the rabbinical estate, on the one side, and the Roman (Byzantine) administration of the Land of Israel, on the other. Rabbis in their role as local authorities derived their authority from the Jewish government of which they formed a mere part (and we do not know how large a propor-tion of the whole). The rabbinical judges and clerks depended for political and legal legitimation of their decisions and orders upon that government beyond themselves, both close at hand, in the patriarchate, and far away, in the Roman government itself.

The only Jew represented by the Talmud as entering into legitimate relationships (as distinct from extra-legal ones) with the Roman authorities is the patriarch. His relationships in particular are represented as honorable. In the following, a Roman official gave a gift to a patriarch.

Y. Abodah Zarah 1:1.II.

    E.   A certain *quaestor* honored Yudan, the patriarch, with a chest filled with *denars* [in celebration of the pagan festival]. [Yudan] took one of them and sent back the rest.

    F.   He asked R. Simeon b. Laqish [whether it was permitted to derive benefit from the *denar* he had accepted, since it was given to him in celebration of a pagan festival.]

    G.   He said to him, "Send any benefit derived from that coin[, that is, whatever you buy with it] to the Dead Sea[, for it is prohibited to benefit from the coin]."

It is generally assumed that Judah the Patriarch, to whom the Mishnah is ascribed, enjoyed a close relationship with a Roman authority, Antoninus. The Talmud of the Land of Israel knows that relationship in the following, essentially nonpolitical (and incredible) context.

Y. Sanhedrin 10:5.II.

    A.   R. Hezekiah, R. Abbahu in the name of R. Eleazar, "If the righteous proselytes come to the world to come, Antolinus will come at the head of them all."

    F.   Antolinus came to Rabbi. He said to him, "Do you foresee that I shall eat from Leviathan in the world to come?"

    G.   He said to him, "Yes."

    H.   He said to him, "Now you did not let me eat from the Passover lamb in this world, and yet will you give me Leviathan's flesh to eat in the coming world?"

    I.   He said to him, "And what can we do for you? Concerning the Passover lamb it is written, '[And when a stranger shall sojourn with you and would keep the passover to the Lord, let all his males be circumcised, then he shall come near and keep it; he shall be as a native of the land.] But no uncircumcised person shall eat of it'" [Ex. 12:48].

    K.   When he heard this, he went and converted. He came to Rabbi, saying to him, "Now look at the mark of my circumcision!"

    L.   He said to him, "In my whole life I never looked at mine! Am I supposed to look at yours!" . . .

P. Antolinus came to Rabbi. He said to him, "Pray for me."

Q. He said to him, "May He protect you from cold, as it is written, '[He casts forth ice like morsels,] who can stand before his cold?'" [Ps. 147:17].

R. He said to him, "Rabbi, this prayer is not much. If you cover yourself, lo, the cold goes away."

S. He said to him, "May he spare you from the hot winds which blow through the world."

T. He said to him, "Now that is a fitting prayer. May your prayer be heard,

U. "for it is written, '[Its rising is from the end of the heavens, and its circuit to the end of them.] And there is nothing hid from its heat'" [Ps. 19:7].

All that can be gleaned from this tale is rabbis' fantastic ideas of what a Roman authority would want to talk about with the great Rabbi. Clearly, the tale-teller regards Rabbi himself as fully one with sages at large, the great master of Torah. He also sees no political aspect at all to Rabbi's dealings with the Roman. If Israel was in the domain of a Roman appointee, a patriarch, and if rabbis, for their part, labored in that appointee's bureaucracy, the story presents not a hint of either matter. If it bears any implications for the politics of the rabbi, it is that the rabbi who believed such a story had no grasp whatsoever of the political realities of his own place and time.

The Talmud also knows Roman administrators in a less honorable, but more practical setting. The Caesarean Jewish authority, Abbahu, hinted to his colleagues that he had bribed some Roman clerks to do his bidding. But a woman's appeal against rabbinical judgment appears to have been sustained.

Y. Megillah 3:2.IV.

F. R. Hiyya, R. Yosé, R. Immi were engaged in judging [the case of a woman named] Tamar. She went and complained against them to Antiputa [governor of Caesarea]. The [rabbis] sent and wrote [about it] to R. Abbahu [who lived in Caesarea].

G. R. Abbahu sent and wrote to them, "We have already won over three advocates, Tob Yeled [Goodchild], Tob Lamed [Well-learned], and Tarsus Ebdocus Eumusus Tallassios. But Tamar ['bitter'] is bitterness. She abides in her bitterness, and we tried to sweeten her [by a bribe] but 'in vain has the smelter smelted' [Jer. 6:29] [for gold could not buy her]."

By contrast to the direct appeal to the Roman governor indicated in the foregoing, when we hear about rabbis' seeking support for their decisions, it usually is to the patriarch.

Y. Ketubot 9:2.II.

   A. To a woman relative of R. Samuel bar Abba they gave [the residuary estate] on grounds that she was the weakest. R. Simeon b. Laqish brought agents [gendarmes] of R. Yudan the Patriarch and took the property away from her.
   B. R. Yohanan was leaning on R. Simeon b. Abba. He said to him, "What shall we do for that poor lady?" He said to him, "R. Simeon b. Laqish brought the agents of R. Yudan the Patriarch, who took the property away from her."
   C. He said to him, "And is that the right way to do things? [That is, how can the property be seized from her after she has acquired ownership of it by court decree?]"

What we see here is that the patriarch's support for the rabbi's decision was forthcoming. This support consisted of the use of gendarmes to transfer property from one claimant to some other. Even though we have only a few stories such as this one, it stands to reason that, in the Talmud's view, when brute force was needed to carry out rabbis' decisions, it was provided by the patriarch.

The Talmud's picture of the patriarchal government makes clear that the power of rabbis to judge cases depended upon their status as legitimate clerks, conferred by the patriarchate, probably more than on the brute force it made available. To begin with, "appointment"—that is, employment in the government and thus recognition as a duly constituted authority—depended (in the Talmud's view) upon the patriarch's concurrence. The patriarch may well have thought he did more than concur, as these stories suggest.

Y. Sanhedrin 1:2.XIV.

   A. They went and paid honor to "this house" [the patriarchate].
   B. They made the rule, "A court which made an appointment without the knowledge and consent of the patriarch—the act of appointment is null.
   C. "And a patriarch who made an appointment without the knowledge and consent of the court—his appointment is void."
   D. They reverted and made the rule that the court should make an appointment only with the knowledge and consent of the patriarch, and that the patriarch should make an appointment only with the knowledge and consent of the court.

Whether or not the patriarch, for his part, accepted his part of the deal we cannot say. In the Talmud's conception the relationship was between equals. What is important is that the Talmud's sages therefore recognized an authority beyond their own, even though, in their conception, their knowledge of the law constituted ample validation for their decisions.

Other stories make it explicit that appointment involved bestowing credentials, from the rabbis' viewpoint, or, we may assume, granting of a position in the patriarchal administration, from the patriarch's. In any event, appointment depended upon the patriarch's "good will." Several stories indicate that a rabbi who crossed the patriarch, not surprisingly, would not receive a position in the Jewish government.

Y. Taanit 4:2.VIII.

A. Rabbi would make two appointments [to his administration, at one time]. If they proved worthy, [the appointees] were confirmed. If not, they were removed.

B. When he was dying he instructed his son [Gamaliel], "Don't do it that way. Rather appoint them all at one time."

C. He appointed R. Hami bar Haninah at the head [of the group].

D. And why had Rabbi not appointed him? It was because the people of Sepphoris were opposed to him.

E. And merely because people raise a cry, do they do the things they want? [Obviously not!]

F. Said R. Eleazar b. R. Yosé, "It was because [Haninah] publicly contradicted [what Rabbi had said]."

G. [This is the story.] Rabbi was in session. He cited the following verse: "Then those of you who escape will remember me among the nations where they are carried captive, when I have broken their wanton heart which has departed from me, and blinded their eyes which turn wantonly after their idols; and they will be loathsome in their own sight for the evils which they have committed, for all their abominations" (Ezek. 6:9).

H. "And if any survivors escape, they will be on the mountains, like doves of the valleys, all of them moaning, every one over his iniquity" (Ezek. 7:16).

I. [Haninah] said to him, "We read the verse as, 'roar.'"

J. [Rabbi] said to him, "Where did you study Scripture?"

K. He said to him, "Before R. Hamnuna of Babylonia."

L. He said to him, "When you go down there, tell him to appoint you a sage." [Haninah] realized that he would not be appointed [a sage in Rabbi's administration] for the rest of his life.

M. After [Rabbi] died, his son [Gamaliel] wanted to appoint him a sage, but [Haninah] did not accept the appointment. He said to him, "I shall accept appointment only after you have appointed R. Epes, the Southerner, before me."

N.   Now there was a certain elder there, who said, "If Haninah is appointed before me, then I shall be second, and if R. Epes, the Southerner, is appointed before me, then I shall be second."

O.   R. Hanina agreed to be appointed third in line.

P.   Said R. Hanina, "I have had the merit of living a long life. I do not know whether it was because of that incident, or because, when I would come up from Tiberias to Sepphoris, I would take the long way round to go and greet R. Simeon b. Halputa in Ein Tinah."

Y. Moed Qatan 3:1.IV.

H.   Rabbi had high regard for Bar Eleasha [his son-in-law]. Bar Qappara said to him, "Everyone brings questions to Rabbi, and you don't bring questions to him."

I.   He said to him, "What should I ask him?"

J.   He said to him, "Ask: 'It looks down from heaven, it searches the corners of the house. All the winged creatures fear.' 'The young men saw me and withdrew, the aged rose and stood; . . . and laid their hand on their mouth' [Job 29:8–9]. Lo, they say, 'Wonderful, wonderful.' 'He who is taken is taken in his sin.'"

K.   [Upon hearing this riddle,] Rabbi turned and saw [Bar Qappara] laughing. Rabbi said, "I do not recognize you, O sage."

L.   And [Bar Qappara] realized that he would not be appointed as an official of Rabbi's court for the rest of his days.

Both stories make the simple point that a sage enjoyed that status independent of his position in the patriarchal administration. At the same time, the patriarch is represented as a sage himself, knowing Scripture, teaching lessons. True, the patriarch withheld appointment because of his personal feelings, despite the merit of the candidate. Hanina, after all, is shown to be humble and respectful of other sages. That fact stands in contrast to Rabbi's reception of Hanina's correction. The second story is like the first, in presenting Judah the Patriarch as vindictive. At the same time, once again, the patriarch appears as someone like a sage in learning, different from a sage in power.

We have now to ask, precisely what could a man do if appointed a member of the patriarchate, which he could not do if without that office? The following story provides part of the Talmud's view of matters. Appointment to the administration was not general. It involved quite specific powers. It conferred particular sorts of authority and withheld others. That is the picture derived from the following.

Y. Hagigah 1:8.III.

    C.   Rabbi appointed Rab to release vows and to examine women's menstrual stains. After he had died, Rab asked his son to appoint him to examine blemishes of firstlings.

    D.   The son said to him, "I am not going to add to what father assigned to you."

    E.   Said R. Yosé b. R. Bun, "[Rabbi] had given him a total assignment, to judge cases all by himself, to release vows, to examine blemishes which are visible. When Rabbi died, Rab asked his son for permission to assess blemishes which are not visible. He said to him, 'I am not going to add to what father assigned to you.'"

    F.   Even though you have said that they do appoint elders to serve for specific purposes alone, that is the case only if the one appointed is suitable to carry out all sorts of tasks.

    G.   It is in line with the following: R. Joshua b. Levi appointed all his disciples [to carry out official duties], but he was distressed in regard to one of them, who had weak eyes, and he could not appoint him. He did assign him to carry out some tasks . . .

    I.   What is the law as to appointing elders for a limited period of time?

    J.   Let us derive the answer from the following:

    K.   R. Hiyya bar Ba came to R. Eleazar, saying to him, "Recommend me to R. Yudan, the Patriarch, so that he will write a letter of recommendation for me as I go abroad to make my living." He recommended him, and [the patriarch] wrote the following letter for him: "Lo, we send you a great man. He is our messenger and stands in our stead until he comes back to us."

    L.   R. Hezekiah, R. Dosetai, R. Abba bar Zamina—and some present the same saying in the name of R. Dosai the Elder: "Thus did he write for him: 'Lo, we send you a great man.' And what is the greatness that is his? That he is not ashamed to say, 'I have not heard [the law].'"

Since Joshua b. Levi, G, was not patriarch, it is not entirely clear why he appointed his disciples and what power he bestowed upon them. The story of Hiyya bar Ba and Eleazar is more apropos. Here the patriarch is represented as enjoying influence among Jewish communities outside the Land of Israel.

As to the service performed for the patriarch, the following story indicates that the Talmud regarded the patriarchal sages as supervisors, inspectors, and administrators of the nation at large. The patriarch assigned to rabbis the task of supervising the life of the villages, not merely to judge cases and administer the law.

Y. Hagigah 1:7.II.

A. R. Yudan the Patriarch sent R. Hiyya, R. Asi, and R. Ami to travel among the towns of the land of Israel to provide for them scribes and teachers. They came to one place and found neither a scribe nor a teacher. They said to the people, "Bring us the guardians of the town." The people brought them the citizens of senatorial class in the town.

B. They said to them, "Do you think these are the guardians of the town? They are none other than the destroyers of the town."

C. They said to them, "And who are the guardians of the town?"

D. They said to them, "The scribes and teachers."

E. That is in line with what is written: "Unless the Lord builds the house those who build it labor in vain. Unless the Lord watches over the city the watchman stays awake in vain" [Ps. 127:1].

Since rabbis formed part of the bureaucracy and entourage of the patriarch, we may hardly be surprised to find stories in which rabbis paid formal respects to the patriarch from day to day, sought to marry his relatives, and engaged in conflict over priority in relationship to him and his office.

Y. Horayot 3:5.III.

QQ. Members of the household of Bar Pazzi and members of the household of Bar Hoshaiah would go up and greet the patriarch every day. And the members of the house of Bar Hoshaiah went in first [before those of the house of Bar Pazzi].

RR. The house of Bar Pazzi went and intermarried with the house of the patriarch. Then they wanted to go in first [to greet the patriarch, before the ones who had traditionally done so first]. So they appealed the matter to R. Immi.

SS. [He said to them,] "'And you shall erect the tabernacle according to its judgment' [Ex. 26:30: According to the plan for it that has been shown you on the mountain]. Now is there such a thing as 'judgment' for pieces of wood? But this beam has acquired the merit of being placed at the north, so let it be placed at the north; the other had the merit of being placed at the south, let it be placed at the south.''

TT. Two families in Sepphoris, Balvati and Pagani, would go up and greet the patriarch every day. And the Balvati family would go in first and come out first. The Pagani family went and attained merit in learning. They came and sought the right to

enter first. The question was brought to R. Simeon b. Levi.
R. Simeon b. Levi asked R. Yohanan. R. Yohanan went and
gave a talk in the schoolhouse of R. Benaiah: *"But if a*
mamzer was a disciple of a sage and a high priest was an ig-
noramus, the mamzer who is a disciple of a sage takes prece-
dence over the high priest who is an ignoramus [M. Hor.
3:5D].

These stories, on a trivial scale, surely conform to the general picture of the
emphasis upon form and procedure in the court of Byzantium, with status
expressed through precedence in rites and relationship to the person of the
head of state. It would be normal to greet the patriarch in his circuits around
the country.

Y. Abodah Zarah 2:4:III.

    F.   R. Yohanan went out to receive R. Yudan the Patriarch in Acre.
        They came and asked him, "As to jars, what is the mode of
        cleaning them?"

Y. Baba Batra 9:6.II.

    A.   R. Perida paid his respects to R. Judah the Patriarch by sending
        him two kinds of radishes between the New Year and the
        Fast. Now it was at the end of the Sabbatical Year, and
        [radishes were so abundant] that one could taste in them [the
        flavor of the scent deriving from their having been] carried by
        a camel.

    B.   Rabbi said to him, "Are they not still forbidden [as produce of
        the Seventh Year]? Are they not the stubble of the field
        [growing in that year, which may not be eaten]?"

    C.   He said to him, "At the end of the Sabbatical Year were they
        sown."

    D.   Forthwith Rabbi permitted purchasing produce immediately at
        the end of the Sabbatical Year [without waiting until the crops
        of the year following the Sabbatical Year had begun to appear
        on the market].

Here again we find striking evidence that the Talmud's authorities regarded
the patriarch as a learned man just like themselves. He was able to decide
questions of law and furthermore did so in an authoritative manner. Since his
counterpart, the exilarch in Babylonia, normally was represented as ignorant
of the law and even indifferent to niceties of observance, the contrast in the
representation of the patriarch is striking.

    The office of patriarch, more than the holder, elicited rabbinical reverence,
and they reminded the patriarch to conduct himself in accordance with the
dignity of that office.

Sanhedrin 2:6.IV.

C. *And others may not see [a king] while he is nude, or when he is getting a haircut, or in the bathhouse [M. San. 2:6L].*

D. This is in line with the following verse: "Your eyes shall see the king in his beauty" (Is. 33:17).

E. R. Haninah went up to R. Yudan the Patriarch. [The latter] came out to greet him, dressed in his undershirt.

F. He said to him, "Go and put on your woolen cloak, on the grounds of, 'Your eyes shall see the king in his beauty' (Is. 33:17)."

G. R. Yohanan went up to call on R. Yudan the Patriarch. He came forth to receive him in a shirt made of cotton.

H. He said to him, "Go back and put on your cloak of wool, on the grounds of: 'Your eyes shall see the king in his beauty.'"

It is hardly surprising that the great sages insisted on being accorded a proper reception by the patriarch.

When the patriarch died, taboos ordinarily in effect were suspended, for example, the prohibition against the priests' contracting corpse-uncleanness except for immediate family.

Y. Nazir 7:1.V.

A. And what is the law as to a priest's contracting corpse-uncleanness to bury a ruler?

B. When R. Yudan the Patriarch died, R. Yannai proclaimed, saying, "There is no consideration of priesthood today, [and everyone must participate in the burial rites, even priests]."

C. When R. Yudan the Patriarch, grandson of R. Yudan the Patriarch, died, R. Hiyya pushed R. Zeira bar Ba into the synagogue which stood among the vineyards in Sepphoris and forced him to contract uncleanness [since the body lay in the synagogue].

D. When Yehudinaia, sister of R. Yudan the Patriarch, died, R. Hanina sent to R. Mana, but the latter did not come up. He said to him, "If when they are alive, one does not contract uncleanness on account of women, is it not an argument *a fortiori* that when they are dead, one should not do so?"

E. Said R. Nisa, "When they are dead, they are to be treated as neglected corpses [and so given all due respect, even by priests]."

As we have repeatedly noted, the framers of the Talmud certainly regarded the patriarch as chief and one of themselves. Members of his household were assumed to know the law and their deeds would be cited as a precedent or suitable illustration of what was required.

Y. Abodah Zarah 2:9.IV.

> V. R. Jacob bar Aha, in the name of R. Yassa, "The slave belonging to a reliable Israelite himself is tantamount to a reliable person."
>
> W. Germana, the slave of R. Yudan the Patriarch, had purple dye [for sale].
>
> X. R. Yassa in the name of R. Yohanan: "The slave belonging to a reliable Israelite himself is tantamount to a reliable person [so it is permitted to purchase this purple dye from Germana]."

Y. Megillah 2:2.II.

> A. If he read it piecemeal in sections, if he read one verse, skipped a verse, [read the third, then came back to the second]—
>
> B. As to the words in Hebrew for "piecemeal" [*serugim*] and for portulaks [*halaglagot*], the rabbis were in doubt as to their meaning. Said R. Haggai, "The associates were wondering about the meaning of the cited words, and also about whether one who is greater in wisdom or one who is greater in years should take precedence.
>
> C. "They said, 'Let us go and ask the house of Rabbi.' They went up to ask. A servant girl of Rabbi's household came out, and she said to them, 'Go in in order of years.'
>
> D. "They said, 'Let So-and-so go in first, let So-and-so go in first.' They began to go in piecemeal [one by one].
>
> E. "She said to them, 'Why are you going in *serugim* [piecemeal]?'
>
> F. "One of the rabbis was carrying portulaks. They fell from him. She said to him, 'Rabbi, your *halaglagot* [portulaks] have fallen.'
>
> G. "She said to her co-worker, 'Bring a broom,' and she brought a bundle of shoots. [This served to explain the language of Is. 14:23.]"

Here even the slaves and servants of the patriarch provide adequate precedent or information. Accordingly, the patriarch is no different from any other sage. Then it is no surprise that the patriarch was portrayed in study sessions with other sages, in entirely nonpolemical contexts.

Y. Qiddushin 4:6.II.

> A. R. Hoshaiah the Elder and R. Judah the Patriarch were in session. R. Yohanan ran in and whispered into the ear of R. Hoshaiah the Elder: "A priest lacking a penis [Deut. 23:1]—what is the law as to his marrying the daughter of proselytes?"
>
> B. [Judah the Patriarch] said to him, "What did he say to you?"
>
> C. He said to him, "Something to which the carpenter, son of a

carpenter [a learned son of a learned man], would not be able to answer."

D. "He did not speak to me about a proselyte woman, who in respect to him [a priest] has the status of a prostitute, nor did he ask me about the daughter of an Israelite, who would be in the status of an impaired priestly woman [if she were to be married to him]. He has asked me only about the daughter of proselytes!"

Y. Qiddushin 3:5.I.

E. R. Hoshaiah the Elder and R. Yudan the Patriarch were in session. They said, "Let us discuss a topic having to do with betrothals."

F. [Someone asked,] "He who says to a woman, 'Here is this *perutah* so that you will be betrothed to me as soon as I divorce you,' what is the law?"

G. They burst out laughing, got up and walked out.

H. Said R. Yosé, "And why did they laugh? Did not R. Ba bar Mamel say, 'When she is freed, she gets a mind of her own'? Here too, when she is divorced, she gets a mind of her own [and may change her mind]."

The patriarch's own decisions were respected and accepted as decisive precedents.

Y. Abodah Zarah 2:9:III.

D. R. Eleazar in the name of R. Haninah: "A fishing vessel belonging to the household of Rabbi had more than three hundred kegs [of fish]. Rabbi inspected all of them. He found only one in which the heads and backbones [of the fish] were visible [in which case this sort of fish, prepared by a gentile, was permitted for Israelite use, and on the strength of that single keg], he permitted the whole lot of them [to be sold to, and eaten by, Israelites]."

Y. Megillah 1:11.I.

D. R. Hoshaiah the Elder asked R. Yudan the Patriarch, "Have you heard from your father the law as to whether it is permitted to carry a chicken?"

E. [He replied,] "How is this a question? If it is prepared in advance of slaughter, it is permitted to carry it about, and if not, it is forbidden."

F. "But are not all chickens regarded as ready for slaughter? It is on that account that it is a question."

G. He told it to him in a whisper, saying to him, "Just as I heard the

tradition in a whisper, so I am repeating it to you in a whisper, [that any chicken not designated for laying eggs may be
carried about, in the theory that it is always designated as
ready for slaughter]."

For his part, the patriarch was represented as subservient to rabbinical decisions on the law, and that representation bears no polemical weight whatever.

Y. Abodah Zarah 5:5.
  I.   A.   Said R. Haninah, "[There was] a wagon belonging to the house-
             hold of Rabbi from which the Israelite driver went away by
             more than four *mil*.
       B.   "The case came before the rabbis, who declared the wine to be
             acceptable to Israelites."
       C.   They say that [this was because] it took place on a road near
             Sidon and the whole of it was filled with Israelites.

Y. Abodah Zarah 5:5.I.
       G.   R. Ammi went up with R. Yudan the Patriarch to the hot springs
             of Gedar.
       H.   They borrowed silver from certain gentile moneylenders [to
             make the silver into utensils].
       I.   They asked R. Jeremiah [whether even the silver had to be
             immersed]. He instructed them to immerse the coins, for they
             had come forth with the uncleanness pertaining to a gentile
             and had entered the sanctification pertaining to an Israelite.

Y. Baba Qamma 2:1.III.
       A.   R. Hoshaiah the Elder and R. Yudan the Patriarch were in
             session. R. Ba bar Mamal came in and asked, "When a beast
             switches its tail, like those asses [which flick off flies that
             way]—what is the law? [Is this deemed a secondary effect in
             the primary category of horn, or is this simply not normal
             behavior and if it happens in the public domain and causes
             damage, the owner would be exempt?]"
       B.   They did not give any answer at all.
       C.   Afterward R. Hoshaiah the Elder said to him, "If we do not rule
             [that it is a normal form of behavior for the beast], we shall
             have to require the owner to walk along holding the tail of
             the beast."

Respect for the person and office of the patriarch, further, is expressed in the
conviction that, if the patriarch was absent from a rite, the rite was null and
did not produce the desired effect.

Y. Taanit 2:1.VI.

    A.   It is written, "Let the bridegroom leave his room, and the bride her chamber" [Joel 2:16].

    B.   "The bridegroom leave his room"—this refers to the ark.

    C.   "And the bride her chamber"—this refers to the Torah.

    D.   Another interpretation: "The bridegroom leave his room"—this refers to the patriarch.

    E.   "And the bride her chamber"—this refers to the head of the court.

    F.   R. Helbo said to R. Yudan the Patriarch, "Come out with us, and what is painful to you will pass. [If the patriarch comes out with us to a public fast, the prayers will be answered. Otherwise we cannot properly carry out the rite.]"

    G.   Said R. Yosé, "That is to say that these fasts that we carry out—they are not really fasts. Why not? Because the patriarch is not with us [so we cannot carry out the rite in the proper way]."

This story is especially important in indicating that the patriarch was not regarded as a merely "political figure," let alone a front man for the Romans. He was not only learned. He also enjoyed the supernatural power that learning in general was supposed to endow upon the learned. Accordingly, the patriarch was received as fully a rabbi in every respect.

Perhaps a criticism of the patriarch was intended by the foregoing story. There can be no doubt that in the next one the patriarch is subject to criticism for a niggardly gift.

Y. Megillah 1:4.XI.

    A.   R. Yudan the Patriarch sent to R. Hoshaiah a piece of meat and a flask of wine.

    B.   He replied, saying to him, "Through us have you carried out the following verse of Scripture: '[As the days on which the Jews got relief from their enemies, and as the month that had been turned for them from sorrow into gladness and from mourning into a holiday; that they should make them days of feasting and gladness, days for sending choice portions to one another and] gifts to the poor' (Est. 9:22)." [This gift is worthy only of a poor man.]

    C.   He went and sent him a calf and a barrel of wine. He sent back to him, "through us you have carried out the following verse of Scripture: 'As the days on which the Jews to relief from their enemies, and as the month that had been turned for them from sorrow into gladness . . . "'

The three important stories about tension between patriarchs and sages take
for granted a commonality of viewpoint between patriarch and sage. In the
first case the patriarch differs from the view of an unusually pious sage about
the latter's strict position on the law.

Y. Taanit 3:1.II.

H. Rabbi wanted to release the prohibitions of the Sabbatical Year.
I. R. Phineas b. Yair came to him. He said to him, "What sort of
    crop is coming up this year?"
J. He said to him, "Endives of good quality."
K. [Again,] "What sort of crop is coming up this year?"
L. "Endives of good quality."
M. Thereupon Rabbi realized that he did not concur with this view.
N. [Rabbi] said to him, "Would the Rabbi [Phineas] not care to eat
    a bite with us today?"
O. He said to him, "Yes."
P. When he went down [to eat], he saw the vast herd of mules
    belonging to Rabbi standing around, [even though it is forbid-
    den to keep herds of small beasts in the Land]. He said, "Do
    Jews feed all of these? It is not possible that he [Rabbi] will
    ever see my face again."
Q. [He went on home. Members of the household of Rabbi] heard
    the report [of what Phineas had said]. They went and told
    Rabbi. He sent [a messenger] to appease R. Phineas.
R. [The messengers] came to the town [of Phineas]. [Phineas] said,
    "The townspeople of my town will stand up for me."
S. The townspeople went out and encircled [Phineas, so that he
    would not be seen by the messengers of Rabbi]. The messen-
    gers said to them, "Rabbi wants to appease him." So they
    allowed them to pass, and [the townfolk] went their way.
T. [Phineas] said, "My sons will stand up for me."
U. A fire descended from heaven and encircled him.
V. They went back and informed Rabbi. He said, "Since we did not
    have the merit of seeing him [again] in this world, we shall
    have the merit of hearing from him in the world to come."

What is striking here is the respect paid by Phineas to the patriarch, even
while Phineas rejected the patriarch's legal opinion and feared his soldiers.
The relationship then was not one between colleagues. But it also was not
one in which the rabbi expressed contempt for the patriarch's learning. True,
he regarded as reprehensible his practice of raising small beasts—an eco-
logical disaster for the country. Further, the storyteller understands that local
folk will try to protect their holy man against Rabbi's soldiers. Yet, through-

out, the patriarch is acknowledged as not only the stronger but legitimately so.

In the second tale the patriarch is offended by a position taken by a sage on a specific point of law. The story has the sage flee the wrath of the patriarch. At the same time, respect for the patriarch's learning and piety is the foundation of the story. So while the threat of force and punishment is implicit in the narrative, the story is possible only in the conviction that the patriarch and the sage belong to essentially the same party, believe the same things, and respond to the same appeals to learning.

Y. Horayot 3:1.II.

A. R. Simeon b. Laqish said, "A ruler who sinned—they administer lashes to him by the decision of a court of three judges."

B. What is the law as to restoring him to office?

C. Said R. Haggai, "By Moses! If we put him back in office, he will kill us!"

D. R. Judah the Patriarch heard this ruling [of Simeon b. Laqish's] and was outraged. He sent a troop of Goths to arrest R. Simeon b. Laqish. [R. Simeon b. Laqish] fled to the Tower, and some say, it was to Kefar Hittayya.

E. The next day R. Yohanan went up to the meeting house, and R. Judah the Patriarch went up to the meeting house. He said to him, "Why does my master not state a teaching of Light [Torah]?"

F. [Yohanan] began to clap with one hand [only].

G. [Judah the Patriarch] said to him, "Now do people clap with only one hand?"

H. He said to him, "No, nor is Ben Laqish here [and just as one cannot clap with one hand only, so I cannot teach Torah if my colleague, Simeon b. Laqish, is absent]."

I. [Judah] said to him, "Then where is he hidden?"

J. He said to him, "In the Tower."

K. He said to him, "You and I shall go out to greet him."

L. R. Yohanan sent word to R. Simeon b. Laqish, "Get a teaching of Light [Torah] ready, because the patriarch is coming over to see you."

M. [Simeon b. Laqish] came forth to receive them and said, "The example that you [Judah] set is to be compared to the paradigm of your Creator. For when the All-Merciful came forth to redeem Israel from Egypt, he did not send a messenger of an angel, but the Holy One, blessed be he, himself came forth, as it is said, 'For I will pass though the land of Egypt that night' [Ex. 12:12]—and not only so, but he and his entire retinue.

N.   "[What other people on earth is like thy people Israel, whom God went to redeem to be his people (2 Sam. 7:23).] 'Whom the divinity went' [sing.] is not written here, but 'Whom God went' [plural—meaning, he and all his retinue].

O.   [Judah the Patriarch] said to him, "Now why in the world did you see fit to teach this particular statement [that a ruler who sinned is subject to lashes]?"

P.   He said to him, "Now did you really think that because I was afraid of you, I would hold back the teaching of the All-Merciful? [And lo, citing 1 Sam. 2:23f.,] R. Samuel b. R. Isaac said, '[Why do you do such things? For I hear of your evil dealings from all the people.] No, my sons, it is no good report that I hear the people of the Lord spreading abroad. [If a man sins against a man, God will mediate for him; but if a man sins against the Lord, who can intercede for him? But they would not listen to the voice of their father, for it was the will of the Lord to slay them' (1 Sam. 2:23–25).) [When] the people of the Lord spread about [an evil report about a man], they remove him [even though he is the patriarch]."

This story is truncated, lacking any sort of clear-cut ending. It is one of a handful of accounts in our Talmud, in which the patriarch is shown to tyrannize over the sages. The concurrence of the stories at hand, that Rabbi would not hesitate to call upon his gendarmes to enforce his will, and that he ruled as something of a despot, shows another side of matters. The patriarch, supposedly yet another sage, in important ways was more than a chief rabbi of sorts. He is represented as a rabbi, but the storytellers contradict that message in their account of an official enjoying command of Gothic or German "slaves."

In the third story, a rabbi taught a matter of lore contrary to the interests of the patriarch, stating that people are so heavily taxed by the patriarch that they cannot in addition give the priestly gifts. Here too the story portrays the patriarch as part of the rabbinical estate and well able to participate in its discourse.

Y. Sanhedrin 2:6.V.

A.   Yosé Meoni interpreted the following verse in the synagogue in Tiberias: "'Hear this, O priests!' [Hos. 5:1]: Why do you not labor in the Torah? Have not the twenty-four priestly gifts been given to you? [So you need not work and can study.]

B.   "They said to him, 'Nothing at all has been given to us.'

C.   "'And give heed, O House of Israel!' [Hos. 5:1].

D.   "'Why do you not give the priests the twenty-four gifts concerning which you have been commanded at Sinai?'

E. "They said to him, 'The king [= the patriarch] takes them all.'

F. "'Hearken, O house of the king! For the judgment pertains to you' (Hos. 5:1).

G. "To you have I said, 'And this shall be the priests' due from the people, from those offering a sacrifice . . . : they shall give to the priest the shoulder, the two cheeks, and the stomach' (Deut. 18:3).

H. "I am going to take my seat with them in court and to make a decision concerning them and blot them [the kings] out of the world."

I. R. Yudan the Patriarch heard [about this attack on the rulers] and was angry.

J. [Yosé] feared and fled.

K. R. Yohanan and R. Simeon b. Laqish went up to make peace with [the Patriarch].

L. They said to him, "Rabbi, he is a great man."

M. He said to them, "Is it possible that everything which I ask of him, he will give to me?"

N. They said to him, "Yes." [So Yosé was called back.]

O. [The Patriarch] said to [Yosé], "What is the meaning of that which is written: 'For their mother has played the harlot' [Hos. 2:5]?

P. "Is it possible that our matriarch, Sarah, was a whore?"

Q. They said to him, "As is the daughter, so is her mother.

R. "As is the mother, so is the daughter.

S. "As is the generation, so is the patriarch.

T. "As is the patriarch, so is the generation.

U. "As is the altar, so are its priests." . . .

W. He said to them, "Is it not enough for him that he dishonors me one time not in my presence, but also in my presence he does so these three times [Q–T]!"

X. He said to him, "What is the meaning of that which is written, 'Behold, every one who uses proverbs will use this proverb about you, 'Like mother, like daughter' [Ez. 16:44].

Y. "Now was our matriarch, Leah, a whore?

Z. "As it is written, 'And Dinah went out [Gen. 34:1] [like a whore, thus reflecting on her mother].'"

AA. He said to him, "It is in accord with that which is written, 'And Leah went out to meet him' [Gen. 30:16].

BB. "They compared one going out to the other [and Leah went out to meet her husband, and Dinah learned from this that it was all right to go out, so she went out to meet the daughters of the land; but she was raped]." [This was an acceptable reply to Yudan.]

Here again the story ends rather abruptly. Its point for our survey is self-evident and requires no comment.

Who Rules Israel?

The Talmud portrays the rabbi as an effective authority over Israel. Yet details of the portrait time and again contradict its main lines. The rabbi was part of the administration of a man who stood at the margins of the rabbinical estate, one foot in, the other out. The sage was further limited in his power by popular will and consensus, by established custom, and by other sorts of Jewish Big Men. Furthermore, the rabbi as clerk and bureaucrat dealt with matters of surpassing triviality, a fair portion of them of no interest to anyone but a rabbi, I should imagine. He might decide which dog a flea might bite. But would the fleas listen to him? Accordingly, the Talmud's voluminous evidence of rabbis' quest for authority over the Jewish nation, as we review its principal expressions, turns out to present ambiguities about inconsequentialities. On the one side, the rabbi could make some practical decisions. On the other, he competed for authority over Israel with the patriarch and with local village heads. And, in general, no Jew decided much.

From the viewpoint of the Roman empire, moreover, the rabbi was apt to have been one among many sorts of invisible men, self-important nonentities, treating as consequential things that concerned no one but themselves, doing little, changing nothing. After all, in the very period in which the tales before us were coming to closure and beginning to constitute our Talmud as we know it, the power of the Jewish nation to govern itself grew ever less. Even the authority of the patriarch supposedly ended within the very period at hand, leaving only rabbis and their Talmud, legal theory in abundance but legal standing slight indeed. So we discern a certain disproportion between the insistence of the Talmud that rabbis really decided things and established important precedents, and the Talmud's context—both the actual condition of Israel, whom rabbis ruled, and the waning authority of the government of Israel, by whom rabbis were employed.

Once more, one of the Talmud's principal points of emphasis turns out, upon closer inspection, to address head-on, but in a perverse way, the reality of Israel within the now-Christian Roman empire. We recall the Talmud's puzzling indifference to the stunning, world-historical events of the age. Yet silence is also a response. It is not possible to suppose that the Talmud's framers, by the end of the fourth century, in the aftermath of nearly a century of Christian rule and pagan disaster, of Jewish messianic fervor followed by a heart-breaking debacle—it is not possible to suppose that the people who made the Talmud did not recognize things had changed for the worse. Nor can we maintain for one moment the outlandish possibility that the rabbis had nothing to say about the events of the day, merely pretending nothing was new. They knew. They cared. They judged. But if so, then we can suppose only one of two alternatives. Either the rabbis of the Talmud framed their document in total disregard of the issues of the day. Or they composed their principal literary monument in complete encounter with those issues and serene certainty of their mastery. By harping on how *they* decided things and inserting into the processes of legal theory precedents established in their courts, and by representing the life of Israel in such a way that the government of the nation was shown to be entirely within the hands of the nation's learned, legitimate authorities, the Talmud's sages stated quite clearly what they thought was going on. Israel remained Israel, wholly subject to its own law, entirely in control of its own destiny, fully possessed of its own land. Testimony to and vindication of the eternity of Israel lay in the continuing authority of Israel's sages, fully in control of God's Light and law for Israel. That is why the Talmud insists upon the quest for authority.

5

The Quest for Salvation

The Issue of Salvation

The Talmud of the Land of Israel speaks mostly about the Mishnah. The framers of the Talmud undertook a vast, sustained quest into the Mishnah's law and its Scriptural foundations, seeking the right principles and practices for Israelite polity and private life alike. To what end?

What we want to know is how the Talmud explains its purpose, tells us what will happen if the laws are kept and the rabbis obeyed. The answer to this question of sanctions lies in the Talmud's theory of salvation. For its ultimate concern is to provide Israel with an account of how to overcome the unsatisfactory circumstances of an unredeemed present, so as to accomplish the movement from here to the much-desired future. When the Talmud's authorities present statements on the promise of the law for those who keep it, therefore, they provide glimpses of the goal of the system as a whole. The primacy of the rabbi, the legitimating power of the Torah—what have these to do with salvation? We now seek evidence of Talmud's theory of the meaning and goal of its system, promise, hope, and purpose.

For both the nation and the individual, the answer had to be the same—to attain salvation. For the individual that meant the life of the world to come, and for the nation, the return to, and restoration of, Jerusalem and its holy Temple. The system's teleology is not stated with great frequency in discourse even on theological issues: It is never expressed in a clear way in discussion of legal ones. Yet, once emerging with force and authority, the purpose of the system as a whole is amply clear. The profundity of the message, its decisive place at the center and heart of matters, its power to impart to the Judaism to which the Talmud attests life-force and meaning—these become self-evident, once a statement of the ultimate and critical points of insistence comes forth.

Looking backward from the end of the fourth century to the end of the first, the framers of the Talmud surely perceived what two hundred years earlier, with the closure of the Mishnah, need not have appeared obvious and unavoidable, namely, the definitive end, for here and now at any rate, of the old order of cultic sanctification. After a hundred years there may have been some doubt. After two centuries more with the fiasco of Julian near at hand, there can have been little hope left. The Mishnah had designed a world in which the Temple stood at the center, a society in which the priests presided at the top, and a way of life in which the dominant issue was the sanctification of Israelite life. Whether the full realization of that world, society, and way of life was thought to come sooner or later, the system had been meant only initially as a utopia, but in the end, as a plan and constitution for a material society here in the Land of Israel. Two hundred years now had passed from the closure of the Mishnah to the completion of the Talmud of the Land of Israel. Much had changed. Roman power had receded from part of the world. Pagan rule had given way to the sovereignty of Christian emperors. The old order was cracking; the new order was not yet established. But, from the perspective of Israel, the waiting went on. The interim from Temple to Temple was not differentiated. Whether conditions were less favorable or more favorable hardly made a difference. History stretched backward, to a point of disaster, and forward, to an unseen and incalculable time beyond the near horizon. Short of supernatural events, salvation was not in sight. Israel for its part lived under its own government, framed within the rules of sanctification, and constituted a holy society. But when would salvation come, and how could people even now hasten its day? These issues, in the nature of things, proved more pressing as the decades rolled by, becoming first one century, then another, while none knew how many more, and how much more, must still be endured.

So the unredeemed state of Israel and the world, the uncertain fate of the individual—these framed and defined the context in which all forms of Judaism necessarily took shape. The question of salvation presented each with a single ineluctable agendum. But it is not merely an axiom generated by our hindsight that makes it necessary to interpret all of a system's answers in the light of the single question of salvation. In the case of the Judaism to which the Yerushalmi attests, the matter is explicitly stated.

For the important fact is that Yerushalmi expressly links salvation to keeping the law. This means that the issues of the law were drawn upward into the highest realm of Israelite consciousness. Keeping the law in the right way is represented as not merely right or expedient. It is the way to bring the Messiah, the son of David. This is stated by Levi, as follows.

Y. Taanit 1:1.IX.

> X. Said R. Levi, "If Israel would keep a single Sabbath in the proper way, forthwith the son of David would come.
>
> Y. "What is the Scriptural basis for this view? 'Moses said, Eat it today, for today is a sabbath to the Lord; today you will not find it in the field' (Ex. 16:25)."

Z.   And it says, "For thus said the Lord God, the Holy One of Israel, 'In returning and rest you shall be saved; in quietness and in trust shall be your strength. And you would not' (Is. 30:15)."

The coming of the Messiah, moreover, was explicitly linked to the destruction of the Temple. How so? The Messiah was born on the day the Temple was destroyed. Accordingly, as the following story makes explicit, the consolation for the destruction of the Temple lay in the coming of the son of David.

Y. Berakhot 2:3 [Zahavy].

A.   The rabbis said, "This messiah king if he comes from among the living, David will be his name; if he comes from among the dead, it will be David himself."

B.   Said R. Tanhuma, "I say that the Scriptural basis for this teaching is, *'And he shows steadfast love to his messiah, to David and his descendants forever' (Ps. 18:50)."*

C.   R. Joshua b. Levi said, "'Sprout' (*semah*) is his name."

D.   R. Yudan, son of R. Aibo, said, "Menahem is his name."

E.   Said Hananiah son of R. Abahu, "They do not disagree. The numerical value of the letters of one name equals the numerical value of the other—*semah* (= 138) is equal to *menahem* (= 138)."

F.   And this story supports the view of R. Yudan son of R. Aibo. "Once a Jew was plowing and his ox snorted once before him. An Arab who was passing and heard the sound said to him, 'Jew, loosen your ox and loosen the plow and stop plowing. For today your Temple was destroyed.'

G.   "The ox snorted again. He [the Arab] said to him, 'Jew, bind your ox and bind your plow. For today the messiah king was born.' He said to him, 'What is his name?' 'Menahem.' He said to him, 'What is his father's name?' He said to him, 'Hezekiah.' He said to him, 'Where is he from?' He said to him, 'From the royal capital of Bethlehem in Judea.'

H.   "He went and sold his ox and sold his plow. And he became a peddler of infants' felt clothes. And he went from place to place until he came to that very city. All of the women bought from him. But Menahem's mother did not buy from him. He heard the women saying, 'Menahem's mother, Menahem's mother, come buy for your child.' She said, 'I want to bring him up to hate Israel. For on the day he was born the Temple was destroyed.' They said to her, 'We are sure that on this day it was destroyed and on this day is will be rebuilt.'

I. "She said to him[the peddler], 'I have no money.' He said to her, 'It is no matter to me. Come and buy for him and pay me when I return.' A while later he returned to that city. He said to her, 'How is the infant doing?' She said to him, 'Since the time you saw him a wind came and carried him off away from me.'"

These two stories provide a glimpse into a far larger corpus of theories about the coming of the Messiah. The former, as we have noted, explicitly links the coming of the Messiah to the proper observance of the law as sages propound it. From our perspective, that story is the more important of the two, for by definition it is particular to the matrix in which our Talmud takes shape. The latter story presents a series of rather generalized messianic sayings and in no way addresses the distinctive concerns of rabbis and clerks. Yet for that reason it is all the more important. For in the Mishnah's entire corpus of ideas, there is scarcely a hint of the paramount idea of the earlier second century, the hope for the imminent advent of the Messiah. The Mishnah's system, whole and complete, remains reticent on the entire theme. By contrast, our Talmud finds ample place for a rich collection of statements on the messianic theme. What this means is that, between the conclusion of the Mishnah and the closure of the Talmud, room had been found for the messianic hope, expressed in images not revised to conform to the definitive and distinctive traits of the Talmud itself. The two stories together, therefore, provide ample testimony both to the entry of the Messiah into the Talmudic structure and to his (if one may use the term) "rabbinization."

The "rabbinization" of the messianic hope required its neutralization, so that peoples' hopes would not be raised prematurely, with consequent, incalculable damage to the defeated nation. This meant, first of all, that rabbis insisted the Messiah would come in a process extending over a long period of time, thus not imposing a caesura upon the existence of the nation and disrupting its ordinary life. Accordingly, the Yerushalmi treats the messianic hope as something gradual, to be worked toward, not a sudden cataclysmic event. That conception was fully in accord with the notion that the everyday deeds of people formed a pattern continuous with the salvific history of Israel.

Y. Yoma 3:2.III.

A. One time R. Hiyya the Elder and R. Simeon b. Halapta were walking in the valley of Arabel at daybreak. They saw that the light of the morning star was breaking forth. Said R. Hiyya the Elder to R. Simeon b. Halapta, "Son of my master, this is what the redemption of Israel is like—at first, little by little, but in the end it will go along and burst into light.

B.   "What is the Scriptural basis for this view? 'Rejoice not over
     me, O my enemy; when I fall, I shall rise; when I sit in dark-
     ness, the Lord will be a light to me' (Mic. 7:8).

C.   "So, in the beginning, 'When the virgins were gathered together
     the second time, Mordecai was sitting at the king's gate'
     (Est. 2:19).

D.   "But afterward: 'So Haman took the robes and the horse, and he
     arrayed Mordecai and made him ride through the open square
     of the city, proclaiming, Thus shall it be done to the man
     whom the king delights to honor' (Est. 6:11).

E.   "And in the end: 'Then Mordecai went out from the presence of
     the king in royal robes of blue and white, with a great golden
     crown and a mantle of fine linen and purple, while the city of
     Susa shouted and rejoiced' [Est. 8:15].

F.   "And finally: 'The Jews had light and gladness and joy and
     honor' (Est. 8:16)."

We may regard the emphasis upon the slow but steady advent of the Messiah's day as entirely consonant with the notion that the Messiah will come
when Israel's condition warrants it. The improvement in standards of observ-
ing the Torah, therefore, to be effected by the nation's obedience to the clerks
will serve as a guidepost on the road to redemption. The moral condition of
the nation ultimately guarantees salvation. God will respond to Israel's
regeneration, planning all the while to save the saved, that is, those who save
themselves.

What is most interesting in Yerushalmi's picture is that the hope for the
Messiah's coming is further joined to the moral condition of each individual
Israelite. Hence the messianic fulfillment was made to depend on the repentance of Israel. The entire drama, envisioned by others in earlier types of
Judaism as a world-historical event, was reworked in context into a moment
in the life of the individual and the people of Israel collectively. The coming
of the Messiah depended not on historical action but on moral regeneration.
So from a force that moved Israelites to take up weapons on the battlefield,
the messianic hope and yearning were transformed into motives for spiritual
regeneration and ethical behavior. The energies released in the messianic
fervor were then linked to rabbinical government, through which Israel
would form the godly society.

Y. Taanit 1:1:IX.

J.   "'The oracle concerning Dumah. One is calling to me from Seir,
     "Watchman, what of the night? Watchman, what of the
     night?" (Is. 21:11).'"

K.   The Israelites said to Isaiah, "O our Rabbi, Isaiah, What will
     come for us out of this night?"

L.   He said to them, "Wait for me, until I can present the question."

M.   Once he had asked the question, he came back to them.

N.   They said to him, "Watchman, what of the night? What did the Guardian of the ages tell you?"

O.   He said to them, "The watchman says: 'Morning comes; and also the night. If you will inquire, inquire; come back again' (Is. 21:12)."

P.   They said to him, "Also the night?"

Q.   He said to them, "It is not what you are thinking. But there will be morning for the righteous, and night for the wicked, morning for Israel, and night for idolaters."

R.   They said to him, "When?"

S.   He said to them, "Whenever you want, He too wants [it to be]—if you want it, He wants it."

T.   They said to him, "What is standing in the way?"

U.   He said to them, "Repentance: 'Come back again' (Is. 21:12)."

V.   R. Aha in the name of R. Tanhum b. R. Hiyya, "If Israel repents for one day, forthwith the son of David will come.

W.   "What is the Scriptural basis? 'If today you would hearken to his voice'" (Ps. 95:7).

When we reflect that the message, "If you want it, He too wants it to be," comes in a generation confronting a dreadful disappointment, its full weight and meaning become clear. The advent of the Messiah will not be heralded by the actions of a pagan king. Whoever relies upon the salvation of a gentile is going to be disappointed. Israel's salvation depends wholly upon Israel itself. Two things follow. First, the Jews were made to take up the burden of guilt for their own sorry situation. But, second, they also gained not only responsibility for, but also power over, their fate. They could do something about salvation, just as their sins had brought about their tragedy. This old, familiar message, in no way particular to the Talmud's bureaucrats, took on specificity and concreteness in the context of the Talmud, which offered a rather detailed program for reform and regeneration. The message to a disappointed generation, attracted to the kin-faith, with its now-triumphant messianic fulfillment, and fearful of its own fate in an age of violent attacks upon the synagogue buildings and faithful alike, was stern. But it also promised strength to the weak and hope to the despairing.

No one could be asked to believe that the Messiah would come very soon. The events of the day testified otherwise. So the counsel of the Talmud's sages was patience and consequential deeds. People could not hasten things, but they could do something. The duty of Israel, in the meantime, was to accept the sovereignty of heavenly government.

Y. Sanhedrin 6:9.III.

A.   R. Abbahu was bereaved. One of his children had passed away from him. R. Jonah and R. Yosé went up [to comfort him].

When they called on him, out of reverence for him, they did
not express to him a word of Torah. He said to them, "May
the rabbis express a word of Torah."

B.   They said to him, "Let our master teach us."

C.   He said to them, "Now if in regard to the government below, in
which there is no reliability, [but only] lying, deceit, favoritism, and bribe taking—

D.   "which is here today and gone tomorrow—

E.   "if concerning that government, it is said, *And the relatives
of the felon come and inquire after the welfare of the judges
and of the witnesses, as if to say, 'We have nothing against
you, for you judged honestly'* [*Y. San.* 6:9],

F.   "in regard to the government above, in which there is reliability,
but no lying, deceit, favoritism, or bribe taking—

G.   "and which endures forever and to all eternity—

H.   "all the more so are we obligated to accept upon ourselves the
just decree [of that heavenly government]."

I.   And it says, "That the Lord . . . may show you mercy, and have
compassion on you . . ." (Deut. 13:17).

As we shall now see, the heavenly government, revealed in the Torah, was
embodied in this world by the figure of the sage. The meaning of the salvific
doctrine just outlined becomes fully clear when we uncover the simple fact
that the rule of Heaven and the learning and authority of the rabbi on earth
turned out to be identified with one another. It follows that salvation for Israel
depended upon adherence to the sage and acceptance of his discipline. God's
will in Heaven and the sage's words on earth—both constituted Torah. And
Israel would be saved through Torah, so the sage was the savior.

Salvation and Torah

The framers of the Talmud regarded "Torah" as the source and guarantor of
salvation. But what they understood by the word "Torah" took on meanings
particular to the rabbis. They took to heart as salvific acts what others,
standing outside of sages' social and mythic framework, will have regarded
as merely routine, on the one side, or hocus pocus, on the other. For to the
rabbis the principal salvific deed was to "study Torah," by which they meant
memorizing Torah sayings by constant repetition, and, as the Talmud itself
amply testifies, (for some sages) profound analytic inquiry into the meaning
of those sayings. This act of "study of Torah" imparted supernatural power.
For example, by repeating words of Torah, the sage could ward off the angel
of death and accomplish other kinds of miracles as well. So Torah formulas
served as incantations. Mastery of Torah transformed the man who engaged

in Torah learning into a supernatural figure, able to do things ordinary folk could not do. In the nature of things, the category of "Torah" was vastly expanded so that the symbol of Torah, a Torah scroll, could be compared to a man of Torah, namely, a rabbi. Once it was established that salvation would come from keeping God's will in general, as Israelite holy men had insisted for so many years, it was a small step for rabbis to identify their particular corpus of learning, namely, the Mishnah and associated sayings, with God's will expressed in Scripture, the universally acknowledged revelation. In consequence "Torah" would include pretty much whatever rabbis knew (inclusive of Scripture) and did—that alone.

Especially striking in the rabbinical doctrine of salvation is the blurring of boundaries between the nation and the individual. Suffering affected both. Catastrophe of a historical and one-time event, such as the destruction of the Temple, was brought into juxtaposition with personal suffering and death. Accordingly, while the things the nation and its people must be saved from were many, the mode of salvation was one. The consequence for the theory of salvation was this. Torah might protect a person from suffering or death, and Torah might in due course save Israel from its subjugation to the nations of the world. In regard to both the individual and society, Torah would save Israel for a life of Torah in Heaven as much as on earth.

Since Heaven was conceived in the model of earth, so that the analysis of traditions on earth corresponded to the discovery of the principles of creation, the full realization of the teachings of Torah on earth, in the life of Israel, would transform Israel into a replica of heaven on earth. We deal, therefore, with a doctrine of salvation in which the operative symbol, namely, Torah, and the determinative deed, namely, Torah learning, defined not only how to reach salvation but also the very nature of the salvation to be attained. The system was whole and cogent. Entering it at any point, we find ourselves at once before the structure as a whole. It is important, then, to recognize, as we do, that the profound issues confronting Israelite existence, national and individual alike, were framed in terms of Torah and resolved through the medium of Torah. Stated simply: Salvation was to come from Torah; the nature of salvation was defined in Torah.

So the single most striking phenomenon, in the matrix of which the Talmud's system of Judaism formed one element, is the vastly expanded definition of the symbol of "Torah." It now was deemed appropriate to compare or apply that symbol to a remarkable range of things. But the principal instance comes first, the claim that a sage (or, disciple of a sage) himself was equivalent to a scroll of the Torah—a material, legal comparison, not merely a symbolic metaphor.

Y. Moed Qatan 3:7.X.

    A.   He who sees a disciple of a sage who has died is as if he sees a scroll of the Torah that has been burned.

Y. Moed Qatan 3:1.XI.

    I.   R. Jacob bar Abayye in the name of R. Aha: "An elder who
        forgot his learning because of some accident which happened
        to him—they treat him with the sanctity owed to an ark [of
        the Torah]."

In both instances actual behavior was affected. The Talmud of the Land of
Israel (among other rabbinic documents) stretched to the limit the bounds of
the concept of Torah by showing that Scripture itself stood behind the extension and amplification of divine revelation through rational inquiry. The
processes of reason, very much like those undertaken in the rabbinical circles
of masters and disciples, themselves were regarded as able to generate Torah
teachings, as one thing led to another through right thinking. Whatever
through systemic logical analysis derived from the Torah, that is, Scripture,
itself was part of Torah, that is, Revelation.

Y. Megillah 1:11.V.

    L.   R. Abba b. R. Pappi, R. Joshua of Sikhnin in the name of R.
        Levi: "Noah through reflection derived a lesson of Torah
        from another lesson of Torah. He said, 'It has been said to
        me, "And as I gave you the green plants, I give you every-
        thing" (Gen. 9:3). For what purpose has the Scripture used
        that inclusive phrase? It serves to indicate that clean animals
        are for offerings.'"

Rabbis of course did the same sort of thinking every day. That the entire
corpus of rabbinical learning and tradition belonged to the category of divine
revelation was made quite explicit, as in the following.

Y. Sanhedrin 10:1.IV.

    A.   It is written, "Because he has despised the word of the Lord,
        [and has broken his commandment, that person shall be ut-
        terly cut off; his iniquity shall be upon him]" (Num. 15:31).
    B.   I know that this applies only when he despised the teaching of
        Torah [entirely].
    C.   How do I know that [this applies] if he denied even a single verse
        of Scripture, a single verse of Targum, a single argument *a
        fortiori?*
    D.   Scripture says, "[Because he has despised the word of the Lord,]
        and has broken his commandment, [that person shall be ut-
        terly cut off; his iniquity shall be upon him]" (Num. 15:31).
    E.   As to a single verse of Scripture: "[The sons of Lotan were Hori
        and Heman;] and Lotan's sister was Timna" (Gen. 36:22).

F.   As to a single verse of Targum: "Laban called it Jegarsahadutha: [but Jacob called it Galeed]" (Gen. 31:47).

G.   As to a single argument *a fortiori:* "If Cain is avenged sevenfold, [truly Lamech, seventy-sevenfold]" (Gen. 4:24).

The notion, moreover, that the sage participated in the work of revelation, both through his memorizing Torah sayings and through his reasoning on them, was made explicit. The sage was holy because he knew Torah. That meant that, in his act of learning Torah, his work of memorizing and repeating sayings, and his dialectical arguments on the amplification and analysis of what he learned, the sage took over the work of Moses in receiving the will of God. This made the sage equivalent to the prophet, indeed, superior to him. Identifying themselves with a (mythic) class of "scribes," sages of the Talmud made explicit the superiority of their learning over the direct revelation received by prophets.

Y. Abodah Zarah 2:7.III.

D.   R. Ishmael repeated the following: "The words of Torah are subject to prohibition, and they are subject to remission; they are subject to lenient rulings, and they are subject to strict rulings. But words of scribes all are subject only to strict interpretation, for we have learned there: *He who rules, 'There is no requirement to wear phylacteries,' in order to transgress the teachings of the Torah, is exempt. But if he said, 'There are five partitions in the phylactery, instead of four,' in order to add to what the scribes have taught, he is liable'* [*M. San. 11:3*]."

E.   R. Haninah in the name of R. Idi in the name of R. Tanhum b. R. Hiyya: "More stringent are the words of the elder than the words of the prophets. For it is written, 'Do not preach'—thus they preach—one should not preach of such things (Micah 2:6). And it is written, '[If a man should go about and utter wind and lies, saying,] "I will preach to you of wind and strong drink," he would be the preacher for this people!'" (Mic. 2:11).

F.   "A prophet and an elder—to what are they comparable? To a king who sent two senators of his to a certain province. Concerning one of them he wrote, 'If he does not show you my seal and signet, do not believe him.' But concerning the other one he wrote, 'Even though he does not show you my seal and signet, believe him.' So in the case of the prophet, he has had to write, 'If a prophet arises among you . . . and gives you a sign or a wonder . . . ' (Deut. 13:1). But here

> [with regard to an elder:] ' . . . according to the instructions which they give you . . . '(Deut. 17:11) [without a sign or a wonder]."

What is important here is the status imputed by the Talmud to "words of scribes," on the one side, and "the elder," on the other. Rabbis knew full well they could not provide many signs or wonders. (As we shall see, that did not prevent them from claiming to do just that.) Their principal validation lay in their role as masters of the law and clerks of the bureaucracy. So they maintained these attainments and tasks enjoyed a status still higher than that accorded to the written Torah and the prophets. We may hardly be surprised, therefore, that in some sayings sages regarded study of Torah as more important than acts of loving-kindness or other sorts of ethical actions. The master of Torah was then irreplaceable.

Y. Hagigah 1:7.IV.

    A.   When R. Judah would see a deceased person or a bride being praised, he would set his eyes on the disciples and say, "Deeds come before learning. [The students should go after the crowd to praise the dead or the bride, for doing so is a religious duty.]"

    B.   They voted in the upper room of the house of Aris: "Learning comes before deeds."

    C.   R. Abbahu was in Caesarea. He sent R. Haninah, his son, to study Torah in Tiberias. They sent and told him, "He is doing deeds of kindness [burying the dead] there [and not studying]."

    D.   He sent and wrote to him, "Is it because there are no graves in Caesarea that I sent you to Tiberias [to go around burying people]? And they have in fact taken a vote in the upper room of the house of Aris in Lud: 'Studying Torah takes precedence over deeds.'"

    E.   Rabbis of Caesarea say, "That which you say applies to a case in which there is someone else who can do the deeds which are required. But if there is no one else available to do the required deeds, then doing the religious deed takes precedence over study of Torah."

    F.   Once R. Hiyya, R. Yosa, R. Ammi were late in coming to see R. Eleazar. He said to them, "Where were you today?"

    G.   They said to him, "We had to do a religious duty."

    H.   He said to them, "And were there no others available to do it?"

    I.   They said to him, "He was an alien in the country, and had no one else to bury him, [his relatives being overseas]."

The issue of the relative importance of good deeds over studying Torah was not a matter of pure theory. Concrete deeds were involved, since a disciple who went off to bury a corpse could not then spend the time reciting his sentences of the Mishnah. Only special circumstances could justify a sage's doing what less important folk could be relied upon to carry out. It must follow that we deal not with ephemeral sayings about the relative merit of one thing over something else, but with declarations of norms. These declarations take us into the center of the Talmud's system and show us, in progression, how from the hope for messianic salvation, realized in Torah, the system moves on to the centrality of learning in Torah and the critical importance of the rabbi in the salvific process.

Y. Berakhot 2:7 [Zahavy].
When R. Simon bar Zebid died, R. Ilia came up and in regard to him expounded as follows, "Four things are essential for the world. But if they are lost they can be replaced [as we see in the following verse]. 'Surely there is a mine for silver, and a place for gold which they refine. Iron is taken out of the earth, and copper is smelted from the ore (Job 28:1–2).' If these are lost they can be replaced.

"But if a disciple of the sages dies who shall bring us his replacement? Who shall bring us his exchange? 'But where shall wisdom be found and where is the place of understanding?' (Job 28:12) It is hid from the eyes of all living (Job 28:21).'"

The Sage as Torah

The sage held in his hand the power to bring salvation to Israel. Torah as he taught it was the source of Israel's salvation. The supernatural power imputed to him even now was a foretaste of what would come when all Israel conformed to the Torah as the sage taught it. So, as I have insisted, tales of the supernatural or magical power of the rabbi have to be read in the larger setting of the salvific process posited by the Talmud's framers. What was the theory behind the identification of rabbinical supernatural power or magical power with Israel's ultimate, historical redemption and not merely with immediate and personal salvation?

It was an axiom of all forms of Judaism that, because Israel had sinned, it was punished by being given over into the hands of earthly empires; when it atoned, it was, and again would be, removed from their power. The means of atonement, reconciliation with God, were specified elsewhere as study of Torah, practice of commandments, and doing good deeds. Why so? The answer is distinctive to the matrix of our Talmud: When Jews in general had mastered Torah, they would become rabbis, just as some now had become rabbis, saints, or holy men. When all Jews had become rabbis, they would no longer lie within the power of the nations, that is, of history. Then the Messiah would come. Redemption then depended upon all Israel's accepting the yoke of the Torah. Why so? Because at that point all Israel would attain a full and complete embodiment of Torah, revelation. Thus conforming to God's will and replicating Heaven, Israel on earth, as a righteous, holy community, would exercise the supernatural power of Torah. They would be able as a whole to do what some few saintly rabbis now could do. With access to supernatural power, redemption would naturally follow.

As I have stressed, the theory of salvation focused upon Torah addressed the circumstance of the individual as much as of the nation. This was possible because the same factor had caused the condition of both, namely sin. Not doing the will of God led to the fall of Israel, the destruction of the Temple. Disobediance to the will of God, that is, sin, is what causes people to suffer and die. The angel of death has power, specifically, over those not engaged in the study of Torah and performing of commandments.

That view is expressed in stories indicating the belief that while a sage is repeating Torah sayings, the angel of death cannot approach him.

Y. Moed Qatan 3:5.XXI.

> F.   [Proving that while one is studying Torah, the angel of death cannot touch a person, the following is told:] A disciple of R. Hisda fell sick. He sent two disciples to him, so that they would repeat Mishnah-traditions with him. [The angel of death] turned himself before them into the figure of a snake, and they stopped repeating traditions, and [the sick man] died.
>
> G.   A disciple of Bar Pedaiah fell ill. He sent to him two disciples to repeat Mishnah-traditions with him. [The angel of death] turned himself before them into a kind of star, and they stopped repeating Mishnah-traditions, and he died.

Repeating Mishnah traditions thus warded off death. It is hardly surprising that stories were told about wonders associated with the deaths of various rabbis. These validated the claim of supernatural power imputed to the rabbis. A repertoire of such stories includes two sorts. First, there is a list of supernatural occurrences accompanying sages' deaths, as in the following.

Y. Abodah Zarah 3:1.II.

> A.   When R. Aha died, a star appeared at noon.
> B.   When R. Hanah died, the statues bowed down.
> C.   When R. Yohanan died, the icons bowed down.

D. They said that [this was to indicate] there were no icons like him [so beautiful as Yohanan himself].

E. When R. Hanina of Bet Hauran died, the Sea of Tiberias split open.

F. They said that [this was to commemorate the miracle that took place] when he went up to intercalate the year, and the sea split open before him.

G. When R. Hoshaiah died, the palm of Tiberias fell down.

H. When R. Isaac b. Elisheb died, seventy [infirm] thresholds of houses in Galilee were shaken down.

I. They said that [this was to commemorate the fact that] they [were shaky and] had depended on his merit [for the miracle that permitted them to continue to stand].

J. When R. Samuel bar R. Isaac died, cedars of the land of Israel were uprooted.

K. They said that [this was to take note of the fact that] he would take branch [of a cedar] and [dance, so] praising a bride [at her wedding, and thereby giving her happiness].

L. The rabbis would ridicule them [for lowering himself by doing so]. Said to them R. Zeira, "Leave him be. Does the old man not know what he is doing?"

M. When he died, a flame came forth from heaven and intervened between his bier and the congregation. For three hours there were voices and thunderings in the world: "Come and see what a sprig of cedar has done for this old man!"

N. [Further] an echo came forth and said, "Woe that Samuel b. R. R. Isaac has died, the doer of merciful deeds."

O. When R. Yosa bar Halputa died, the gutters ran with blood in Laodicea.

P. They said [that the reason was] that he had given his life for the rite of circumcision.

Q. When R. Abbahu died, the pillars of Caesarea wept.

R. The [gentiles] said [that the reason was] that [the pillars] were celebrating. The Israelites said to them, "And do those who are distant [such as yourselves] know why those who are near [we ourselves] are raising a cry?"

Y. Abodah Zarah 3:1.II.

BB. One of the members of the patriarchate died, and the [burial] cave folded over [and received the bier], so endangering the lives [of those who had come to bury him]. R. Yosé went up and took leave [of the deceased], saying "Happy is a man who has left this world in peace."

CC. When R. Yosa died, the castle of Tiberias collapsed, and mem-

bers of the patriarchate were rejoicing. R. Zeira said to them,
"There is no similarity [between this case and the miracle described at BB]. The peoples' lives were endangered, here no
one's life was endangered. In that case, no pagan worship
was removed, while here, an idol was uprooted [so, consequently, the event described in BB was not a miracle, while
the event described here was a miracle and a sign of divine
favor]."

What is important in the foregoing anthology is the linkage between the holy
deeds of the sage and the miracles done at their demise. The sages' merit,
attained through study of Torah or through acts of saintliness and humility
(despite mastery of Torah), was demonstrated for all to see. So the sage was
not merely a master of Torah. But his mastery of Torah laid the foundations
for all the other things he was.

Second, specific miracles, as distinct from natural wonders, were related
with regard to the death of the Patriarch.

Y. Ketubot 12:3.IV.

    E.   R. Nathan in the name of R. Mana: "There were miracles done
that day. It was the eve of the Sabbath, and all the villagers
assembled to make a lamentation for him. They put down the
bier eighteen times en route to burial to mourn him, and they
accompanied him down to Bet Shearim. The daylight was
protracted until each one of them had reached his home [in
time for the Sabbath] and had time to fill up a jug of water
and light the Sabbath lamp. When the sun set, the cock
crowed, and the people began to be troubled, saying, 'Perhaps we have violated the Sabbath.'

    F.   "But an echo came to them, 'Whoever did not refrain from
participation in the lamentations for Rabbi may be given the
good news that he is going to enjoy a portion in the world to
come

    G.   "'except for the launderer [who used to come to Rabbi day by
day, but did not bother to participate in his funeral].' When
he heard this, he went up to the roof and threw himself down
and died. Then an echo went forth and said, 'Even the laun-
dryman [will enjoy the life of the world to come].'"

Y. Ketubot 12:3.VII.

    J.   When R. Huna, the exilarch, died, they brought his bones up
here. They said, "If we are going to bury him properly, let us
place him near R. Hiyya, because he comes from there."

    K.   They said, "Who is worthy of placing him there?"

L. Said to them R. Haggai, "I shall go up and place him there."

M. They said to him, "You are looking for an excuse, for you are an old man, so you want to go up there and die and be buried there next to Hiyya."

N. He said to them, "Tie a rope to my feet, and if I delay there too long you can drag me out."

O. He went in and found three biers.

P. [He heard,] "Judah, my son, is after you, and no one else. Hezekiah, my son, is after you, and no one else. Joseph, son of Israel, and no one else."

Q. He raised his eyes and looked. One said to him, "Lower your face."

R. Said R. Hiyya the Elder, "Judah, my son, make room for R. Huna."

S. He made a place for him, but [Huna] did not accept being buried [next to Hiyya the Elder, out of modesty].

T. [Haggai] said, "Just as [out of modesty] he did not accept being buried next to him, so may his seed never die out."

U. R. Haggai left that place at the age of eighty years, and they doubled the number of his years, [so that he lived another eighty years].

It is hardly in the context only of death scenes that miracles were imputed to rabbis. Their power was compared to that of other wonder-workers. Rabbis were shown more effective than other magicians, specifically in those very same settings in which, all parties conceded, other wonder-workers, as much as rabbis, were able to perform magical deeds. What is important in the following is the fact that in a direct contest between a rabbi and another sort of magician, an Israelite heretic, the rabbi was shown to enjoy superior magical power.

Y. Sanhedrin 7:12.III.

A. When R. Eleazar, R. Joshua, and R. Aqiba went in to bathe in the baths of Tiberias, a *min* saw them. He said what he said, and the arched chamber in the bath [where idolatrous statues were put up] held them fast, [so that they could not move].

B. Said R. Eleazar to R. Joshua, "Now Joshua b. Haninah, see what you can do."

C. When that *min* tried to leave, R. Joshua said what he said, and the doorway of the bath seized and held the *min* firm, so that whoever went in had to give him a knock [to push by], and whoever went out had to give him a knock [to push by].

D. He said to them, "Undo whatever you have done [to let me go]."

E. They said to him, "Release us, and we shall release you."

F. They released one another.

G. Once they got outside, said R. Joshua to that *min*, "Lo, you have learned [from us whatever you are going to learn]."

H. He said, "Let's go down to the sea."

I. When they got down to the sea, that *min* said whatever it was that he said, and the sea split open.

J. He said to them, "Now is this not what Moses, your rabbi, did at the sea?"

K. They said to him, "Do you not concede to us that Moses, our rabbi, walked through it?"

L. He said to them, "Yes."

M. They said to him, "Then walk through it."

N. He walked through it.

O. R. Joshua instructed the ruler of the sea, who swallowed him up.

IV. A. When R. Eliezer, R. Joshua, and Rabban Gamaliel went up to Rome, they came to a certain place and found children making little piles [of dirt]. They said, "Children of the Land of Israel make this sort of thing, and they say, 'This is heave offering,' and 'That is tithe.' It's likely that there are Jews here."

B. They came into one place and were received there.

C. When they sat down to eat, [they noticed] that each dish which they brought into them would first be brought into a small room, and then would be brought to them, and they wondered whether they might be eating sacrifices offered to the dead. [That is, before the food was brought to them, it was brought into a small chamber, in which, they suspected, sacrifices were taken from each dish and offered to an idol.]

D. They said to [the host], "What is your purpose, in the fact that, as to every dish which you bring before us, if you do not bring it first into a small room, you do not bring it in to us?"

E. He said to them, "I have a very old father, and he has made a decree for himself that he will never go out of that small room until he will see the sages of Israel."

F. They said to him, "Go and tell him, 'Come out here to them, for they are here.'"

G. He came out to them.

H. They said to him, "Why do you do this?"

I. He said to them, "Pray for my son, for he has not produced a child."

J. Said R. Eliezer to R. Joshua, "Now, Joshua b. Hananiah, let us see what you will do."

K. He said to them, "Bring me flax seeds," and they brought him flax seeds.

L. He appeared to sow the seed on the table; he appeared to scatter the seed; he appeared to bring the seed up; he appeared to take hold of it, until he drew up a woman, holding on to her tresses.

M. He said to her, "Release whatever [magic] you have done [to this man]."

N. She said to him, "I am not going to release [my spell]."

O. He said to her, "If you don't do it, I shall publicize your [magical secrets]."

P. She said to him, "I cannot do it, for [the magical materials] have been cast into the sea."

Q. R. Joshua made a decree that the sea release [the magical materials] and they came up.

R. They prayed for [the host], and he had the merit of begetting a son, R. Judah b. Bathera.

S. They said, "If we came up here only for the purpose of begetting that righteous man, it would have been enough for us."

T. Said R. Joshua b. Haniniah, "I can take cucumbers and pumpkins and turn them into rams and hosts of rams, and they will produce still more."

These long extracts leave no doubt that the Talmud imputed to Israel's sages precisely the powers generally assigned to magicians. There was no important distinction between the one and the other. We see no claim that the superior merit of the rabbi, based on his knowledge of Torah, accounted for his remarkable magical power. On the contrary, the sage did precisely what the magician did, only he did it better. When the magician then pretended to do what Moses had done, it was his end. The story about Joshua's magic in Rome is similar, in its explicit reference to sympathetic magic, K–L. The result was the discovery that the childless man had been subject to a spell. There can be no doubt that distinctions between magic and supernatural power meant nothing to the Talmud's storytellers. The clerks were not merely holy men; they were a particular kind of holy men.

In consequence of the belief that rabbis had magical powers, it was quite natural to impute to rabbis the ability both to bless those who favored them and to curse those who did not. As to the latter:

Y. Sanhedrin 10:2.VII.

II. Said R. Yosé, "This is in line with what the proverb says: A person has to scruple about the curse of a great master, even if it was for nought."

Y. Abodah Zarah 2:2.IV.

I. A snake bit Eleazar b. Dama. He came to Jacob of Kefar Sama for healing. Said to [Ben Dama] R. Ishmael, "You have no right to do so, Ben Dama."

J.   He said to him, "I shall bring proof that it is permitted for him
     to heal me."·

K.   But he did not suffice to bring proof before he dropped dead.

L.   Said to him R. Ishmael, "Happy are you, O Ben Dama, for you
     left this world in peace and did not break through the fence
     of the sages, and so in dying you have carried out that which
     has been said: 'A serpent will bite him who breaks through a
     wall' (Qoh. 10:8)."

So much for a curse. As to the power of rabbis to impart a blessing, it was
represented in a more subtle way.

It was not merely that rabbis themselves could do magical deeds. Heaven
itself would intervene in favor of people who did good to rabbis, even though
rabbis, for their part, did nothing. The next story shows how magic was done
in behalf of a man and his wife who gave generous support to rabbis, even
though the beneficiaries themselves are not represented as participating in the
miracle done for their friend.

Y. Horayot 3:4.III.

A.   R. Eliezer, R. Joshua, R. Aqiba went up to Holat Antokhiya in
     a connection with collecting funds for sages.

B.   Now there was a certain man there, by the name of Abba Judah.
     He would fulfill the commandment [of supporting the sages]
     in a liberal spirit. One time he lost all his money, and he saw
     our rabbis and despaired [of helping them]. He went home,
     and his face was filled with suffering.

C.   His wife said to him, "Why is your face filled with suffering?"

D.   He said to her, "Our rabbis are here, and I simply do not know
     what I can do for them."

E.   His wife, who was even more righteous than he, said to him,
     "You have a single field left. Go and sell half of it and give
     the proceeds to them . . ."

F.   He went and did just that. He came to our rabbis, and he gave
     them the proceeds.

G.   Our rabbis prayed in his behalf. They said to him, "Abba Judah,
     may the Holy One, blessed be He, make up all the things you
     lack."

H.   When they went their way, he went down to plough the half-field
     that remained in his possession. Now while he was ploughing
     in the half-field that remained to him, his cow fell and broke
     a leg. He went down to bring her up, and the Holy One,
     blessed be He, opened his eyes, and he found a jewel. He
     said, "It was for my own good that my cow broke its leg."

I. Now when our rabbis returned, they asked about him. They said, "How are things with Abba Judah?"

J. People replied, "Who can [even] gaze upon the face of Abba Judah—Abba Judah of the oxen! Abba Judah of the camels! Abba Judah of the asses!" So Abba Judah had returned to his former wealth.

K. Now he came to our rabbis and asked after their welfare.

L. They said to him, "How is Abba Judah doing?"

M. He said to them, "Your prayer in my behalf has yielded fruit and more fruit." They said to him, "Even though to begin with other people gave more than you did, you were the one whom we wrote down at the top of the register."

N. They took and seated him with themselves, and they pronounced upon him the following Scriptural verse: "A man's gift makes room for him and brings him before great men" (Prov. 18:16).

The story takes for granted that the one whose name is at the top of the rabbis' register of donors is the most blessed on the list. Its emphasis upon the sure reward for those who contribute to the support of masters and their disciples only restates the point of that minor detail. Those who disobey rabbis are cursed and die; those who give them money are blessed and get rich. This same point is made explicit in the following.

Y. Sotah 7:4.IV.

F. R. Aha in the name of R. Tanhum b. R. Hiyya: "If one has learned, taught, kept, and carried out [the Torah], and has ample means in his possession to strengthen the Torah and has not done so, lo, such a one still is in the category of those who are cursed." [The meaning of "strengthen" here is to support the masters of the Torah.]

G. R. Jeremiah in the name of R. Hiyya bar Ba, "[If] one did not learn, teach, keep, and carry out [the teachings of the Torah], and did not have ample means to strengthen [the masters of the Torah] [but nonetheless did strengthen them], lo, such a one falls into the category of those who are blessed."

H. And R. Hannah, R. Jeremiah in the name of R. Hiyya: "The Holy One, blessed be he, is going to prepare a protection for those who carry out religious duties [of support for masters of Torah] through the protection afforded to the masters of Torah [themselves].

I. "What is the Scriptural basis for that statement? 'For the protection of wisdom is like the protection of money'" (Qoh. 7:12).

J.   "And it says, '[The Torah] is a tree of life to those who grasp it; those who hold it fast are called happy'" (Prov. 3:18).

Thus far we have shown that the Talmud maintains the sage exercised magical-supernatural powers and could reward his friends and punish his enemies. We have now to show that the supernatural status accorded to the person of the sage endowed his deeds with normative, therefore revelatory power. What the sage did had the status of law; the sage was the model of the law, thus the human embodiment of the Torah. That mundane view has to be joined to the otherworldly notion, just now illustrated, that the sage was a holy man. For what made the sage distinctive was his combination of this-worldly authority and power and otherworldly influence. The clerk in the court and the holy man on the rooftop in the Talmud's view were one and the same. Given the fundamental point of insistence of the Talmud, that the salvation of Israel will derive from keeping the law, the Talmud had no choice but to preserve the tight union between salvation and law, the magical power of the sage and his lawgiving authority. We turn now to spell out this definitive trait of the system as a whole, as it is exemplified in the Yerushalmi. To state matters simply: If the sage exercised supernatural power as a kind of living Torah, his very deeds served to reveal law, as much as his word expressed revelation.

The capacity of the sage himself to participate in the process of revelation is illustrated in two types of materials. First of all, tales told about rabbis' behavior on specific occasions immediately are translated into rules for the entire community to keep. Accordingly, he was a source not merely of good example but of prescriptive law.

Y. Abodah Zarah 5:4:III.

X.   R. Aha went to Emmaus, and he ate dumpling [prepared by Samaritans].

Y.   R. Jeremiah ate leavened bread prepared by them.

Z.   R. Hezekiah ate their locusts prepared by them.

AA. R. Abbahu prohibited Israelite use of wine prepared by them.

These reports of what rabbis had done enjoyed the same authority, as statements of the law on eating what Samaritans cooked, as did citations of traditions in the names of the great authorities of old or of the day. What someone did served as a norm, if the person was a sage of sufficient standing.

Far more common in the Talmud are instances in which the deed of a rabbi is adduced as an authoritative precedent for the law under discussion. It was everywhere taken for granted that what a rabbi did, he did because of his mastery of the law. Even though a formulation of the law was not in hand, a tale about what a rabbi actually did constituted adequate evidence on how to formulate the law itself. So from the practice of an authority, a law might be framed quite independent of the person of the sage. The sage then functioned as a lawgiver, like Moses. Among many instances of that mode of generating law are the following.

Y. Abodah Zarah 3:11.II.

 A. Gamaliel Zuga was walking along, leaning on the shoulder of R. Simeon b. Laqish. They came across an image.

 B. He said to him, "What is the law as to passing before it?"

 C. He said to him, "Pass before it, but close [your] eyes."

 D. R. Isaac was walking along, leaning on the shoulder of R. Yohanan. They came across an idol before the council building.

 E. He said to him, "What is the law as to passing before it?"

 F. He said to him, "Pass before it, but close [your] eyes."

 G. R. Jacob bar Idi was walking along, leaning upon R. Joshua b. Levi. They came across a procession in which an idol was carried. He said to him, "Nahum, the most holy man, passed before this idol, and will you not pass by it? Pass before it but close your eyes."

Y. Abodah Zarah 2:2.III.

 FF. R. Aha had chills and fever. [They brought him] a medicinal drink prepared from the phallus of Dionysian revelers. But he would not drink it. They brought it to R. Jonah, and he did drink it. Said R. Mana, "Now if R. Jonah, the patriarch, had known what it was, he would never have drunk it."

 GG. Said R. Huna, "That is to say, 'They do not accept healing from something that derives from an act of fornication.'"

What is important is GG, the restatement of the story as a law. The example of a rabbi served to teach how one should live a truly holy life. The requirements went far beyond the measure of the law, extending to refraining from deeds of a most commonplace sort. The example of rabbinical virtue, moreover, was adduced explicitly to account for the supernatural or magical power of a rabbi. There was no doubt, in people's imagination, therefore, that the reason rabbis could do the amazing things people said they did was that they embodied the law and exercised its supernatural or magical power. This is stated quite openly in what follows.

Y. Taanit 3:11.IV.

 C. There was a house that was about to collapse over there [in Babylonia], and Rab set one of his disciples in the house, until they had cleared out everything from the house. When the disciple left the house, the house collapsed.

D. And there are those who say that it was R. Adda bar Ahwah.

E. Sages sent and said to him, "What sort of good deeds are to your credit [that you have that much merit]?"

F. He said to them, "In my whole life no man ever got to the synagogue in the morning before I did. I never left anybody there when I went out. I never walked four cubits without speaking words of Torah. Nor did I ever mention teachings of Torah in an inappropriate setting. I never laid out a bed and slept for a regular period of time. I never took great strides among the associates. I never called my fellow by a nickname. I never rejoiced in the embarrassment of my fellow. I never cursed my fellow when I was lying by myself in bed. I never walked over in the marketplace to someone who owed me money.

G. "In my entire life I never lost my temper in my household."

H. This was meant to carry out that which is stated as follows: "I will give heed to the way that is blameless. Oh when wilt thou come to me? I will walk with integrity of heart within my house" (Ps. 101:2).

The correlation between learning and teaching, on the one side, and supernatural power or recognition, on the other, is explicit in the following.

Y. Ketubot 12:3.VII.

A. R. Yosa fasted eighty fasts in order to see R. Hiyya the Elder [in a dream]. He finally saw him, and his hands trembled and his eyes grew dim.

B. Now if you say that R. Yosa was an unimportant man, [and so was unworthy of such a vision, that is not the case]. For a weaver came before R. Yohanan. He said to him, "I saw in my dream that the heaven fell, and one of your disciples was holding it up."

C. He said to him, "Will you know him [when you see him]?"

D. He said to him, "When I see him, I shall know him." Then all of his disciples passed before him, and he recognized R. Yosa.

E. R. Simeon b. Laqish fasted three hundred fasts in order to have a vision of R. Hiyya the Elder, but he did not see him.

F. Finally he began to be distressed about the matter. He said, "Did he labor in learning of Torah more than I?"

G. They said to him, "He brought Torah to the people of Israel to a greater extent than you have, and not only so, but he even went into exile [to teach on a wider front]."

H. He said to them, "And did I not go into exile too?"

    I.   They said to him, "You went into exile only to learn, but he went into exile to teach others."

This story shows that the storyteller regarded as a fact of life the correlation between mastery of Torah sayings and supernatural power—visions of the deceased, in this case. That is why Simeon b. Laqish complained, E–F, that he had learned as much Torah as the other, and so had every right to be able to conjure the dead. The greater supernatural power of the other then was explained in terms of the latter's superior service to "Torah." It seems to me pointless to distinguish supernatural power from magic. The upshot is that the sage was made a magician by Torah learning and could save Israel through Torah, source of the most powerful magic of all.

The Sage beyond the Torah

While all Jews said prayers and carried out the requirements of Israel's holy way of life, by definition only sages "studied Torah," for that act is what distinguished the sage from everybody else. Accordingly, mastery of Torah separated the sage from common Jews and imposed upon them special responsibilities to carry out requirements beyond the minimal ones of the law. The sage had to do more than others, forego advantages accruing in the normal course of events to ordinary folk. At the same time the sage also enjoyed respect beyond the requirements of the courtesy ordinarily to be paid by one person to another. As a holy and righteous man, he was to be treated with dignity congruent to his standing. He made sure that he was, and he was. It follows that, just as the sage transcended the limits of the law, so in his stories he enjoyed far more than routine standing in the community. In these respects we see how the Talmud reports the earthly effects of the mythic and heightened standing imputed to the sage as a supernatural figure.

    Since the reason the sage transcended the limits of the law was that he was a master of Torah, it must follow, in the sages' view, knowledge and study of Torah were more important than any other form of service to God, including, specifically, praying. We already have observed instances of that view. It would further follow that people owed support for sages' labor more, even, than for building synagogues. One's time should be spent in study, in preference to engaging in trade. These are the points of the following two statements.

Y. Sheqalim 5:4.II.
    A.   R. Hama bar Haninah and R. Hoshaia the Elder were strolling in the synagogues in Lud. Said R. Hama bar Haninah to R. Hoshaia, "How much money did my forefathers invest here [in building these synagogues]!"

B.   He said to him, "How many lives did your forefathers invest here! Were there not people who were laboring in Torah [who needed the money more]?"

C.   R. Abun made the gates of the great hall [of study]. R. Mana came to him. He said to him, "See what I have made!"

D.   He said to him, "'For Israel has forgotten his Maker and built palaces'! (Hos. 8:14). Were there no people laboring in Torah [who needed the money more]?"

Y. Sotah 9:13.VI.

C.   A certain rabbi would teach Scripture to his brother in Tyre, and when they came and called him to do business, he would say, "I am not going to take away from my fixed time to study. If the profit is going to come to me, let it come in due course [after my fixed time for study has ended]."

So synagogue worship took second place, as (obviously) did profit in business, behind Torah learning. Instances of the sort of exemplary behavior demanded of the sage included attention to the perfect objectivity of the sage as a judge. No advantage whatsoever was to be gained through the sage's this-worldly power. In applying the law to himself with greater rigor than to third parties, the sage thus demonstrated that he accepted demands beyond the minimal measure of the law. In so doing, of course, he once more demonstrated his status as coequal with the Torah, his special capacity, because of what he knew, to do more for the sake of Heaven than was even demanded in the strict law. These two stories illustrate how the saints transcended the Torah observance of ordinary people by imposing upon themselves a higher requirement.

Y. Baba Batra 2:13.I.

A.   R. Jonathan was an exemplary judge. He had as a neighbor an Aramaean [pagan], who lived cheek by jowl in the field and in the village. Now R. Jonathan had a tree planted [so that it overshadowed the property] of the Aramaean. A case along the lines [of the situation prevailing for Jonathan and his Aramaean neighbor] came before [Jonathan]. He said to them, "Go and come back tomorrow."

B.   Now the Aramean thought to himself, "It is on my account that he made no ruling. Tomorrow I shall go and chop off the branch which overshadows my property on my own, and I shall see how he decides the other case. If he judges other people but does not apply the judgment to himself, he is not a decent person."

C.   At evening R. Jonathan sent instructions to his carpenter, say-
      ing, "Go, cut off the part of the tree which is overshadowing
      the Aramaean's land."

D.   In the morning, the litigant came before R. Jonathan. He said to
      him, "Go, cut the branch which is overhanging into your
      land."

E.   The Aramaean then said to him, "And what is the law about your
      branches?"

F.   He said to him, "Go and see how my branches are treated in your
      property [for they already had been cut off]."

G.   He went out and saw the pruning which had taken place, and he
      said, "Blessed be the God of the Jews."

H.   A certain woman [having a case before Jonathan] brought him a
      present of figs. He said to her, "By your leave, if you
      brought them in uncovered, bring them out uncovered, and if
      you brought them in covered up, bring them out covered up,
      so that people won't say that you brought in money when in
      fact you brought a gift of figs [which in any case I shall not
      accept]."

I.   R. Haninah came to visit R. Jonathan in his garden and he [that
      is, Jonathan] brought him figs to eat. When he went out, he
      saw that [elsewhere in the garden] he had white Bath Sheba
      figs [that is, figs of a far higher quality]. He said to him,
      "Now why did you not feed me some of these [which are of
      better quality]?"

J.   He said to him, "They are my son's."

K.   R. Haninah scrupled about not taking them without permission
      from the son and so committing an act of theft against him.

To the framers of the Talmud, the notion of deeds beyond the limits of the law
proved far more subtle than merely the requirement to apply the law scru-
pulously. A more profound notion, with which rabbis identified, was contained in stories of a different order altogether. In these stories, not told about
rabbis, a single remarkable deed, exemplary for its deep humanity, sufficed
to win for an ordinary person the supernatural favor enjoyed by some rabbis.
Even though a man was degraded, one action sufficed to win for him that
heavenly glory to which rabbis in general aspired. The rabbinical storyteller
identifies with this lesson. In the third story, a different form of unusually
reflective behavior again is adduced to exemplify the same notion, that the
law states a minimum, but the saintly person explores the outer limits of true
piety. In all three instances the point is that the deeds of the heroes of the story
make them worthy of having their prayers answered, that is, deeds beyond
the limits of the law transform the hero into a holy man just like a sage.

Y. Taanit 1:4.I.

F. A certain man came before one of the relatives of R. Yannai. He said to him, "Rabbi, attain merit through me [by giving me charity]."

G. He said to him, "And didn't your father leave you money?"

H. He said to him, "No."

I. He said to him, "Go and collect what your father left in deposit with others."

J. He said to him, "I have heard concerning property my father deposited with others that it was gained by violence [so I don't want it]."

K. He said to him, "You are worthy of praying and having your prayers answered."

L. A certain ass driver appeared before the rabbis [in a dream] and prayed, and rain came. The rabbis sent and brought him and said to him, "What is your trade?"

M. He said to them, "I am an ass driver."

N. They said to him, "And how do you conduct your business?"

O. He said to them, "One time I rented my ass to a certain woman, and she was weeping on the way, and I said to her, 'What's with you?' and she said to me, 'The husband of that woman [me] is in prison [for debt], and I wanted to see what I can do to free him.' So I sold my ass and I gave her the proceeds, and I said to her, 'Here is your money, free your husband, but do not sin [by becoming a prostitute to raise the necessary funds].'"

P. They said to him, "You are worthy of praying and having your prayers answered."

Q. In a dream of R. Abbahu, Mr. Pentakaka ["Five sins"] appeared, who prayed that rain would come, and it rained. R. Abbahu sent and summoned him. He said to him, "What is your trade?"

R. He said to him, "Five sins does that man [I] do every day, hiring whores, cleaning up the theater, bringing home their garments for washing, dancing, and performing before them."

S. He said to him, "And what sort of decent thing have you ever done?"

T. He said to him, "One day that man [I] was cleaning the theater, and a woman came and stood behind a pillar and cried. I said to her, 'What's with you?' And she said to me, 'That woman's [my] husband is in prison, and I wanted to see what I can do to free him,' so I sold my bed and cover, and I gave the proceeds to her. I said to her, 'Here is your money, free your husband, but do not sin.'"

U. He said to him, "You are worthy of praying and having your prayers answered."

V. A pious man from Kefar Imi appeared [in a dream] to the rabbis. He prayed for rain and it rained. The rabbis went up to him. His householders told them that he was sitting on a hill. They went out to him, saying to him, "Greetings," but he did not answer them.

W. He was sitting and eating, and he did not say to them, "You break bread too."

X. When he went back home, he made a bundle of faggots and put his cloak on top of the bundle [instead of on his shoulder].

Y. When he came home, he said to his household [wife], "These rabbis are here [because] they want me to pray for rain. If I pray and it rains, it is a disgrace for them, and if not, it is a profanation of the Name of Heaven. But come, you and I will go up [to the roof] and pray. If it rains, we shall tell them, 'We are not worthy to pray and have our prayers answered.'"

Z. They went up and prayed and it rained.

AA. They came down to them [and asked], "Why have the rabbis troubled themselves to come here today?"

BB. They said to him, "We wanted you to pray so that it would rain."

CC. He said to them, "Now do you really need my prayers? Heaven already has done its miracle."

DD. They said to him, "Why, when you were on the hill, did we say hello to you, and you did not reply?"

EE. He said to them, "I was then doing my job. Should I then interrupt my concentration [on my work]?"

FF. They said to him, "And why, when you sat down to eat, did you not say to us 'You break bread too'?"

GG. He said to them, "Because I had only my small ration of bread. Why would I have invited you to eat by way of mere flattery [when I knew I could not give you anything at all]?"

HH. They said to him, "And why when you came to go down, did you put your cloak on top of the bundle?"

II. He said to them, "Because the cloak was not mine. It was borrowed for use at prayer. I did not want to tear it."

JJ. They said to him, "And why, when you were on the hill, did your wife wear dirty clothes, but when you came down from the mountain, did she put on clean clothes?"

KK. He said to them, "When I was on the hill, she put on dirty clothes, so that no one would gaze at her. But when I came home from the hill, she put on clean clothes, so that I would not gaze on any other woman."

LL.   They said to him, "It is well that you pray and have your prayers answered."

What is striking in these stories is their contradiction of the generality of statements we have reviewed about the lifelong adherence to the doing of religious duties and study of Torah. Yet a second glance shows us how in these tales the system provides remissions to reenforce its integrity. For those who gain their world to come in a single stunning act are at the extremes of society, people of no standing at all. To them roads are open that are closed to ordinary folk, living out their lives of substance in the respectable community. So the storyteller expresses a principal conviction of the Talmud as a whole. The truly saintly man exceeds the minimal requirements of the law. At the same time, in the first two accounts, he presents a dramatic picture of the law's own provision for remission from its rigors.

As noted above, the special position of the sage as supernaturally favored figure also imposed on Israelite society the requirement to accord him special dignity. The disciple of a sage himself had to exemplify what was required by his behavior toward his own master, who taught him Torah. The disciple's acts of respect for the master, devotion to his standing and honor, ongoing concern for his comfort were principal expressions of the respect for Torah upon which the entire system rested. Accordingly, the respect paid to the Torah also was due to the sage, a view quite natural in light of the established identification of sage and Torah. In the context of this kind of Judaism, the act of respect paid to a sage transcended merely social and conventional bounds. What to us may look like sycophancy was understood as a religious deed to which Heaven would respond. What was rightly done to a sage produced a Heavenly blessing, and predictably, what was wrongly done, a curse.

Y. Sheqalim 5:4.I.

U.   The teacher of the son of R. Hoshaiah the Elder was blind, and he was accustomed to eat with him every day. One day he had guests, and he did not come to eat with him in the evening. He came to him, saying to him, "May my master not be angry with me, for I had guests today, and I thought that I would not allow my master's honor to be cheapened today, so I did not eat with my master today."

V.   He said to him, "You have thereby appeased one who is seen but does not see. May the one who sees but is not seen accept your excuse."

W.   He said to him, "Whence did you learn this [saying]?"

X.   He said to him, "From R. Eliezer b. Jacob. For to the town of R. Eliezer b. Jacob a blind man came. R. Eliezer b. Jacob sat below him, so that people would say, 'If it were not that this

man was a great man, R. Eliezer b. Jacob would not have
seated himself lower than he.' They paid the blind man great
honor [and supplied his needs]. The blind man asked, 'Why
thus?' They said to him, 'R. Eliezer b. Jacob sat below you.'

Y. "So the blind man prayed this prayer: 'You have dealt faithfully
with one who is seen but does not see. May he who sees but
is not seen deal faithfully with you.'"

Special courtesy between sage and disciple, in particular, was mutual. The
disciple honored the sage as he honored his father, and the sage treated the
disciple as his son. This mythic transformation of ordinary relationships
found full expression, in particular, in rites of mourning and burial, in which
the disciple was expected to conduct himself just as he would if his father had
died.

Y. Baba Mesia 2:11.I.

G. A certain man started Rab off in his studies, and when Rab heard
that he had died, he tore his garment on his account [as a
sign of mourning, even though Rab had studied with him
only at the elementary phase of his education].

H. R. Yohanan was going up from Tiberias to Sepphoris. He saw
someone coming down from there. He said to him, "What do
you hear in town [in Sepphoris]?"

I. He said to him, "A rabbi has died, and everyone in town is
running about arranging for his burial."

J. R. Yohanan knew that it was R. Hanina. So he sent and brought
his best Sabbath garments and tore them [as a sign of mourn-
ing].

K. Now has it not been taught: Any act of tearing which not done
at the monent of most intense grief is not a valid act of tearing [in mourning]? [It must be spontaneous.]

L. R. Yohanan wanted to do it in a big way, because [Hanina had
been his master, and he honored him.]

M. Nonetheless, we still do not know whether R. Yohanan did it this
way because he had been his master, or because it was simply bad news [that the head of the court had died, and even if
Hanina had not been his master, Yohanan would have be-
haved in the same way].

N. From the following story about R. Hiyya bar Wa in Sepphoris
[we find the answer]. [Hiyya] saw everyone running about.
He said, "Why is everyone running about?"

O. They said to him, "R. Yohanan is in session and expounding
[Torah] in the schoolhouse of R. Benaiah, and everyone is
running to hear him."

P.   [Hiyya, who had been Yohanan's principal master, said,] "Blessed is the All-Merciful, who allowed me to see everyone running to hear [my disciple, Yohanan], while I am yet alive." [This indicates that Yohanan, for his part, had studied principally not with Hanina but with Hiyya, as we shall now see.]

Q.   "Now I have taught him [all] matters of *aggadah,* except for Proverbs and Qohelet."

R.   This indicates that one [must tear his garment in mourning] for each encounter of discipleship [with a teacher, not merely with the principal teacher]. [Consequently, Yohanan is not in accord with Judah. He tore his garments at Hanina's death because of the bad news that the head of the Sephhoris court had died, not because Hanina had been his principal teacher.]

Y. Berakhot 2:7 (Zahavy).

When R. Hiyya bar Adda, the nephew of Bar Qappara died Resh Laqish [accepted condolences] on his account because he [Resh Laqish] had been his teacher. We may say that a person's student is as beloved to him as his son.

The behavior of gentiles, particularly of powerful ones, was invoked to confirm the special respect and dignity owed to the sage as a figure of supernatural importance. Great lords of state were represented as acknowledging the heavenly character of sages. Even sources of power and danger in the natural world, for example, snakes, were supposed to take account of the sage's study of Torah and to protect him on that account.

Y. Berakhot 5:1 (Zahavy).

R. Yohanan was sitting and reciting before a congregation of Babylonians in Sepphoris. An official passed by but Yohanan did not stand before him. The [official's guard] went to strike him. He said to them, "Leave him be! He is absorbed in his Creator's laws."

R. Haninah and R. Joshua b. Levi went before the proconsul of Caesarea. When he saw them he stood up. [His courtiers] said to him, "Why do you stand up for these Jews?" He said to them, "I see in them the faces of angels."

R. Jonah and R. Yosé went before Ursicinus, governor of Antioch. When he saw them he stood up. They said to him, "Why do you stand up for these Jews?" He said to them, "I saw their faces in a vision during a battle and I was victorious."

R. Abin went before the king. When he was leaving, he turned his back [on the king to go]. They sought [on acount of this affront] to execute him. But they saw two bands of fire emanating from his back, and they let him alone. This fulfills that which Scripture says, "And all the peoples of the earth shall see that you are called by the name of the Lord; and they shall be afraid of you" (Deut. 28:10).

R. Simeon b. Yohai taught, "'And all the people of the earth shall see' [*ibid.*], all—even the spirits and even the demons."

R. Yanai and R. Yohanan were walking down the street when they saw one [demon]. It greeted them and said to them, "May your peace be increased." They said, "It even addressed us in friendly terms! It cannot do us any harm!"

Y. Berakhot 9:1 (Zahavy).

R. Phineas [told of] this incident: Rab was coming up from the hot spring of Tiberias. He met some Romans. They asked him, "Who are you?" He said to them, "I am a member of Vespasian's [the governor's] entourage." They let him pass. That night they came to the governor and said to him, "How much longer will you stand up for these Jews?" He said to them, "What do you mean?" They said to him, "We encountered one Jew, asked him who he was, and he said he was a part of your entourage."

He [the governor] said to them, "What did you do for him?" They said to him, "Isn't it enough that we let him alone?"

He said to them, "You acted properly."

[The lesson of this story is:] one who relies on the protection of mere flesh and blood may be saved. How much more so will one who relies on the protection of God [be saved from harm] . . .

Y. Berakhot 5:1 (Zahavy).

R. Yudan b. R. Ishmael was accustomed to becoming deeply absorbed in thoughts of the Torah. His cloak fell off him and a serpent stood guard over it. His students said to him, "Master your cloak has fallen." He said to them, 'Is not this deadly serpent guarding it [that no one steal it]?"

We should not lose sight of the point of these diverse stories. It is that the sage's relationships with gentiles, on the one side, and with nature, on the other, were subject to supernatural intervention. So all things acknowledged the sage's special position in the larger scheme of things. The sage's disciples entered into a nonnatural relationship with him, as if he were their father. This notion is carried to the extreme view that even if one has studied only a trivial part of his education with a sage, when that man dies, the one-time disciple must go into mourning. Gentile officials, likewise, are represented as paying respect to the sage, the ultimate cachet in a subordinated community. It showed that the sage had attained remarkable status in the world. The gentile rulers thereby conceded two things. First, what the sage knew was of the highest consequence. Second, the sage himself was an angelic or supernatural figure. In all of these ways God's favor was shown to the sage.

In the mind of the sage, the community's institutions existed for the benefit of sages and disciples. The special status of the rabbinical estate was to be recognized, in particular, in synagogues. That was not a matter of special role in the rites, as we noted, but involved extraordinary privileges in use of the sacred property. Sages owned the Torah, so they claimed dominion over the synagogue as well. This claim extended far beyond the right of a judge to dispose of communal property.

Y. Megillah 3:3:V.

    A.   R. Joshua b. Levi said, "Synagogues and schoolhouses belong to sages and their disciples."

    B.   R. Hiyya bar Yosé received [guests] in the synagogue [and lodged them there].

    C.   R. Immi instructed the scribes, "If someone comes to you with some slight contact with Torah learning, receive him, his asses, and his belongings."

    D.   R. Berekhiah went to the synagogue in Beisan. He saw someone rinsing his hands and feet in a fountain [in the courtyard of the synagogue]. He said to him, "It is forbidden to you [to do this]."

    E.   The next day the man saw [Berekhiah] washing his hands and feet in the fountain.

    F.   He said to him, "Rabbi, is it permitted to you and forbidden to me?"

    G.   He said to him, "Yes."

    H.   He said to him, "Why?"

    I.   He said to him, "Because this is what R. Joshua b. Levi said: 'Synagogues and schoolhouses belong to sages and their disciples.'"

The extraordinary privileges accruing to sages' special status were material as well as symbolic. Sages in theory should not be paid for their learning. But they could accept a fee in compensation for the time they gave to teaching. In a setting in which people claimed lost property by having to describe what they had lost, sages were exempted from that requirement. Merely saying the property was theirs sufficed; they were assumed to be honest in all respects. Sages could indulge themselves by stretching the law to provide for their own ease and comfort. These three quite disparate elements point to the simple fact that the special standing of sages carried with it this-worldly benefits.

Y. Nedarim 4:3.II.

    A.   It is written, "Behold, I have taught you statutes and ordinances" [Deut. 4:5].

    B.   Just as I do so without pay, so you must do so without pay.

C. Is it possible that the same rule applies to teaching Scripture and translation [cf. M. Ned. 4:3D]?

D. Scripture says, "Statutes and ordinances."

E. Statutes and ordinances must you teach without pay, but you need not teach Scripture and translation without pay.

F. And yet we see that those who teach Mishnah collect their pay.

G. Said R. Judah b. R. Ishmael, "It is a fee for the use of their time [which they cannot utilize to earn a living for themselves] which they collect."

Y. Baba Mesia 2:8.III.

A. R. Judah said, "Disciples of sages do not have to indicate distinguishing characteristics."

Y. Besah 1:7.I.

K. R. Abbahu went down to bathe in the spring of Tiberias, and he would lean on two Goths as his guards. When they started to fall, he helped them up, and that happened twice. They said to him, "What's going on? [Why do you have to lean on us at all?]"

L. He said to them, "I am saving my strength for my old age, [by leaning on you now]."

M. R. Huna did not go down to the meetinghouse [on the festival day, wanting to save his strength, since he did not wish to walk].

N. R. Qatina asked, "And has it not been taught: 'They may carry infirm folk'?"

It should not be supposed that we deal merely with the theory of how sages wished to conduct themselves and to be treated. Some stories indicate that, while meticulous about objectivity in decisions on property, sages were prepared in their courts to use their power to enforce their own demands for dignity and honor. Insulting or offending a sage therefore bore material, not merely spiritual, penalties, as in the following

Y. Ketubot 4:7.IV.

A. R. Simeon b. Laqish in the name of R. Judah bar Haninah: "They voted in Usha in the case of him who insulted a sage [elder] and who hit him that one pays him compensation for the humiliation *in toto* [which is more than the compensation paid for damages to him]."

B. There was a case of someone who insulted a sage and hit him, and he [was required to] pay him compensation for the humiliation *in toto*.

Y. Baba Qamma 8:6.I.

B.   Someone taught in the name of R. Simeon b. Laqish, "He who humiliates a sage pays him the full compensation to be paid for his humiliation."

C.   Someone lost his temper with R. Judah b. Hanina. The case came before R. Simeon b. Laqish. He imposed on him a fine of a *litra* of gold.

We need hardly remind ourselves that sages prided themselves on the honesty and objectivity of their courts. They would not make use of their position for private gain. But they most certainly used their power to exact the high degree of respect they thought their due.

A socially sanctioned penalty imposed by sages on their own involved ostracism or excommunication. Under these circumstances a sage could declare someone who had displeased him to be beyond the pale of the community. As the arbiter of society, the sage thus invoked a powerful penalty indeed. How a decree of ostracism worked in the setting of ordinary life, as distinct from the context of formal court action, is illustrated in the following.

Y. Moed Qatan 3:1.X.

G.   A serving woman who worked for Bar Pata was passing by a synagogue, and she saw the teacher hit a child more than was necessary. She said to him, "That man [you] should be in excommunication." He came and asked R. Aha [how to deal with what she had said]. He said to him, "You must take account of yourself [in the light of what she said]."

H.   That is to say, He who does something which is improper is to be excommunicated.

I.   R. Simeon b. Laqish was guarding figs in a garden. Thieves came and stole them by night. In the end he found out who they were. He said to them, "Let them be excommunicated." They said to him, "Let that man [you] be subject to a decree of excommunication."

J.   He paid attention to what they had said. He said, "They owe me money, but did they owe me their life [that I put them into excommunication]? [Surely not. What I did was wrong.]"

K.   He went and ran after them. He said to them, "Release me [from the decree of excommunication]."

L.   They said to him, "Release us, and we shall release you."

M.   That is to say, He who excommunicates him who should not be subject to excommunication—his act of excommunication still is valid.

The foregoing picture is how, in general, sages wished to see things. But the Talmud preserves a picture at sharp variance with the fantasy we have outlined. The following story tells us that, beyond the realm of disciples and sages, ordinary Israelites had their own view of matters and did not hesitate to carry out their wishes, even in the face of the sages' displeasure.

Y. Megillah 4:4.III.

A. To R. Simeon, teacher of Trachonitis, the townspeople said, "Cut your reading short, so that our children may learn to read [by following it slowly]."

B. He came and asked R. Haninah. He said to him, "Even if they cut off your head, do not listen to them." So he did not listen to them, and they fired him from his job as teacher.

C. After a while he came down here [to Babylonia, where the story was told]. R. Simon b. Yusinah dealt with him. He said to him, "What did you do in that town?" And he told him the story.

D. He said to him, "Why did you not listen to them, [and do what they wanted]?"

E. He said to him, "And do you do it that way?"

F. He said to him, "And do we not cut a verse into parts in the study session [so as to translate it bit by bit and learn it that way]?"

G. He said to him, "But do we not then go back and say the whole thing as one piece?"

H. Said R. Zeira, "If that teacher were alive in my time, I should appoint him as a sage."

Once more we conclude our review with evidence that the Talmud's rather lifeless picture of a society humbling itself to the sage is to be set alongside a quite separate and astringent fact that the sages were by no means the sole authorities in Jewry. The Big Men of the town controlled the town. The sage did not. Accordingly, when it came down to the wire, the local authorities could not be excommunicated, there being no social sanction effective against them. They fired the sage for not following their instructions, and he stayed fired. Accordingly, the rather ample account of the sages' special privileges is to be set in the balance against the Talmud's striking evidence of the tale-tellers' anxiety in the world beyond the pages of the text.

The Sage's Special Torah

The dignity and standing claimed by the sage from the Israelite community at large may or may not have come to him. In his own circle, by contrast, he reigned supreme. And in the intersecting circles of masters and disciples, rites and rituals expressing the supernatural status of the rabbi produced considerable, heated conflict. The rules of courtesy and conduct particular to the rabbinical estate governed the conduct of disciple toward the masters, on the one side, and the masters toward one another, on the other.

The former rules were ambiguous. The disciple was kept in a state of subservience and could do only what the master permitted him to do. That status was expressed in stories on a number of topics, including the right of a sage's disciple to give instruction, on the one side, and his role in assignments assigned to carry out specific tasks, on the other.

Y. Gittin 1:2.I.

D. Rabbi was in Acre. He saw people eating clean bread. He said to them, "How do you knead the dough? [If it is with a liquid capable of imparting susceptibility to uncleanness, then the bread also is susceptible to uncleanness, and hence, located in Israelite territory it must be kept cultically clean.]"

E. They said, "A disciple of a sage came here and taught us that egg water does not impart susceptibility to uncleanness." [The issue of cleanness is pertinent only if Acre is part of the Land of Israel.]

F. Now they thought that he had said that water in which eggs had been boiled [will not impart susceptibility to uncleanness], while he had meant only the whites of the eggs themselves. [The words differ only in one vowel.]

G. Said R. Jacob b. Idi, "From that moment they decreed that a disciple of a sage should not give rulings."

H. R. Huna in the name of R. Huna said, "A disciple who gave a decision, even in accordance with decided law—his ruling is null."

I. It was taught: A disciple who gave instruction in the presence of his master is liable to the death penalty.

Y. Gittin 1:2.I.

P. R. Tanhum bar Jeremiah was in Happar, and a question was brought to him, and he gave a ruling. Someone said to him, "And did you not teach us, Rabbi, 'It is forbidden for a disciple to teach a law in the presence of his master—until he has moved twelve *mil* away from him, the breadth of the camp of Israel'? Now lo, R. Mana, your master, dwells in Sepphoris!"

Q. He said to him, "May a curse come upon me, if I knew it!" From that moment he gave no further instruction [in that place, at that time].

The striking element here is not the error deriving from the disciple's improper pronouncement of a ruling. It is the view of H, I. A disciple is closely restricted and may not give a decision, even when his opinion is completely sound.

If the disciple did not pay the expected obeisance, the master was quick to demand an explanation.

Y. Sanhedrin 1:2.V.

Q. R. Hiyya bar Wa was standing and saying his prayer. R. Kahana came in and stood behind him and prayed. R. Hiyya completed the prayer but could not take his seat because he did not want to pass in front of the other [who was still praying]. R. Kahana carried on and tarried at his prayer. Once he finished, the other said to him, "Is that your customary behavior, to cause trouble for your master?"

R. He said to him, "Rabbi, I come from the house of Eli, concerning whom it is written, 'Therefore I swear to the house of Eli that the iniquity of Eli's house shall not be expiated by sacrifice or offering for ever' [1 Sam. 3:14]. That is to say, through sacrifice and offering it will not be expiated, but it will be expiated through prayer."

S. He prayed in his behalf, and the latter had the merit of living so long that his fingernails turned red like those of an infant.

This story has two sides. First, we see, the disciple had to accept without complaint the master's criticism. But, second, the master then exercised his supernatural power to remove the curse from which the disciple's family had suffered. So it was all part of a single fabric.

For his part, a disciple of a sage could not claim the dignity owed to a sage, though he could on his own adopt the special forms of obligatory observance characteristic of the rabbinical estate.

Y. Berakhot 2:8 [Zahavy].I.

A. In all matters [of religious obligations] entailing pain [such as a fast], anyone who wishes to single himself out [to observe them] may do so. A disciple of the sages may observe them and will receive a blessing.

B. And in all matters [of religious obligation] entailing benefit [such as wearing a special prayer shawl] not anyone who wishes to single himself out [to observe them] may do so.

C. A disciple of the sages may do so unless they appointed him an administrator of the community [lest people suspect him of graft].

The main point is that the sage bore full and complete responsibility for the state of the disciple's mastery of Torah, and, it follows, the disciple acquired merit even from the least form of subservient relationship to the sage, as expressed in the following (to us) extreme instances:

Y. Besah 5:2.VI.

> K. Rabbi said, "I have had the merit of learning Torah only because I saw R. Meir's naked neck from the back."
>
> L. R. Yohanan and R. Simeon b. Laqish both said, "We have had the merit of learning Torah only because we saw the toes of Rabbi reaching out of his slippers."

It was one thing to demand subservience from disciples. In paying respect to the master, the disciple thereby humbled himself before the Torah. But it was quite another thing for one sage to exact from another sage, of the same standing, a measure of respect sufficient to satisfy the former's sense of what was due to him. The following stories convey the heightened tensions in matters of dignity among the great sages.

Y. Moed Qatan 3:7.XIX.

> A. R. Yohanan was leaning on R. Jacob bar Iddi, and R. Eleazar [a Babylonian] saw him and avoided him. [Yohanan] said, "Lo, now there are two things that that Babylonian has done to me! One is that he didn't even bother to greet me, and the other is that he didn't cite a tradition of mine in my name."
>
> B. [Jacob] said to him, "That is the custom over there, that the lesser party does not greet the more important authority. For they carry out the following verse of Scripture: 'The young men saw me and withdrew, and the aged rose and stood'" [Job 29:8].
>
> C. As they were going along, they saw a certain schoolhouse.
>
> D. [Jacob] said to him, "Here is where R. Meir used to go into session and expound the law. And he stated traditions in the name of R. Ishmael, but he did not state traditions in the name of R. Aqiba."
>
> E. [Yohanan] said to him, "Everybody knows that R. Meir was the disciple of R. Aqiba [so he did not have to cite him]."
>
> F. [Jacob] said to him, "Everybody knows that R. Eleazar is the disciple of R. Yohanan."
>
> G. As they were going along, [they passed by a procession in which an idol was carried, and Jacob asked Yohanan,] "What is the law as to passing a procession in which an idol is being carried?"

H. He said to him, "And do you pay respect to the idol? Go before it and blind its eyes."
I. [Jacob] said to him, "Well did R. Eleazar do to you, for he did not pass by you [since that would have required an inappropriate gesture]."
J. [Yohanan] said to him, "Jacob bar Iddi, you know very well how to make peace [between quarreling people]."

A further version of the foregoing story adds important details, in particular stressing the unseemliness of strife among sages and the consequences to be feared from that hatred.

Y. Sheqalim 2:4.V.
H. R. Ami and R. Asi entered the discussion before him. They said to him, "Rabbi, this is the story of what happened in the synagogue of the Tarsians, concerning a debate on a door bolt which has on its top a movable fastening contrivance [that may serve as a pestle]. In this matter R. Eliezer and R. Yosé argued, until, in their anger, they tore a scroll of the Torah."
I. They actually tore a scroll of the Torah?
J. Rather: A scroll of the Torah was torn.
K. Now there was present a certain elder, and his name was R. Yosé b. Qisma. He said, "I shall be surprised if this synagogue is not turned into a Temple for idolatry."
L. [Yohanan] said, "Are you comparing my matter to the case you have described?"
M. R. Jacob bar Idi entered the discourse. He said to him, "'As the Lord commanded Moses his servant, so Moses commanded Joshua, and so Joshua did; he left nothing undone of all that the Lord had commanded Moses' (Joshua 11:15). Now when Joshua was in session and expounding the law, did he say this, 'Thus did Moses say'? But Joshua was in session and expounding the law, and every one knew that the Torah was that of Moses. Now with you too, Eliezer goes into session and expounds the law, but everyone knows that [his] Torah is yours."
N. He said to them, "How is it that you don't know how to appease, the way the son of Idi, our colleague, does?"

This rather protracted extract gives us a glimpse of relationships among the great authorities of the law. There was jealousy; slights were remembered for a long time; matters of honor were bitterly fought out. The Talmud once more conveys the consensus of the community of sages on these matters, in its emphasis upon the unseemly and potentially dangerous character of the hatred affecting the sages. But at the same time, the Talmud is prepared to compare the relationships among the sages to those between Moses and Joshua, with the clear implication that sages in their own day were at a comparable level of dignity.

Matters of dignity extended not merely to important issues, such as the jurisdiction of a court or the application of an opinion. On the contrary, trivial details, such as selection of the color of a burial shroud, on the one side, or precedence in going through a door or failure to rise and pay respect, on the other, could provoke fierce resentment.

Y. Ketubot 12:3.III.

    A.   R. Yohanan gave instructions, "Shroud me in scarlet, which is neither white nor black. If I end up among the righteous, I shall not be ashamed, and if I end up among the wicked, I shall not be ashamed."

    B.   R. Josiah gave instructions, "Shroud me in hemmed white shrouds."

    C.   They said to him, "Are you better than your master [Yohanan]?"

    D.   He said to them, "And should I be ashamed of the things I have done?"

Y. Ketubot 12:3.VI.

    N.   Rabbi began to pay respect to Hiyya.

    O.   When he would come into the meeting house, he would say, "Let R. Hiyya the Elder go in before me."

    P.   Said to him R. Ishmael b. R. Yosé, "Even before me?"

    Q.   He said to him, "Heaven forfend! But R. Hiyya the Elder may be within, but R. Ishmael b. R. Yosé is innermost."

    R.   Rabbi was praising R. Hiyya the Elder in the presence of R. Ishmael b. R. Yosé. One time he saw him in the bathhouse and [Hiyya] did not rise to pay his respects [to Ishmael].

    S.   Ishmael said to [Rabbi], "Is this the one whom you were praising to me?"

    T.   He said to him, "What did he do to you?"

    U.   He said to him, "I saw him in the bathhouse, and he did not rise to pay his respects to me."

    V.   He said to [Hiyya], "Why did you behave in such a way?"

    W.   He said to him, "May a terrible thing happen to me, if I even noticed him. I knew nothing about it. At the time I was reviewing the aggadic traditions of the whole book of Psalms."

    X.   From that time [Rabbi] assigned to him two disciples to accompany him so that he would not get into trouble because of his concentration on his own thoughts.

The clear sense of this story is that the mark of a true sage was the respect he paid to someone higher in rank. Ishmael's complaint is accepted as legitimate, and Hiyya is called to account. And why not, when, in an ascending scale, the dignity paid from disciple to sage, and from sage to an older or greater sage, ultimately extended in a chain leading onward to Heaven. For the sage was in his person not different from the Torah scroll, from Moses "our rabbi," from supernatural figures in Heaven. One of the marks of true sagacity lay in adherence to the canons of courtesy through which, in part, learning was expressed.

The Sages of the Written Torah

The clearest picture of the theory of salvation contained within the Judaism to which the Talmud of the Land of Israel testifies is to be found in the sages' reading of Scripture. Specifically, the world view projected by them upon the heroes of ancient Israel most clearly reveals the Talmud's sages view of themselves and their world. The Talmud's framers naturally took for granted that the world they knew in the fourth century had flourished a thousand and more years earlier. The values they embodied and the supernatural powers they fantasized for themselves predictably were projected backward onto biblical figures. The ubiquitous citation of biblical proof texts in support of both legal and theological statements shows the mentality of the Talmud's framers. In their imagination, everything they said stood in direct continuity with what Scripture had stated. Biblical and Talmudic authorities lived on a single plane of being, in a single age of shared discourse; the Mishnah and associated documents amply restated propositions held for all time and proved in Scripture too.

But it is inappropriate to dwell merely on the (to us) anachronistic reading of Scripture characteristic of Talmudic sages. That is a natural fact of the age. What is important is the theory of salvation thereby given its clearest statement. What was the rabbis' view of salvation? Seeing Scripture in their own model, they took the position that the Torah of old, its supernatural power and salvific promise, in their own day continued to endure—among themselves. In consequence, the promise of salvation contained in every line of Scripture was to be kept in every deed of learning and obedience to the law effected under their auspices. So while they projected backward the things they cherished in an act of (to us) extraordinary anachronism, in their eyes they carried forward, to their own time, the promise of salvation for Israel contained within the written Torah of old.

In this aspect the mode of thought and the consequent salvific proposition conformed to the model revealed likewise in the Gospel of Matthew. The reason Scripture was cited, for both statements on Israel's salvation, was not to establish authority alone. Rather, it was to identify what was happening just then with what had happened long ago. The purpose then was not merely to demonstrate and authenticate the *bona fide* character of a new figure of salvation, but to show the continuity of the salvific process. The point then is that the figure at hand was not new at all. He stood as a renewed exemplar and avatar of Israel's eternal hope, now come to full realization—a very different thing. Authenticity hardly demanded demonstration of the Scriptural authority. That was the datum of the more extreme claim laid down in the profoundly anachronistic reading accorded to Scripture. In finding sages in the (written) Torah, therefore, the Talmud's sages implicitly stated a view of themselves as the continuation of the sanctified way of life of the written Torah. It followed that the pattern and promise of salvation contained therein lay within their way of life. That is the meaning of the explicit reading of the present into the past—the implicit arrogation of the hope of the past to the salvific heroes of the present: themselves.

To state matters simply, if David, King of Israel, was like a rabbi today, then a rabbi today would be the figure of the son of David who was to come as King of Israel. It is not surprising, therefore, that among the many biblical heroes whom the Talmudic rabbis treated as sages, principal and foremost was David himself, now made into a messianic rabbi or a rabbinical Messiah. He was the sage of the Torah, the avatar and model for the sages of their own time. That view was made explicit, both specifically and in general terms. If a rabbi was jealous to have his traditions cited in his own name, it was because that was David's explicit view as well. In more general terms, both David and Moses are represented as students of Torah, just like the disciples and sages of the current time.

Y. Sanhedrin 2:6.IV.

    A.   It is written, "And David said longingly, 'O that someone would give me water to drink from the well of Bethlehem [which is by the gate]'" (1 Chron. 11:17).

    B.   R. Hiyya bar Ba said, "He required a teaching of law."

    C.   "Then the three mighty men broke through [the camp of the Philistines]" (1 Chron. 11:18).

    D.   Why three? Because the law is not decisively laid down by fewer than three.

    E.   "But David would not drink of it; [he poured it out to the Lord, and said, 'Far be it from me before my God that I should do this. Shall I drink the lifeblood of these men? For at the risk of their lives they brought it']" (1 Chron. 11:18–19).

    F.   David did not want the law to be laid down in his own name.

    G.   "He poured it out to the Lord"—establishing [the decision] as [an unattributed] teaching for the generations, [so that the law should be authoritative and so be cited anonymously].

Y. Sheqalim 2:4.V.

O. David himself prayed for mercy for himself, as it is said, "Let me dwell in thy tent for ever! Oh to be safe under the shelter of thy wings, *selah*" (Ps. 61:4).

P. And did it enter David's mind that he would live for ever?

Q. But this is what David said before the Holy One, blessed be he, "Lord of the world, may I have the merit that my words will be stated in synagogues and schoolhouses."

R. Simeon b. Nazira in the name of R. Isaac said, "Every disciple in whose name people cite a teaching of law in this world— his lips murmur with him in the grave, as it is said, 'Your kisses are like the best wine that goes down smoothly, gliding over lips of those that sleep' (Song 7:9).

S. "Just as in the case of a mass of grapes, once a person puts his finger in it, forthwith even his lips begin to smack, so the lips of the righteous, when someone cites a teaching of law in their names—their lips murmur with them in the grave."

Y. Berakhot 1:1 (Zahavy).XII.

O. "I will awake the dawn" (Ps. 5:7, 8)—I will awaken the dawn; the dawn will not awaken me.

P. David's [evil] impulse tried to seduce him [to sin]. And it would say to him, "David. It is the custom of kings that dawn awakens them. And you say, I will awake the dawn. It is the custom of kings that they sleep until the third hour [of the day]. And you say, At midnight I rise." And [David] used to say [in reply], "[I rise early] because of thy righteous ordinances (Ps. 119:62)."

Q. And what would David do? R. Phineas in the name of R. Eleazar b. R. Menahem [said], "[He used to take a harp and lyre and set them at his bedside. And he would rise at midnight and play them so that the associates of Torah should hear. And what would the associates of Torah say? 'If David involves himself with Torah, how much more so should we.' We find that all of Israel was involved in Torah [study] on account of David."

Y. Horayot 3:5.I.

E. R. Yohanan, "All these forty days that Moses served on the mountain, he studied the Torah but forgot it. In the end it was given to him as a gift. All this why? So as to bring the stupid students back to their studies [when they become discouraged]."

This long extract has shown us how the Talmud's authorities readily saw their concerns in biblical statements attributed to David. "Water" meant "a teaching of Torah." "Three mighty men" were of course judges. At issue was whether or not the decision was to be stated in David's own name—and so removed from the authoritative consensus of sages. David exhibits precisely those concerns for the preservation of his views in his name that, in earlier sections, we saw attributed to rabbis. All of this, as we have noted, fully reveals the rabbis' deeper convictions when we remember that David, *the rabbi,* also was in everyone's mind David, *the Messiah.*

The projection of the present onto the past encompassed details as well as general propositions. One striking instance is that the quarrels of Israelite history were read as disputes remarkably like those of contemporary masters, for example, disputes about primacy in the order of precedence due to masters of Torah. Jeroboam's break with Rehoboam was interpreted in precisely this setting.

Y. Abodah Zarah 1:1.I.

RR.   Said R. Yosé bar Jacob, "It was at the conclusion of a sabbatical year that Jeroboam began to rule over Israel. That is the meaning of the following verse: '[And Moses commanded them.] At the end of every seven years, at the set time of the year of release, at the feast of booths, when all Israel comes to appear before the Lord your God at the place which he will choose,   . you shall read this law before all Israel in their hearing' (Deut. 31:10–11).

SS.   "[Jeroboam] said, 'I shall be called upon to read [the Torah, as Scripture requires]. If I get up and read first, they will say to me, "The king of the place [in which the gathering takes place, namely, Jerusalem] comes first." And if I read second, it is disrespectful to me. And if I do not read at all, it is a humiliation for me. And, finally, if I let the people go up, they will abandon me and go over to the side of Rehoboam the son of Solomon.'"

The tale once again shows how contemporary conventions of courtesy owed to sages naturally applied, in the imaginations of the Talmud's framers, to the olden times. The parallels have already come before us.

That the rules governing relationships among sages or between masters and disciples were read into biblical times and relationships among biblical figures is illustrated in the following.

Y. Horayot 3:5.II.

A.   R. Joshua b. Levi said, "[If there] are a head [not a sage] and an elder [a sage], the elder takes precedence. For there is no head if there is no elder."

B. What is the scriptural evidence for this position?

C. "You stand this day all of you before the Lord your God; the heads of your tribes, your elders, and your officers, all the men of Israel (Deut. 29:10)."

D. And it is written, "Then Joshua gathered all the tribes of Israel to Shechem, and summoned the elders, the heads, the judges, and the officers of Israel (Joshua 24:1)."

E. Thus Moses gave precedence to the heads over the elders, while Joshua gave precedence to the elders over the heads.

F. Moses, because all of them were his disciples, gave precedence to the heads over the elders. Joshua, because all of them were not his disciples, gave precedence to the elders [who were sages] over the heads [who were not sages].

G. Moses, because he did not yet have need of them for conquering the land, gave precedence to the heads over the elders. Joshua, because he needed them for conquering the land, gave precedence to the elders over the heads.

H. Moses, because he was not fatigued by the study of the Torah [having divine help], gave precedence to the heads over the elders. Joshua, because he was fatigued by study of the Torah, gave precedence to the elders over the heads.

I. R. Joshua of Sikhnin in the name of R. Levi: "Moses, because he foresaw through the Holy Spirit that the Israelites were destined to be imprisoned by the [gentile] kingdoms, and their heads would be standing over them [to deal with the gentiles], gave precedence to the heads over the elders."

What is striking here is not only the glimpse we gain into the imagination of the Talmud's voice. It is also the certainty that reasons for contemporary organization of the rabbinical estate derived from the founding of Israel's political institutions at the very beginning. This is explicit at H. I then offers a different approach to the matter, reflecting the issue of who dealt with the gentiles, and who did not. The elders were sages of Torah, the heads were not. So the point in the end is not much different.

The institutions imagined by the framers of the Mishnah, chief among them a Sanhedrin, ruling on disputed matters of law, were naturally envisioned in times past. The master-disciple circles of the day had their counterpart in ancient Israel. Saul supported members of the Sanhedrin, and King Hezekiah was subject to sages' opinions.

Y. Nedarim 9:9.I.

A. It is written, "Ye daughters of Israel, weep over Saul, who clothed you daintily in scarlet, who put ornaments of gold upon your apparel" (2 Sam. 1:24).

B. As to the views of R. Judah and R. Nehemiah, one of them said, "The reference is actually to the daughters of Israel, for when their husbands would go to war, [Saul] would provide them with food.'

C. "Why does Scripture say, 'Who put ornaments of gold upon your apparel'?

D. "The meaning is that an ornament is beautiful only on a lovely body."

E. And the other said, "The reference is not to the daughters of Israel but to the builders of Israel, the Israelite Sanhedrin. For Saul would spy out of a group of associates and give them food and drink.

F. "And what is the meaning of the statement of Scripture, 'Who put ornaments of gold upon your apparel'?

G. "For he would listen to the reasoning for a law from a sage and would praise him for it."

Y. Nedarim 6:1.III.

W. Six things did Hezekiah, the king of Judah, do. In three of them [sages] agreed with him, and in three of them they did not agree with him.

X. He dragged his father's bones on a rope bier, he pulverized the brazen serpent, and he hid away the notebook of remedies, and they agreed with him.

Y. And in three things they did not agree with him: He closed off the waters of Upper Gihon, he cut [the gold off] the doors of the Temple, and he intercalated the month of Nisan in Nisan itself [calling Nisan the second Adar after Nisan had already begun], and they did not agree with what he had done.

Not only did the Talmud's sages take for granted that the imaginary institutions of their own system, if not fully realized in their own time, surely functioned in olden times. More strikingly still, they also knew as fact that precisely the ways in which they reasoned about the law characterized the minds of their ancestors. Accordingly, their characteristic modes of thought simply carried forward those established in ancient Israel, deriving from God's revelation to Moses at Sinai. The dispute of Korah and Moses was a dispute not only about the law, but also about how to reason within the law.

Y. Sanhedrin 10:1.VII.

I. Rab said, "Korah was an Epicurean. What did he do? He went and made a prayer shawl which was entirely purple [although the law is that only the fringe was to be purple]."

J. He went to Moses, saying to him, "Moses, our rabbi: A prayer shawl which is entirely purple, what is the law as to its being liable to show fringes?"

K. He said to him, "It is liable, for it is written, 'You shall make yourself tassles [on the four corners of your cloak with which you cover yourself]'" (Deut. 22:12).

L. [Korah continued,] "A house which is entirely filled with holy books, what is the law as to its being liable for a *mezuzah* [containing sacred scripture, on the doorpost]?"

M. He said to him, "It is liable for a *mezuzah,* for it is written, 'And you shall write them on the doorposts of your house [and upon your gates]' (Deut. 6:9)."

N. He said to him, "A bright spot the size of a bean—what is the law [as to whether it is a sign of uncleanness in line with Lev. 13:2ff.]?"

O. He said to him, "It is a sign of uncleanness."

P. "And if it spread over the whole of the man's body?"

Q. He said to him, "It is a sign of cleanness."

R. At that moment Korah said, "The Torah does not come from Heaven, Moses is no prophet, and Aaron is not a high priest."

S. Then did Moses say, "Lord of all worlds, if from creation the earth was formed with a mouth, well and good, and if not, then make it now!"

This colloquy represents Moses and Korah as disputing about the requirements of Scriptural law and interpretation, just as any set of rabbis might do in the third and fourth centuries. Korah led Moses into a series of absurd positions, leading to the conclusion specified at R. Accordingly, a single mode of thought and analysis joined Israel's sages from Moses onward—and reaching false conclusions could be punished again as it was in the day of Korah.

For all their veneration of Scripture and its (rabbinical) heroes, the Talmud's authorities still regarded knowledge of the Mishnah as more important than knowledge of Scripture, citing biblical proof texts in support of that proposition. The relative value of learning in various collections of Torah teachings is worked out in the following extended unit of discourse.

Y. Horayot 3:5.III.

D. This is what has been said: The Mishnah takes precedence over Scripture.

E. And the following supports this tradition:

F. For R. Simeon b. Yohai taught, "He who takes up studies in Scripture—it is a good quality that is no good quality."

G. Rabbis treat Scripture as equivalent to the Mishnah . . .

W.   R. Aha interpreted the following verse: "'A just balance and scales are the Lord's; all the weights in the bag are his work' (Prov. 16:110).

X.   "'A balance'—this refers to Scripture.

Y.   "'Scales' refers to the Mishnah.

Z.   "'Just' refers to the Talmud.

AA. "'Are the Lord's' refers to the Supplement [Tosefta].

BB. "'All the weights in the bag are his work'—all of them take their reward from one bag."

CC. R. Abba bar Kahana went to a certain place. He found R. Levi sitting and interpreting the following verse: "'A man to whom God gives wealth, possession, and honor, so that he lacks nothing of all that he desires, yet God does not give him power to enjoy them, but a stranger enjoys them' (Qoh. 6:2).

DD. "'Wealth'—this refers to Scripture.

EE. "'Possessions'—these are the laws.

FF. "'Honor'—this is the Supplement."

Christians as much as Jews, ordinary folk as much as sages, knew Scripture. So striking is one point not to be missed in the statement at hand. Given that Torah is the source of supernatural power and salvation, what *part* of Torah is the source of supernatural power and salvation, what part of Torah is to enjoy precedence? It quite obviously will be the Mishnah and its associated bodies of discussion, that is, the component of Torah in the hands of Israel, and Israel's sages, alone. Assigning to knowledge of Mishnah precedence over knowledge of Scripture therefore serves to declare that those who master Mishnah possess a power to attain salvation greater than those who know (merely) Scripture. That I take to be the deeper sense of D–F.

The contrary view, G, W–BB, should not be missed. Both parties of course must be right. No one could really maintain that knowledge of the Scripture was secondary to knowledge of the Mishnah. Nor would any sage concur that knowledge of Scripture alone sufficed. So the sense of the passage allows for two correct, if distinct, positions to be juxtaposed. For our purpose the fundamental assertion of the identity of Scripture learning and Mishnah learning with "Torah" is the main thing. That commonplace suffices here, as everywhere else in our Talmud, to state that for which the Talmud's clerks and bureaucrats labored: the salvation of Israel, now and at the end of days.

From Ancient to Medieval

Historians of the West conventionally regard the two centuries with which we deal as the point at which ancient times end and the medieval age begins.

The *Cambridge Ancient History,* volume 12, for example, closes at 325, and the *Cambridge Medieval History,* volume 1, begins at that same year. Along these same lines, Salo Baron, the great historian of the Jewish people, titles his opening discussion on Talmudic history, "Incipient Medievalism," followed then by his descriptions of "World of the Talmud" and "Talmudic Law and Religion" (*A Social and Religious History of the Jews,* vol. 2, *Ancient Times,* pt. II). Accordingly, when we regard the Yerushalmi as a document of an age of transition, from ancient to medieval times, our judgment fully accords with established perspectives on both the age and the document itself. But that general observation does not guide us to the particular respect in which this age of transition is unusually interesting. What is distinctive to the history of Judaism, the Talmud itself, and what is general, the age of its creation and the ethos of the time, so correspond as to illuminate one another.

The Talmud of the Land of Israel turns out to lay its principal emphases upon precisely those things that the traits of the age and social imagination of the setting should have led us to expect. The Talmud's message speaks of how to attain certainty and authority in a time of profound change. The means lie in the person of the Talmudic sage. Salvation consists in becoming like him. We shall now see that, in a unique idiom of its own, the Talmud says what people in general were saying in those days.

Let me explain. As we now realize, the principal development attested by the Yerushalmi is the figure of the rabbi, his centrality in the social and salvific world of the Jewish nation. The rabbi, after all, is the definitive phenomenon of the Judaism produced by him, called either by his title, Rabbinic Judaism, or by his book, Talmudic Judaism, or by his theological authority, Classical Judaism, the authoritative or normative "classics" being the Talmuds and the other writings of rabbis. Yet, as I just said, what appears particular and definitive turns out upon second glance to be typical of its day and so quite unremarkable. This is because we have pointed to a phenomenon noticed in the same time but in quite other settings by people who never saw the particular sources before us. Peter Brown, for example, aptly describes, first, the transitional character of the age, and, second, the critical role of a new type of man in that age. Because of the centrality to my argument of what he says, I provide a sizable extract (*Religion,* p. 13):

> The Late Antique period has too often been dismissed as an age of disintegration, an age of other-worldliness in which sheltered souls withdrew from the crumbling society around them, to seek another, a Heavenly, city. No impression is further from the truth. Seldom has any period of European history littered the future with so many irremoveable institutions. The codes of Roman Law, the hierarchy of the Catholic Church, the idea of the Christian Empire, the monastery—up to the eighteenth century, men as far apart as Scotland and Ethiopia, Madrid and Moscow, still turned to these imposing legacies of the institution-building of the Late Antique period for guidance as to how to organize their life in this world. I find it increasingly difficult to believe that these great experiments in social

living were left there inadvertently by an age of dreamers, or that they happened through some last, tragic twitching of a supposed 'Roman genius for organization'. They were, many of them, the new creations of new men; and the central problem of Late Roman religious history is to explain why men came to act out their inner life through suddenly coagulating into new groups, and why they needed to find a new focus in the solidarities and sharp boundaries of the sect, the monastery, the orthodox Empire. The sudden flooding of the inner life into social forms: this is what distinguished the Late Antique period, of the third century onwards, from the Classical world.

It is not difficult to list the enduring and normative institutions of Judaism created between the end of the second century and the end of the fourth. But why bother to make a long list—when the most important were the two Talmuds! Still, even at this late stage of my argument, I ought to spell out how the matrix to which the Talmuds testify, the Judaism at hand, constituted the creation of a new kind of Israelite figure. So let us speak once more of this rabbi, this new man.

Standing at the end of Bar Kokhba's war and looking backward, we discern in the entire antecedent history of Israel no holy man analogous to the rabbi. There were diverse sorts of holy men. But the particular amalgam of definitive traits—charismatic clerk, savior-sage, lawyer-magician, and supernatural politician-bureaucrat—represented by the rabbi is not to be located in any former type of Israelite authority. Looking forward, from the formation of the Talmud onward, on the other hand, we rarely perceive a holy man wholly *unlike* the rabbi. None is out of touch with the rabbis' particular books. All present the knowledge of them as a source of legitimation at least until we reach (for a brief moment) the earliest phase of Hassidism in the eighteenth century. From the Talmud onward, Jewish authorities were authoritative because, whatever else they knew, they knew the Talmud and conformed to its laws and modes of thought. The heretic opposed the Talmud and violated its laws. So whoever exercised power did so because, whatever other basis for authority he may have enjoyed, he was made holy by knowledge of the writings of rabbis of this period. So the Talmud was the creation, in Brown's word, of "new men." But what the new men made then endured as a foundation of the Jewish nation's social life from their time to our own. The rabbi as a distinctive Jewish authority persisted virtually alone for a millennium and a half and then, from the nineteenth century, in competition with other kinds of leaders, framed in competing modes of social and imaginative structure, for another two hundred years thereafter, to the present day. Accordingly, when I call "transitional" both the period at hand and the document under study, I mean, in particular, the period in which the Mishnah was made over into the Talmuds and in which the Mishnah's system was revised into the one the Talmuds put forth. These revolutionaries of late antiquity created something which stands, in its influence within its chosen society, equivalent to a Papacy, a Christian Empire, and a Caliphate—the other great institutions of late antiquity.

If I may now specify the single most interesting question presented to us by the formation of the rabbi as the definitive figure in Judaism, it is how to describe and interpret the relationship between the social events and conditions of the age, on the one side, and the development of the figure and authority of the rabbi, on the other. Peter Brown (*Religion*, p. 16) defines the problem of study as an inquiry into "the nexus that links the inner experiences of men to the society around them." In the present context we should want to know two things. First, what made people want to become, or at least submit to the authority of, rabbis, as a particular kind of Jewish holy man–politician? Second, how did the rabbi interpret shared disciplines and sagacity, his program of accountable behavior and public responsibility, as the expression of his own inner life? We should like to relate content to context, public theology to inner anguish.

The sole source of facts in hand, unhappily, prevents us from answering either question. For the only evidence we have is the Talmud, not a private document but in essence and by definition the collective evidence of the generality of rabbis themselves. So we cannot deal with the former question. And, again by definition, rabbis never wrote their own individual books or spoke for themselves in particular. So we cannot take up the latter question either. The rabbi conforms to a single ideal type. In the sources, a rabbi scarcely reveals individual traits of mind or expression except within the collectively permitted framework of trivial points of difference. Not only does the rabbi emerge, therefore, as a completely public and available figure, lacking traits of individuation and substantial differentiation. He also is never represented except as an *example* of social and hence common virtue.

This judgment requires some qualification. For while the rabbi of the Talmud is never an individual, he also is never merely a conventional or convenient name on which to hang a random opinion. True, he is one of a type, not wholly individuated. But he also is not merely a genus, but, in himself, a specimen of a genus—a genius. A contrast is to be drawn between the Mishnah and the Talmud. One may differentiate Mishnaic rabbis only by idiosyncratic opinions on unimportant things. By contrast, we can easily distinguish one Talmudic authority from another on a much broader range of points of difference and individuation. Each one typifies. But the range of choice is broader and more interesting. So the Talmud differs from the Mishnah in this important aspect too. Its authors, and not only the things they say, play a major role in the document. Thus while sages in the Mishnah have names but no faces, opinions but no biographies, rabbis in the Talmud not only say things but also do things. They are given flesh-and-blood lives and, in the anachronistic nature of things, so are their Mishnaic predecessors. The power to change the world, not merely judge or describe it, was the rabbi's. The power of the rabbi extended backward to Moses' Scripture, forward to the Messiah. He was the link, his word the guarantee. The lifeless names of the Mishnah can scarcely compete.

The Mishnah came forth confidently on its own, only to be chained to a mass of Scriptural proof texts. So the new Mishnah was made old, a new version of ancient Scripture, and the fresh transformed into avatar and continuator of the solely authoritative. Perhaps that is how matters had to be in the logic of things. But it is also how things were in the age itself. For, as Brown describes matters (*Religion,* p. 11), the shift from the second century to the fourth was a time in which people confronted "a mounting tension between their inner and their outer life, between the demands of their personal experience and the patterns of life so confidently handed down to them by an ancient society." If we now take account of Brown's description of the time, we find much familiar from our survey of the Talmud's account:

> Nothing is quite what it appears in the Later Roman Empire. This is the first and most lasting attraction of that age of change. Seldom were the externals of traditional Roman life so strenuously maintained; seldom did the aristocracy feel so identified with their inherited classical tradition and with the myth of Eternal Rome. Seldom had the authority of the Roman Emperors been supposed to reach so far—into the definition of their subject's beliefs, into what oaths they swore when gambling, into the "irrepressible avarice" that might lead a man, if undeterred by beheading, to seek edible dormice above the market price. When we enter a museum, we peer at the fourth-century ivories to catch some hint of the profound changes that raced beneath their surface: the smooth, neo-classical faces stare us down. Yet we know that the surface of ancient life was being betrayed at every turn: it was being abandoned in the clothes men wore, in the mosaics they walked on, in the beliefs they held, or in the beliefs of the women they married, in the very sounds that filled their streets and churches with the strange chants of Syria. Like bizarre reflections of a building in troubled water, the facade of Greco-Roman life shifts and dissolves.

If we substitute "Scripture and Mishnah" for "traditional Roman life," we find Brown's description remarkably apropos. The externals of Scriptural authority and Mishnaic teaching alike were, in Brown's words, "strenuously maintained." The Mishnah was made over into a mere amplification and specification of general rules of Scripture, supplied with proof texts for most of its propositions. The Mishnah, for its part, defined the program of the Talmud. The exegesis of its specific laws form the focus of interest and discourse; in the Talmud little else takes place. The authority of Scripture through the specification of the Mishnah then was made to reach into the obscure and unimportant details of the life of Israel everywhere, under all imaginable conditions and circumstances. If the Mishnah speaks mainly of the Temple, on the one side, and public life, on the other, the Talmud addresses an inner world of privacy, both in petty transactions and in peoples' dreams and fears, to which the Mishnah is oblivious. So, in line with

Brown's conception, the movement from the Mishnah to the Talmud belies the formal design of the Talmud as a mere commentary to, and extension of, the Mishnah. In fact, what takes shape is a new construction, in literary and conceptual terms alike, built with the bricks and mortar of the old. The Talmud is indeed an amplification and extension of the Mishnah. But the net result of the Talmud is a kind of Judaism asymmetrical with the Mishnah, off-center, or as Brown says, "reflections of a building in troubled water."

The Mishnah governs what the rabbi knows. But it is *the rabbi* who speaks about the Mishnah. He imposes his voice by breaking the Mishnah down into bits and pieces, then doing what he wants with some of them. Like a good apprentice to an artist, the rabbi copied carefully. He faithfully memorized the Mishnah and subserviently mastered its principles and details. Then he went and made his own freehand picture. In his masterpiece one discerns the technique of color and brushstrokes of his master. But seeing it whole, we gaze upon what is original to the apprentice, now shown to be an artist in his own right.

The most important fact in the Talmud is its anonymous, monotonous, uniform voice, its "rabbi." The critical actor is the rabbi as authority on earth and intermediary of supernatural power. If we did not know that the Talmud came from the time and place from which it comes, knowledge of those two definitive facts of this document, joined with familiarity with the world of late antiquity, should have made us guess so. For, as I said at the outset, the rabbi, so particular to Judaism and distinctive to the Talmud, also is typical of his age. He presents a version, for Judaism, of what was wholly commonplace in the world at large. This is how Peter Brown, describes matters (*World,* pp. 102–103):

> The idea of the holy man holding the demons at bay and bending the will of God by his prayers came to dominate Late Antique society. In many ways, the idea is as new as the society itself. For it placed a man, a "man of power," in the centre of people's imagination. Previously, the classical world had tended to think of its religion in terms of *things*. Ancient religion had revolved round great temples, against whose ancient stones even the most impressive priest had paled into insignificance; the gods had spoken impersonally at their oracle-sites; their ceremonies assumed a life in which the community, the city, dwarfed the individual. In the fourth and fifth centuries, however, the individual, as a "man of power," came to dwarf the traditional communities . . . . In the popular imagination, the emergence of the holy man at the expense of the temple marks the end of the classical world.

In his *Making of Late Antiquity* (pp. 11–16, *pass.*), Brown elaborates on this matter in the following way.

> What changed in no uncertain manner . . . between the second and the fifth centuries, were men's views as to where exactly this "divine power" was to be found on earth and, consequently, on what terms access to it could be achieved . . . .

In the period between 200 and 400, Mediterranean men came to accept, in increasing numbers and with increasing enthusiasm, the idea that this "divine power" did not only manifest itself directly to the average individual or through perennially established institutions: rather "divine power" was represented on earth by a limited number of exceptional human agents, who had been empowered to bring it to bear among their fellows by reason of a relationship with the supernatural that was personal to them, stable and clearly perceptible to fellow believers . . . .

What gives Late Antiquity its special flavor is precisely the claims of human beings . . . . to vest a fellow human being with powers and claims to loyalty associated with the supernatural, and especially a human being whose claim was not rendered unchallengeable by obvious coercive powers, is a momentous decision for a society made up of small face-to-face groups to make.

There is scarcely need to point out how the Talmud's figure of the rabbi conforms to Brown's account of the prevailing imagination of the age. The rabbi, mediating divine power, yet highly individual, became the center and the focus of the supernatural life of Israel. In the age at hand, that was his view, perhaps not widely held, and not shared at all by other Big Men. But in the time to come, the rabbi would become Israel's model of sanctification, the Jews' promise of ultimate salvation. That is why from then to nearly now, whatever Judaism there would ever be properly came to be called rabbinic.

To conclude, let us turn from the quest for salvation back to our observation that, in their search of certainty, the framers of the Talmud appeal to Scripture. But the certainty they discovered is contingent. For, as we noted in our study of the politics of certainty, it is the rabbi who rules uncontingently, with perfect certainty to begin with, meaning, confidence in his authority. So the Judaism of the Talmud invents Scripture as source of certainty (some thing of which, we remember, the Mishnah scarcely dreamed) and at the same time makes the rabbi authority and arbiter of what is true and certain. So the Talmud effects an astonishing parallelism between Scripture and sage. In a word, the Talmud brings forth the rabbi as Scripture incarnate, therefore (completing the trilogy) the hope and salvation of Israel. Out of the union of the Torah and the person of the rabbi, the messianic and salvific faith, Rabbinic Judaism, was born.

What worldly use has this faith, created in the matrix of late antiquity, served, and how has the Jewish sector of the civilization of the West drawn nourishment and hope from it? What the rabbi of our Talmud bequeathed to Israel and the West in the end is a vision of man in the image of God, a model for what a man can be: not mud alone but mind as well. His legacy served to exalt man's unique powers of thought, to order his daily routine and endow it with a wonderful sense of its formal perfection. So the national historical life of Israel was matched by and joined to the local and private life of the village. The whole served as a paradigm of ultimate perfection, sanctification—hence—salvation. (True, from his time to ours, the Talmud's rabbi as model served for only half of Israel, the male half. Yet that is our problem, not the Talmud's, which, in this regard, alas, proved no better than its day, if not much worse.) The power of the Talmud's vision endures for an age with a lesser view of humanity. Ours is diminished faith in the human capacity of rationality to attain orderly rules for sanctification in the everyday and so to gain salvation in the end of days.

For who in our time, challenged to frame a protracted statement of what we should do and can make of ourselves, would answer, as did the Talmud's rabbis in an age of unreal hope and despair: So receive the heritage of the ages as to make sense of yourselves this day. So use your minds as to act in accord with the rules of reason. Be secure therefore in the certainty of what is done, in the authority of the one who guides what is done, and in the ultimate salvation of those who persist in doing what God wants.

Important Events of the Third and Fourth Centuries A.D.

235	Murder of Severus Alexander, beginning of fifty year's chaos
219–251	Decius' persecution of the Christians
268–269	Goths defeated in the Balkans
270–275	Reign of Aurelian, Rome fortified, Dacia evacuated, Gaul and East reconquered, currency reform
285	Defeat of Carinus; Diocletian in control
303–305	Diocletian's persecution of the Christians
306	Constantine proclaimed emperor at York
320	Pachomius' first monastery
321	Constantine defeats Licinius and reunites the empire
325	The Council of Nicaea
330	Constantinople becomes the imperial residence
331	Pagan temples' properties expropriated
361–363	Julian the Apostate restores the privileges of paganism
391	Theodosius I prohibits pagan worship
406–429	Gaul and Spain overrun by Alans, Sueves, and Vandals
440	Rome sacked by the Visigoths; Britain abandoned
448	Visigoths settle in Gaul
429	Vandals invade Africa (Carthage taken 439)

Source: Smith, p. 184.

Abbreviations and Bibliography

Avi-Yonah
>   M. Avi-Yonah. *The Jews of Palestine: A Political History from the Bar Kokhba War to the Arab Conquest*. New York, 1976.

A.Z.   Abodah Zarah

b.   ben, "son of"

Bailyn
>   Bernard Bailyn. "The Challenge of Modern Historiography." *American Historical Review*, vol. 87, no. 1 (1982).

Baron
>   Salo Baron. *A Social and Religious History of the Jews*. Vol. 2, *Ancient Times*. Philadelphia, 1952.

B.B.   Baba Batra

Bes.   Besah

B.M.   Baba Mesia

Bowersock
>   G.W. Bowersock. *Julian the Apostate*. Cambridge, 1978.

Brown, *Making of Late Antiquity*
>   Peter Brown. *The Making of Late Antiquity*. Cambridge, 1978.

Brown, *Religion*
>   Peter Brown. *Religion and Society in the Age of Saint Augustine*. New York, 1972.

Brown, *World*
>   Peter Brown. *The World of Late Antiquity*. New York, 1971.

Chron.   Chronicles

Deut.   Deuteronomy

Ed.   Eduyyot

Est.   Esther

Ex.   Exodus

Ezek.   Ezekiel

Gen.   Genesis

Git.   Gittin

Hor.   Horayot
Hos.   Hosea
Is.   Isaiah
Jastrow
    Marcus Jastrow. *A Dictionary of the Targumim, the Talmud Babli and
    Yerushalmi, and the Midrashic Literature.* 2 vols. New York,
    1895–1903. Reprinted: New York, 1975.
Jer.   Jeremiah
Jones
    A.H.M. Jones. *The Decline of the Ancient World.* London, 1966.
Jones in Momigliano
    A.H.M. Jones. "The Social Background of the Struggle between Pa-
    ganism and Christianity." In Arnaldo Momigliano, ed., *The Conflict
    between Paganism and Christianity in the Fourth Century.* Oxford,
    1964.
Josh.   Joshua
Ket.   Ketubot
Lev.   Leviticus
Lieberman
    Saul Lieberman. "Palestine in the Third and Fourth Centuries." *Jewish
    Quarterly Review,* vol. 36, no. 4 (1946); and vol. 37, no. 1 (1946).
Lot   Ferdinand Lot. *The End of the Ancient World and the Beginning of the
    Middle Ages.* New York, 1961.
M.   Mishnah
Meg.   Megillah
Mic.   Micah
Naz.   Nazir
Ned.   Nedarim
Neusner, *Evidence*
    Jacob Neusner. *Judaism: The Evidence of the Mishnah.* Chicago, 1981.
Neusner, *Purities*
    Jacob Neusner. *A History of the Mishnaic Law of Purities.* Vols. 1–22.
    Leiden, 1974–1977.
Neusner, vol. 35
    Jacob Neusner. *The Talmud of the Land of Israel.* Vol. 35, *Introduction:
    Taxonomy.* Chicago, 1983.
Nid.   Niddah
Num.   Numbers
Peters
    E.E. Peters. *The Harvest of Hellenism.* New York, 1970.
PM   Pene Moshe, Moses Margolies (d. 1780). Commentary to the Jeru-
    salem Talmud. Amsterdam, 1754; Leghorn, 1770. Reprinted in the
    Jerusalem Talmud.
Prov.   Proverbs
Ps.   Psalms

Qid.   Qiddushin
Qoh.   Qoheleth
R.   Rabbi
Sam.   Samuel
San.   Sanhedrin
Shab.   Shabbat
Sheb.   Shebuot
Shebi. Shebiit
Smith
    Elias Bickerman and Morton Smith. *The Ancient History of Western Civilization.* New York, 1976.
Smith, *Imagining Religion*
    Jonathan Z. Smith. *Imagining Religion.* Chicago, 1982.
Smith, *Map Is Not Territory*
    Jonathan Z. Smith. *Map Is Not Territory: Studies in the History of Religions.* Leiden, 1978.
T.   Tosefta
Y.   Yerushalmi, Talmud of the Land of Israel
Yeb.   Yebamot
Zahavy
    T. Zahavy. *The Talmud of the Land of Israel: A Preliminary Translation and Explanation.* Vol. 1, *Berakhot.* Chicago, forthcoming.
Zech.   Zechariah

Index of Biblical and Talmudic References

General Index